VICTORIAN MASTERS AND THEIR ART

Russell Ash

PAVILION

First published by Pavilion Books Ltd as *Sir Lawrence Alma-Tadema* (1989); *Sir Edward Burne-Jones* (1993); *Lord Leighton* (1995); *Sir John Everett Millais* (1996); *Dante Gabriel Rosetti* (1995) and *James Tissot* (1992)

This combined edition first published in Great Britain in 1999 by
PAVILION BOOKS LIMITED
London House, Great Eastern Wharf
Parkgate Road, London SW11 4NQ

Produced, edited and designed by Russell Ash & Bernard Higton
Text copyright © Russell Ash
Editorial research by Vicki Rumbell
Picture research by Mary-Jane Gibson
Design and layout © Pavilion Books Ltd.

The moral right of the author
has been asserted

Designed by Bernard Higton

A CIP catalogue record for this book is available
from the British Library.

ISBN 1 86205 304 9

Set in Monotype Perpetua
Printed in Singapore by Kyodo

2 4 6 8 10 9 7 5 3 1

This book can be ordered direct from the publisher. Please contact
the Marketing Department. But try your bookshop first.

Frontispiece: Sir Edward Burne-Jones, *The Bath of Venus* (1873–88),
Calouste Gulbenkian Foundation, Lisbon
Opposite: Dante Gabriel Rossetti, *Joli Coeur* (1867)

CONTENTS

SIR LAWRENCE ALMA-TADEMA 6

SIR EDWARD BURNE-JONES 99

LORD LEIGHTON 193

SIR JOHN EVERETT MILLAIS 285

DANTE GABRIEL ROSSETTI 379

JAMES TISSOT 473

Picture Acknowledgements 568

SIR LAWRENCE
ALMA-TADEMA

Sir Lawrence Alma-Tadema

1839–1912

Fellow artists pay tribute to Alma-Tadema on the occasion of his knighthood in 1899.

Who knows him well he best can tell
  That a stouter friend hath no man
Than this lusty knight, who for our delight
  Hath painted Greek and Roman.
Then here let every citizen,
Who holds a brush or wields a pen,
Drink deep as his Zuyder Zee
  To Alma-Tad –
  Of the Royal Acad –
  Of the Royal Academee.

This, the refrain of a song composed especially for Sir Lawrence Alma-Tadema, was performed at the banquet held to celebrate his knighthood, awarded to him on Queen Victoria's eightieth birthday in 1899. The timing was coincidental, but perhaps not inappropriate, for Alma-Tadema, born the year before Victoria came to the throne, and Victorian England had grown old and prospered together. Alma-Tadema, more than any other painter of the High Victorian period, had intuitively sensed the spirit of the age and, clever businessman that he was, had achieved unrivalled success by producing the most popular, the most reproduced and the most expensive pictures of his day. Yet already, as the end of the century neared and Victoriana was becoming despised and sloughed off, he was an artist out of his time. Within twenty years one would have been hard-pressed to find a buyer for an Alma-Tadema painting, and if one did change hands, a work that might once have commanded £10,000 could have been picked up for £20. Along with the decline in interest in his work, his fame was steadily eclipsed: his knighthood, his rôle as a leading Royal Academician, his

friendship with Society figures from the Prince of Wales to the young Winston Churchill, all were forgotten. Barely forty years after his death, the author of an article on him felt compelled to explain that, despite his strange name, Alma-Tadema was not a woman.

Since the 1960s, however, alongside a general resurgence of interest in the best of Victorian art (as well as some of the worst), Alma-Tadema's star has been shining again. In 1973 the art world gasped when *The Finding of Moses* made £30,000 at auction; in 1980 *Caracalla and Geta* fetched £145,000, while more recently paintings are known to have been sold privately for more than £500,000. Now, nearly eighty years after his death, no one would be surprised if a first-rate picture fetched £1m or more.

Alma-Tadema's story is not a rags to riches tale. His was not the angst-filled life of the penniless artist starving in a garret, never selling a painting until after his death; he was not rejected by the establishment – on the contrary, he was the establishment's favourite artist; nor, in Oscar Wilde's phrase, was his 'a life crowded with incident'. He was twice happily married and, as far as anyone knows, he never engaged in torrid affairs with his models. But lacking high drama, the life of this comfortable, successful and above all internationally popular painter reveals more about Victorian life, Victorian taste and 'Victorian values' than that of almost any other artist of the era.

Alma-Tadema was Dutch, and his name was originally Lourens Tadema; Alma was his middle name. He was born on 8 January 1836 in Dronryp, Friesland, the son of the local notary, Pieter Tadema, and his second wife, Hinke Brouwer. The family moved two years later to the provincial capital, Leeuwarden, where, in 1840, Pieter Tadema died. As he grew up, Lourens showed some artistic ability and the beginnings of his methodical nature: in

Lourens Tadema's proficient self-portrait, painted at the age of 16.

1851, in his own catalogue, he assigned to a portrait of his sister the Roman numeral 'I' preceded by 'Op.' [Opus] – a practice that he continued throughout his life (though he included the numbers on his paintings alongside his signature only from 1872), ending with 'Op. CCCCVIII' at the time of his death.

In 1852 he enrolled as a student at the Antwerp Academy, where he worked briefly under Gustav Wappers and then his successor, Nicaise de Keyser. Both were exponents of the Romantic movement, de Keyser in particular encouraging his pupils to paint genre subjects on nationalistic themes. Tadema later became an assistant to the historical painter Baron Hendryk Leys and lived in the household of an archaeologist, Louis de Taye (under whose roof were also the noted Hague School painters, Jacob and Willem Maris). From Leys and de Taye Tadema began to develop his interest in and knowledge of archaeology and history, which was further fostered by contact with the German Egyptologist, Georg Ebers (later one of Tadema's biographers), and assisted Leys in painting historical murals in the Antwerp Town Hall. His cousin Willem Mesdag, himself a painter of note, became one of his pupils and one of the first collectors of Tadema's work.

The themes for his early paintings derived from the history of the Merovingians, rulers of Gaul from the sixth to the eighth century. This little-known and in many respects bleak period preoccupied him until 1862 when he visited London

Tadema's study of Merovingian history resulted in subjects such as *The Education of the Children of Clovis* (1868).

for the first time, during the International Exhibition. He was deeply impressed by the Elgin Marbles and especially by the Egyptian artefacts he saw in the British Museum and turned increasingly to Egyptian themes in his work (an area he had already explored in his *The Sad Father* of 1859). In 1863 he married a Frenchwoman, Marie Pauline Gressin de Boisgirard, and spent his honeymoon in Italy. There he intended studying the architecture of early Christian churches; instead he became so fascinated by the Roman remains, marble and the newly-excavated ruins of Pompeii that he immediately added ancient Roman subjects to his repertoire. Within a few years such works, 'reanimating the life of the old Romans', as one critic described them, took prominence. Soon afterwards, Tadema and his wife, Pauline, moved to Paris, where he met 'Prince' Ernest Gambart, an eminent art dealer with pan-European connections, entering into a long-term contract with him and soon transferring his studio to Brussels.

In the Peristyle (1866), a portrait of Tadema's first wife in a flowery Pompeian courtyard.

Tadema inspecting the newly-excavated ruins of Pompeii.

The 1860s were marked by a double tragedy: his only son died of smallpox in 1865 and his wife died in 1869, leaving him to support their two daughters, Anna and Laurence. By the end of the decade, however, Tadema's work was being exhibited in London and was attracting a growing following. In 1869 two of his paintings, *A Roman Art Lover* and *Phyrric Dance*, were shown at the Royal Academy. The second of these later prompted the critic John Ruskin to remark that

The Phyrric Dance (1869), one of Tadema's first paintings to be exhibited in London.

'the general effect was exactly like a microscopic view of a small detachment of black-beetles, in search of a dead rat'. Ruskin's was, though, one of the few dissenting voices: so well were Tadema's paintings received that, visiting England in this year (to consult a doctor, Sir Henry Thompson), and with the threat of the Prussian invasion of France, he made the decision to move his base to London in 1870 (as did such artists as Monet and Pissarro). The following year he married his seventeen-year-old pupil, Laura Epps, the daughter of a doctor and member of a family celebrated in the Victorian period for the manufacture of cocoa.

In 1873, Tadema became a naturalized British citizen. A verse accompanying a caricature went:

> Great are your gifts; we in England have had 'em
> Good many years, and we value them much, man.
> Lucky the day when you cried, Alma Tadema,
> Briton I'll turn; if I don't, I'm a Dutchman!

As well as establishing that Alma-Tadema had 'arrived' sufficiently to be the subject of a magazine cartoon, it indicates the correct pronunciation of his name 'Tad-em-a', to rhyme with 'had 'em a', and not 'Tad-ee-ma'. From the time of his settling in London, he also consciously joined his

This is Our Corner (1873), Alma-Tadema's daughters, Laurence and Anna.

middle name, Alma, to his surname. As well as making it more memorable, it had the effect of elevating him to an early position in alphabetical catalogues. He never hyphenated it himself, but almost everyone else did and this has become the convention.

Soon after his remarriage, the Alma-Tademas moved from a rented home in Camden Square to Townshend House, a villa at the north gate of Regent's Park. Elegantly and eclectically decorated in cosmopolitan style, it rapidly became a popular venue for gatherings of fellow artists.

Back in 1866, when Alma-Tadema was visiting Gambart in London, his host's home had been shattered by a gas explosion from which he and Pauline were lucky to escape with their lives. In 1874 he was again the victim of a bizarre explosion. At dawn on 2 October on the Regent's Canal a steam tug towing five barges carrying petroleum and five tons of gunpowder exploded with such force that the bridge was entirely destroyed and houses over about a square mile were gutted. Thousands of windows were shattered and shock waves were felt thirty miles away. The most severely damaged house was the Alma-Tademas', but luckily he and his wife were in Scotland at the time and miraculously no one apart from the crew of the tug was killed. While Townshend House was being repaired, he took his family to Italy for the winter.

The studio entrance to Alma-Tadema's house in St John's Wood, drawn while under construction.

Steadily, Alma-Tadema was achieving fame and wealth: he became an Associate of the Royal Academy in 1876 and a full Royal Academician in 1879. In 1882 the Grosvenor Gallery staged an exhibition of 287 of his paintings. Now one of the most famous painters in Britain, he felt sufficiently confident to develop plans for a yet more spectacular home. The house he found was in Grove End Road, St John's Wood – an area once noted for the number of houses occupied by high-class courtesans. This was the former home of the French artist Jean-Jacques Tissot, who in 1882 had abandoned it after the death of his mistress, Kathleen Newton. It was modest, but had a number of classical features that appealed to Alma-Tadema, such as the colonnade beside a garden pond that featured in several of Tissot's works. Alma-Tadema greatly expanded the house, making of it an extraordinary palace, designing every detail himself, from the artist's palette weather-vane and the doorway, modelled on one from Pompeii, with 'Salve' – 'Welcome' – above the door, down to the rainspouts in the shape of lions' heads. The hall was lined with panels painted by fellow artists, and the vast galleried marble-floored studio was sur-mounted by a polished aluminium dome. The brightness of the light it reflected noticeably affected Alma-Tadema's painting from this time onwards.

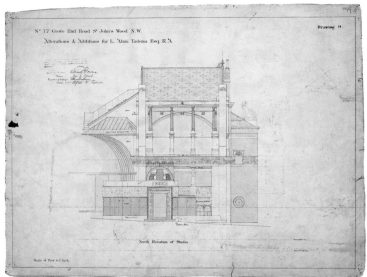

The architect's plan for the imposing conversion of Alma-Tadema's 'palace'.

Both Alma-Tadema's London houses were famous for his well-attended 'At Homes' and elaborate parties. He loved dressing up for fancy-dress balls – sometimes, appropriately, as a Roman emperor. Music was always on the menu, and his many distinguished visitors included Tchaikovsky and Enrico Caruso. Those who performed at his magnificently decorated piano were then asked to sign a vellum panel inside the lid. (Sadly, it was destroyed by bombing during the Second World War, but in 1980 a piano designed by Alma-Tadema for Henry Marquand of New York made £177,273 at auction, making it to that date not only the most expensive musical instrument ever sold, but also the most costly example of nineteenth-century applied art.)

Interior of the domed studio showing its exotic furnishings and often-painted studio sofas.

Dominating the 'At Homes' was Alma-Tadema the host. His genial personality and sense of humour were legendary – notorious, some said. He was an avid collector of clockwork toys and could be found sitting, childlike, on the floor roaring with laughter over a tin monkey beating a drum. He embarrassed Sir Georg Henschel (the conductor of the Boston Symphony Orchestra) by insisting whenever they met that he sing the music hall song, 'Daddy Wouldn't Buy Me a Bow-Wow'. He had a passion for dreadful puns and jokes which he delivered in the thick Dutch accent that he never completely lost. On one occasion he met Angela Thirkell (Burne-Jones's granddaughter and a well-known novelist). He was gabbling volubly, and she could not understand what he was saying but assumed it must be one of his appalling stories and laughed uproariously, only to be asked by the astonished Alma-Tadema, 'What for you laugh when I tell you that

Alfred Parsons' mother is dead?' Some found him overpower-ing and it cannot be denied he was a flamboyant and self-obsessed extrovert. The initials 'LAT' (which, to be fair, were those of his wife as well as himself) were interwoven into the floors and walls of his houses, and even engraved on the screws of his famous piano. He was undoubtedly the sort of man who would today have a custom-built Rolls-Royce with the 'prestige' car registration plate, 'LAT 1'.

Though he was without honour in his own country, where artists such as those of the Hague School took the fancy of patrons while his work was unappreciated, he was hugely popular almost everywhere else, from the United States to Australia. He received awards and honorary titles by the dozen from European and American institutions, with the final accolades in Britain of his knighthood in 1899 and the rarely-awarded Order of Merit in 1905. His clients included members of the British Royal Family and Russian Imperial Family, and his pictures found their way into important private collections as far afield as India and New Zealand. He became a noted Society portraitist – some sixty of his paintings are routine commissioned portraits of subjects ranging from the British Prime Minister Arthur Balfour to the Polish pianist (and later Polish Prime Minister) Ignacy Paderewski.

Lady Laura Alma-Tadema died in 1909 and was buried at Kensal Green cemetery. Alongside her grave, he reserved a plot for himself. Following her death, Alma-Tadema's *joie de vivre* was noticeably declining, but he produced several re-markable pictures before his own death on 25 June 1912 in the German spa of Wiesbaden. He was not buried with his wife: so high had he risen in the artistic pantheon that nothing less than St Paul's Cathedral was thought appropriate. Soon afterwards, his house and contents were sold. The house was later divided into apartments and few architectural details survive. In 1975 it ac-quired a Greater London Council 'blue plaque', installed to commemorate the residences of celebrated people. Alma-Tadema's is unusual: as the house is almost invisible from the road, the plaque is attached to the garden wall. His daughters Laurence and Anna lived on until 1940 and 1943 respectively, dying as elderly spinsters.

The establishment artist: Alma-Tadema at work in the 1890s.

During his sixty productive years, Alma-Tadema had produced over four hundred paintings. In this period, his technical virtuosity, as even Ruskin acknowledged, increased year by year. His work also underwent several dramatic changes of style and content. Firstly the historical location moved successively through obscure Merovingian subjects and Egyptian themes to Pompeian and Roman settings. In content he developed progressively away from defined historical scenes into cosy, often sentimental domestic settings. Most striking of all was his move from the dark into the light: gradually his subjects, originally placed in gloomy interiors, passed through doorways and on to terraces, finally emerging into dazzlingly brilliant light reflected off shimmering white marble in broad, open spaces – often on coastal promontories flooded with sunlight. The extraordinary luminosity of his paintings is all the more remarkable when one notes that he never used glazes or varnish. His technique depended on painting dark pigments on to white canvas, rather than the then conventional technique of adding highlights to a dark background. His palette was not unlike that of his contemporaries, the Impressionists, but in few other respects did he follow their technique. He was also clearly a consummate master of the chemistry of his paint, since works he painted over a century ago still appear fresh and bright, rarely showing any signs of deterioration. Most of his paintings are oils, but he was equally competent in watercolour and pencil; diverse examples exist, from crude sketches to incredibly detailed finished drawings.

Though he was able to convey almost any texture, from fur to feathers, it was his painting of marble that singles Alma-Tadema out from his rivals. His original inspiration came, it is said, from an 1858 visit to a club in Ghent in which there was a marble-lined smoking-room. Recalling an early criticism of his teacher, Leys, who remarked that one of his first attempts at depicting marble 'looked like cheese', he studied it at every opportunity, visiting the quarries at Carrara, and made himself the world's leading exponent of marble painting: 'Marbellous!', quipped *Punch*. In an address to the Royal Institute of British Architects, he informed his audience, ' . . . marble is beautiful stuff of deal with.' Even those artists who had little sympathy with his work acknowledged his skill: 'No man has ever lived who has interpreted with Alma-Tadema's power the incidence of

sunlight on metal and marble,' wrote the Pre-Raphelite painter Sir Edward Burne-Jones.

Having achieved this pre-eminence, he featured marble at every opportunity. The marble bench, or *exedra*, on which lovers sit in bright sunshine, lost in their reveries, was a characteristic theme to which he often returned. In these and in many other works he frequently 'recycled' successful elements, perhaps taking an incidental detail from one and working it up into a full-scale painting. Alternatively, he might produce several versions of a work, ringing the changes by producing one in watercolour and one in oils, altering the size, or modifying certain features. Occasionally he could be self-mocking about this technique, as when, following the success of *An Audience at Agrippa's*, he painted *After the Audience*, in which we see the backs of the same figures as they exit. Some archaeological props also recur again and again – a studio sofa (now in the Victoria & Albert Museum), for example, appears in many pictures.

Alma-Tadema was the foremost depicter of the daily life of the ancient world; unlike such artists as Lord Leighton or Poynter, he did not attempt to portray Greek legends, nor, as his work progressed, did he pay much attention to named historical personages or events – or almost anything that involved action. His were set pieces, scenes in which a moment in time was frozen almost photographically, and the moments themselves were ones in which not much is going on. Bacchantes are seen calling people to participate in revels that we never witness, or lying exhausted after they are over; lovers sit idly on sofas gazing dreamily into the distance; sometimes his subjects are actually asleep.

Alma-Tadema was often criticized for painting decorative objects, marble and skies with greater conviction than that

The perfect blend of women, marble and the Mediterranean in *At Aphrodite's Cradle* (1908).

which he applied to the flesh of the human beings who inhabited his pictures. In Ruskin's view, Tadema's technical perfection was in inverse ratio to the importance of the subject he was portraying. Others saw his figures, with their lack of movement or emotion, as no more than soulless dummies, mere compositional accessories. Alma-Tadema would have been the first to admit that there was little spiritual dimension to his works; no social or moral lessons were being conveyed, as in the paintings of the Pre-Raphaelites, his view being that art should elevate, not teach. Even the historical and psychological backgrounds to many of his works were submerged in the

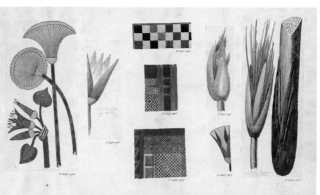

Egyptian motifs from Alma-Tadema's vast collection of reference pictures.

spectacle – *The Roses of Heliogabalus* actually shows the psychopathic Roman emperor suffocating his guests under a shower of rose petals, but it was the quality of Alma-Tadema's skill at depicting roses (brought to his studio weekly for the purpose from the South of France), not the cruelty of the maniac ruler, that excited the critics. While most genre paintings in contemporary costume or allegorical historical subjects tended to dwell on moral questions, Alma-Tadema's art was devoid of 'messages' – but then it was also free of the constraints of 'high art': his, if art it was, was art on an anecdotal level. He had no aspiration beyond that of being a painter of beautiful things – of flowers and decorative objects in picturesque settings, peopled by women and men in attractive costumes.

An Apodyterium, voted 'Picture of the Year' in 1886.

But if his art lacked substance, no one could complain that he short-changed his public on the technical skill and archaeological exactitude with which he depicted the ancient world – to the extent that several generations of school history books featured his paintings as the most accurate representations of daily life in Rome. Widely read, he was the possessor of a substantial library of reference books as well as 167 massive albums of drawings, prints and photographs (donated to the Victoria & Albert Museum, but now held by the Birmingham University Library). To these he would turn for precise visual information. In addition, he had a phenomenal memory for details gleaned on his travels in Italy, Egypt and elsewhere. Almost every object, every vase, statue or bas-relief, derives from some museum exhibit.

Only very rarely is there an anachronism – as when he placed sunflowers in a Roman picture without appreciating that they were indigenous to the Americas.

His scholarship could be turned into paintings only through enormous effort. Take, for example, *Caracalla and Geta*: in a segment comprising one-seventh of the Coliseum, which held 35,000 spectators, he calculated that there would be 5,000 people, half of whom, he estimated, were concealed behind pillars and garlands of flowers. Undaunted, he proceeded to paint 2,500 figures. This is, for Alma-Tadema, a relatively large painting, measuring 4 ft by 5 ft, but many seeing his pictures for the first time are astonished to discover how tiny many of them are. He was proud of his talent as a miniaturist, and often gave a visitors a magnifying-glass with which to inspect some miniscule detail.

Alma-Tadema's perspective is often unconventional, a work like *A Coign of Vantage* presenting strikingly vertiginous angles. In his paintings the viewer is often guided through a doorway. The subject might be framed by bold horizontal or diagonal elements, or figures truncated at the edges of the frame, after the fashion of a Japanese print. Nothing is accidental; every single element is worked out to fit into the whole. Never completely satisfied with his pictures, he repeatedly reworked them – sometimes after they had been sold. Some of his early works were hacked up into sections and made into several smaller paintings; one rejected painting even ended up as a tablecloth. His meticulous supervision of the engravers who reproduced his work was often exasperating. He was a hard-working perfectionist who could not tolerate anything less in his associates.

With varying degrees of success, Alma-Tadema dabbled in many creative endeavours, which he described as 'the sister arts'. He executed a number of book illustrations and stage sets, also designing theatrical costumes, such as that worn by Ellen Terry as Imogen in *Cymbeline*, which became an overnight fashion, as did Liberty's Roman dresses 'à la Tadema'. His chief contribution outside painting, however, was in the field of architecture. In 1906 he won the Gold Medal from the Royal Institute of British Architects for his promotion of architecture through his painting, the only artist ever to receive the award. Alma-Tadema's architectural obsessions ensured that even if it never existed *in toto*, every building he depicted could have been built – his paintings were almost blueprints for fantasy Roman buildings.

'The Year's at the Spring, All's Right with the World' (1902) – late Victorian sentimentality in a vaguely antique setting.

Tadema specialized in painting depictions of esoteric historical events only until he found the niche in which he stayed for the rest of his prolific life. This was the portrayal of the luxury, tranquillity and mores of the upper-middle-class circles in which he himself mixed – their love of art treasures, dining and fashionable parties, their courtship rituals, sentimentality and even their repressed sexuality. The fact that his audience expressed its desire to be represented as elegant 'Victorians in togas', as one art critic has called them, is less easy to comprehend today. What was the secret of the appeal of Alma-Tadema's paintings of his contemporaries in antique fancy dress?

In his incredibly detailed reconstructions of the ancient world, Alma-Tadema provided his public with an uncomplicated, acceptable, and occasionally risqué image of rich patricians, art-lovers and wooing couples; and in particular he was the first to show that the Roman middle class was not unlike the Victorian middle class – 'I have always endeavoured to express in my pictures that the old Romans were human flesh and blood like ourselves, moved by the same passions and emotions,' he explained in an interview in the year of his knighthood. Alma-Tadema was the first artist to use the wealth of archaeological evidence that was being uncovered and published to reconstruct the daily life of ancient Rome in a form that was infinitely more accessible than the loftier works of those artists who attempted to portray significant historical events or obscure myths and legends.

In the Victorian self-image there were obvious parallels between the attainments, the values and the social stratification of the Roman Empire and those of the 'golden age' of the British Empire. Alma-Tadema's public may or may not have consciously appreciated this mirroring of their own society in his paintings, but to modern eyes his reflections of Victorian bourgeois values are obvious enough: property ownership, art connoisseurship, infinite leisure time – especially exemplified in the idleness of the wives of successful men – servants catering to every whim, sentimentality relating to courtship, children who were seen but not heard.

It would not be an exaggeration to state that Alma-Tadema was the most successful and popular of all Victorian painters. All his works, highly priced though they were, found eager buyers; engraved reproductions of his pictures sold in their thousands, while Frederick Stephens' booklet describing one of his paintings, *A Dedication to Bacchus*, was reputed to have sold 40,000 copies. Alma-Tadema was able to support his lavish lifestyle – his palace of a house, extravagant entertaining and extensive travels – purely from the income from the sale of his pictures and copyrights for reproduction. He was one of the most highly-paid artists of his day: *A Reading from Homer*, sold to an American buyer for $30,000 in 1903, was the most expensive painting of the year. For the copyright of *The Baths of Caracalla*, widely reproduced as a print, he received a staggering £10,000. A century ago a less complex but characteristic work might fetch over £2,000, while a portrait commission would command £600 to £800 – figures that should be multiplied by at least thirty to compare them with modern values. It should also be noted that income tax in his peak years was threepence in the pound.

The simple explanation of this achievement is that for over sixty years, like any shrewd entrepreneur, he cleverly calculated precisely what his audience wanted, and gave it to them. Alma-

The melodrama of such works as *Proclaiming Claudius Emperor* (1867) was later supplanted by simple scenes of daily life.

To a materialistic public he provided true value for money – finely detailed paintings crammed with figures, decorative archaeological paraphernalia, and multitudes of flowers, as cluttered as a Victorian drawing-room. He gave glimpses into the past – endlessly fascinating conversation pieces to tempt the jaded palates of a society that constantly sought new pleasures. Recognizing the appeal of Mediterranean colour and sunlight to northern Europeans and Americans, in his most popular works he focused on the Bay of Naples. He also offered an underlying escapism: never is there anything unpleasant or dirty, rarely a tinge of sadness; everything is elevated to a refined and pleasurable plane. Above all, he was the right man at the right time: the Victorian public was complacent (Alma-Tadema's painting, *The Year's at the Spring, All's Right with the World*, could have served as a motto for the entire era) and self-assured with its own place in world history. It was also obsessed with the past, with revivals, discoveries and novelties, and Alma-Tadema's vision struck a perfect balance between erudition and entertainment.

Alma-Tadema realized that the mercantile class that provided most of his patrons included many *nouveaux riches* who lacked the benefit of a classical education. Like the popular singer of today who offers a medley of popular arias without the complexity or tedium of the whole opera, he preferred respectably historical paintings with simple and straightforward anecdotal backgrounds, eschewing convoluted legends and characters with unpronounceable names. This attitude extended even to the simplicity of the titles of his paintings: he soon moved away from history book captions such as *Queen Fredegonda at the Deathbed of Bishop Praetextatus* to short phrases such as *Midday Slumbers* or *The Voice of Spring*, or such memorable quotations as *'Her Eyes Are With Her Thoughts, and They Are Far Away'*

An undeniable element in the appeal of Alma-Tadema's works (especially since those who bought them were usually men) was that they often contained tasteful erotica. Alma-Tadema's subjects may be 'Victorians in togas', but as often as not they are caught in the act of slipping out of their togas or cavorting naked in Roman baths. How deliberate Alma-Tadema's choice of sexually arousing subjects might have been is not hard to assess: time and time again he returned to themes with coyly erotic potential – or, in the case of a work like *In the Tepidarium*, not so coy. We are repeatedly offered an almost voyeuristic glimpse inside baths and changing rooms, while the Roman world is populated by bacchantes exhausted after a wild orgy, nude sculptors' models and languid women barely covered by loosely draped towels or diaphanous, figure-clinging gowns. There are even suggestions of lesbianism as we meet Sappho and discover women

A Sculptor's Model (1877), the painting that shocked the Bishop of Carlisle.

hugging and lounging intimately together in boudoirs.

A letter from the Bishop of Carlisle to the portrait painter George Richmond encapsulated what the more puritanical among his audience must have felt:

My mind has been considerably exercised this season by the exhibition of Alma-Tadema's nude Venus [*A Sculptor's Model*] . . . [there might] be artistic reasons which justify such exposure of the female form. . . . In the case of the nude of an Old Master, much allowance can be made, but for a living artist to exhibit a life-size life-like almost photographic representation of a beautiful naked woman strikes my inartistic mind as somewhat if not very mischievous.

It was rumoured that Alma-Tadema had been commissioned by Edward VII to produce a series of more avowedly pornographic works; some even said he had painted murals discreetly hidden behind curtains in Windsor Castle. The verdict on this must remain 'unproven'. As far as the public at large (*pace* the Bishop of Carlisle) was concerned, Alma-Tadema never overstepped the mark: to ensure that his publicly shown paintings were respectable and hence acceptable, he placed his models in strictly classical settings (after all, every school-boy knew that the Romans spent hours in Roman baths, and no one bathes with their clothes on); to the scene he added a wealth of meticulous archaeological detail. Without question, these were serious historical paintings, successors of a long tradition of such works in which the presence of a nude, if justified by the context, was perfectly within the bounds of decency.

Several writers have seen in Alma-Tadema's more complex compositions an anticipation of the grandeur of the wide-screen Hollywood epic, and films such as D. W. Griffith's *Intolerance* (1916), *Ben Hur* (1926), and Cecil B. De Mille's *Cleopatra* (1934) and *The Ten Commandments* (1956) may well owe something to Alma-Tadema's vision of Rome in all its glory. *Spring* and other Roman crowd scene paintings were already in American collections and were well known through reproductions. (Many of his works were bought by American connoisseurs, and today almost half his *oeuvre* is in public and private collections in the United States.) Jessie Lasky Jr, co-writer on De Mille's *The Ten Commandments*, has described how the producer would customarily spread out reproductions of Alma-Tadema paintings to indicate to his set-builders the design he wanted to achieve, so Alma-Tadema's appellation as 'The Painter Who Inspired Hollywood' may not be too far-fetched.

'Her Eyes are With Her Thoughts, and They Are Far Away' (1897),
a wistfully decorative subject typical of the 1890s.

The 1913 Royal Academy memorial exhibition devoted to Alma-Tadema attracted only 17,000 visitors (Landseer's, a generation earlier and at the pinnacle of his fame, drew over 100,000). Those who had known him were polite enough, but the tide of opinion was already turning, one critic acidly commenting that his pictures were 'about worthy enough to adorn bonbon boxes'. It was the beginning of an anti-Alma-Tadema phase that was to last fifty years. Its chief exponents were Augustus John and his contemporaries in the Bloomsbury Group, to whom Alma-Tadema and his ilk were anathema. The backlash is understandable: Alma-Tadema was the most representative Academy painter of the nineteenth century, the personification of High Victorian art, and when this was rejected out of hand, Alma-Tadema, once the highest of them all, had the furthest to fall.

He was so much a product of his age that, when Victoriana came to be despised, Alma-Tadema's reputation steadily sank. It eventually reached such an all-time low that art galleries were literally throwing his paintings out. Some were sold for insultingly low prices: in 1954 Exeter City Art Gallery got rid of *'The Year's at the Spring, All's Right with the World'* for 130 guineas, while *In a Rose Garden* left the Lady Lever Art Gallery in 1958 for £241 10s. In 1960 *The Roses of Heliogabalus*, commissioned in 1888 for £4,000, and *The Finding of Moses* (£5,250 in 1904) failed to find buyers willing to pay more than £105 and £252 respectively.

The turning-point came about 1962, when the Robert Isaacson Gallery in New York audaciously celebrated the fiftieth anniversary of Alma-Tadema's death by exhibiting twenty-six of his paintings. Prices began to rise along with the general revival of interest in Victorian art – but in Alma-Tadema's case the escalation was curiously spurred by the enthusiasm of Allen Funt, the American film producer and creator of the popular television programme, 'Candid Camera'. Funt perversely built up the world's largest collection of Alma-Tadema paintings, originally to furnish a room decorated in Roman style, but with increasing momentum after he discovered that Ruskin had declared Alma-Tadema to have been the worst painter of the nineteenth century. Funt sprang to his defence, later commenting, 'Soon I found myself with a houseful of Alma-Tadema paintings and a warm feeling of sympathy for

this painter who received rather critical treatment.' Funt came to appreciate the collection of thirty-five paintings he assembled over the next eight years. In 1972, however, Mr Funt's accountant, when discovered to have been embezzling his funds, committed suicide, leaving him, as he described his situation, with 'everything a rich man has – except cash'. The Alma-Tademas had to go, but their potential at auction was encouraging, *Spring* having been sold in that year for $55,000. After a swan-song exhibition at the Metropolitan Museum of Art in New York, they crossed the Atlantic to be sold at Sotheby's, where they realized a total of £234,000. Interestingly, the sale included both *The Roses of Heliogabalus* and the *The Finding of Moses*: just thirteen years after they had been rejected at £105 and £252, they fetched £28,000 and £30,000 respectively – the latter a new record for an Alma-Tadema painting.

In the same year the present author's short biography of Alma-Tadema was published – the first book on him for over sixty years. This was followed by exhibitions organized at the Princessehof Museum in Leeuwarden in 1974 and at Sheffield City Art Gallery in 1976. In 1978 Vern Swanson's *Alma-Tadema: The Painter of the Victorian Vision of the Ancient World* was published in Britain and the United States as well as in French and Dutch. Mr Swanson has been working for many years on the *catalogue raisonné* of Alma-Tadema's paintings, and has been responsible for the acquisition and promotion of his work, particularly at Brigham Young University Art Museum in Provo, Utah.

Rather than being pilloried for being a man of his time, Alma-Tadema is today acknowledged as representing in his works the epitome of High Victorian taste. Once criticised for the lack of 'soul' in his work, or as an arch exponent of kitsch, he is now again admired as one of the most incredibly skilled technicians of all time, in whose pictures no intricate detail, however minute, is left to the imagination. His richly coloured, sumptuous and stunningly lit scenes have a freshness and impact that even now, over a century after some of them were painted, still have the power to amaze.

THE PLATES

1 A SCULPTURE GALLERY

2 PHEIDIAS AND THE FRIEZE OF THE PARTHENON, ATHENS

3 EGYPTIAN JUGGLER

4 THE VINTAGE FESTIVAL

5 JOSEPH, OVERSEER OF PHARAOH'S GRANARIES

6 NINETY-FOUR DEGREES IN THE SHADE

7 FLORA: SPRING IN THE GARDENS OF THE VILLA BORGHESE

8 A HEARTY WELCOME

9 STRIGILS AND SPONGES

10 SAPPHO AND ALCAEUS

11 IN THE TEPIDARIUM

12 THE PARTING KISS

13 ANTONY AND CLEOPATRA

14 WELCOME FOOTSTEPS

15 EXPECTATIONS

16 A READING FROM HOMER

17 THE WOMEN OF AMPHISSA

18 THE ROSES OF HELIOGABALUS

19 THE FAVOURITE POET

20 A DEDICATION TO BACCHUS

21 THE FRIGIDARIUM

22 PROMISE OF SPRING

23 AN EARTHLY PARADISE

24 A KISS

25 COMPARISONS

26 UNCONSCIOUS RIVALS

27 GOD SPEED!

28 SPRING

29 A COIGN OF VANTAGE

30 A DIFFERENCE OF OPINION

31 THE BATHS OF CARACALLA

32 VAIN COURTSHIP

33 UNDER THE ROOF OF BLUE IONIAN WEATHER

34 SILVER FAVOURITES

35 THE FINDING OF MOSES

36 A WORLD OF THEIR OWN

37 ASK ME NO MORE

38 CARACALLA AND GETA

39 A FAVOURITE CUSTOM

40 THE VOICE OF SPRING

—— PLATE 1 ——

A SCULPTURE GALLERY

Opus XLIX, 1867
Oil on panel, 24½ × 18½ in/62.2 × 47 cm
Musée des Beaux Arts de Montréal

The studios of Roman painters and sculptors and the galleries
in which their work was displayed to art connoisseurs
feature strongly in Alma-Tadema's early paintings. Here, in a
picture the full title of which is *A Sculpture Gallery
in Rome at the time of Augustus*, we see a group viewing a bronze
statue of the Greek dramatist, Sophocles. Like many of
his paintings in which sculpture appears, it was based on an
original work of art, in this instance a marble statue
found at Terracina in 1839 and now in the Vatican Museum.
In the background is the group depicting Laocoön and
his sons being killed by snakes, which is also in the Vatican.
On the right in profile is the seated figure of Agrippina
from the Capitoline Museum. Between the garlands,
suspended from the decorative ceiling, is an *oscillum*, or
decorative roundel. As was Alma-Tadema's usual custom, he
signed the painting on a suitable expanse of marble, but
he had not yet begun his practice of adding Opus numbers
alongside his signature.

—— PLATE 2 ——

Pheidias and the Frieze of the Parthenon, Athens

Opus LX, 1868
Oil on panel, 28⅜ × 43½ in/72 × 110.5 cm
Birmingham Museum and Art Gallery

Alma-Tadema had seen the Elgin Marbles in the British
Museum when he first visited London in 1862. At this time, a
debate was raging in academic and artistic circles as to
whether the ancient Greeks actually painted their statues and
whether contemporary sculptors should emulate them –
a concept that proved a severe culture shock to those who
equated Greek sculpture with pure whiteness. Taking
as his theme a 'private view' of the north-west corner of the
Parthenon frieze during the construction of the temple
in the 430s BC, Alma-Tadema, who had closely observed the
surviving colours, faithfully represents the frieze in all
its polychromatic glory. On the elaborate scaffolding
inspecting Pheidias's masterpiece, we see the eminent
Athenian personalities of the day: Pericles, the Athenian
magistrate, and his courtesan Aspasia; his nephew, the *enfant
terrible* Alcibiades; and behind the rope barrier, scroll in
hand, the sculptor Pheidias himself.

—— PLATE 3 ——

Egyptian Juggler

Opus LXXVII, 1870
Oil on canvas, 31 × 19¼ in/78.7 × 48.9 cm
Private collection

We are here invited to attend an elegant 'At Home'
in an elaborate Pompeian house, where the focus of the
entertainment is in the shade of a splendid peristyle
courtyard, the ornate Corinthian capitals and richly painted
wall and ceiling decoration pointing to the rank of the
host. The performance of the itinerant Egyptian entertainer
who gives the painting its title scarcely seems to be
exciting his audience, and, as in many of Alma-Tadema's
works, the human cast appears almost incidental to
the luxury of the surroundings. In the background there is a
picture of Bacchus and his followers; truncated by the
columns is a statue of a stag from the Villa of Papyri near
Herculaneum, and on the left a bronze group (now in
the National Archaeological Museum, Naples) showing the
infant Hercules wrestling with snakes. Alma-Tadema
visited Naples every year, and his sketchbooks were filled
with reference pictures of such treasures. Here too we
see one of his cleverly designed studio sofas, with Pompeian
motifs on one side, and Egyptian on the other, that
reappears in many works. After Alma-Tadema's death one
was sold with the contents of his house and is now in
the Victoria & Albert Museum.

——— PLATE 4 ———

The Vintage Festival

Opus LXXXI, 1870
Oil on canvas, 30¼ × 68½ in/76.8 × 174 cm
Hamburger Kunsthalle

With ever-increasing confidence, by the 1870s Alma-Tadema
was painting some of his most complex pictures,
brimming with archaeological paraphernalia. *A Vintage
Festival*, one of the last paintings he completed before
he moved permanently to London, shows a procession in
Pompeii devoted to Dionysos or Bacchus, the god of
wine. The inscription on the floor relates to 'Marcus
Holconius' – the Holconii family was one of the
foremost in Pompeii. On a bacchic altar stands a bronze
tripod with a blazing offering, below which a silver
bucket, or *situla*, contains the sacrifice of wine. Hanging on
the pilaster to the left is a wall-painting of Bacchus and
his followers, identical to that in *An Egyptian Juggler*, beneath
which is a metal plaque representing a curious votive
offering in the hope of a cure for a diseased leg. To the far
left of the picture there is a marble statue of a drunken
satyr and, behind, a large ornamental marble *volute-krater*
embellished with scenes of bacchic revelry. On the
far right a group of silver wine vessels includes an *askos*
(pouring vessel) of exaggerated size, near which lies
a *thyrsus*, the pine cone-topped ivy-rod carried by devotees of
Bacchus. The procession is led by a priestess crowned
with vine leaves and grapes, behind whom is a troupe of
musicians – females with double-pipes or *auloi*, and
behind them two dancers with *tympana*. The men carry
amphorae of wine, followed by a *liknon*, or winnowing
basket, which customarily contained grapes and the mystic
phallus of the bacchic rites. As with many of Alma-Tadema's
procession scenes, there is little impression of movement,
but in the background there are hints of the more frenzied
celebrations to come.

—— PLATE 5 ——

JOSEPH, OVERSEER OF PHAROAH'S GRANARIES

Opus CXXIV, 1874
Oil on panel, 13 × 17 in/33 × 43.2 cm
Private collection

By 1874 Alma-Tadema had become a naturalized British
citizen, had settled in the first of his London palaces, and was
increasingly acknowledged as one of Britain's leading
artists. It was to be one of his most prolific years, in which he
produced no fewer than twenty-one paintings – an
output that was not even stalled by the disaster in October
that wrecked his house. Egyptian subjects featured
in Alma-Tadema's repertoire after his *The Sad Father* (1859),
but were steadily eclipsed as he concentrated increasingly
on Roman themes. Apart from several later representations
of Cleopatra, *Joseph, Overseer of Pharaoh's Granaries* was
one of the last of his paintings set in Egypt until he returned
to it with *The Finding of Moses* thirty years later. When
this work was exhibited at the Royal Academy in 1874, the
art critic of the *Athenaeum* described it thus: 'Joseph,
wearing one of those wonderful Egyptian wigs, sits in state,
giving orders, and taking note of the labours of the
servants; his costume is of white tissue, painted with
charming fidelity, richness and brilliancy. A secretary
squats on the floor reading from a scroll: a capital figure.'
The writer Gerard Manley Hopkins visited the Royal
Academy and wrote in his notebook that *Joseph* was
'. . . merely antiquarian, but excellent in that way'. It
clearly draws heavily on the innumerable sketches of
Egyptian motifs that Alma-Tadema had been
systematically collecting in his scrapbooks. By now, it may be
noted, he was adding the Opus number rather than
the date beside his signature – a practice that made his
exhibited paintings 'timeless' and, since every work
now bore a unique serial number, forgery became virtually
impossible.

——— PLATE 6 ———

Ninety-four Degrees in the Shade

Opus CLXIV, 1876
Oil on canvas, 14 × 8½ in/35.6 × 21.6 cm
Fitzwilliam Museum, Cambridge

Alma-Tadema had visited London in 1869 to be operated on
by Sir Henry Thompson (a specialist in urological
complaints who also operated on King Leopold I of Belgium
and Napoleon III). Thompson had aspirations as an
artist, and Alma-Tadema became his teacher and a close
friend. When they holidayed together on the doctor's
houseboat in 1875, Alma-Tadema painted portraits of
Sir Henry and his son, Herbert (later an eminent
Egyptologist), on the door panels. Only very occasionally did
he depart from his lifelong concern with the ancient
world, his portraits of contemporary figures being among his
only works in which his subjects appear in modern
dress. He painted *Ninety-four Degrees in the Shade* after harvest
on the edge of a cornfield near Godstone, Surrey.
A small and untypically Impressionistic picture (painted
within two years of the Impressionists' first Paris
exhibition), it depicts seventeen-year-old Herbert Thompson
as a young lepidoptcrist in Victorian summcr kit of
sola topi-style hat and linen suit, intently consulting a
reference book, his butterfly net lying beside him on
the ground. As with many of his more characteristic
paintings, Alma-Tadema has adopted an unconventional
viewpoint, looking down on the prostrate figure.

—— PLATE 7 ——

FLORA: SPRING IN THE GARDENS
OF THE VILLA BORGHESE

Opus CLXXXVII, 1877
Watercolour, 11 ¾ × 8 in/29.9 × 20.3 cm
Private collection

In 1877 Alma-Tadema painted a series of paintings, one on
each of the four seasons, taking as his setting the gardens
of the Villa Borghese, Rome. As well as demonstrating his
considerable skill in the alternative medium of watercolour,
Flora exemplifies two of his working methods that are
increasingly encountered. Firstly, he often executed several
versions of the same work, usually with variant details,
in different sizes or media. This was in fact the fourth of four
versions of the subject; the other three were all in oils,
the first of them destroyed during the Second World War,
the second now in the Madison Art Center, Wisconsin,
and the third, painted on a door panel for Hendrik Willem
Mesdag, and to be seen today in the Mesdag Museum
in The Hague. Secondly, one small element of a painting was
often taken, adapted and worked up into another picture
in its own right – in this instance, the scene in the right
background where a woman sits upon a marble bench
or *exedra*, while a man lies alongside, his head cupped in one
hand. Under the title, *Pleading*, the composition had
already appeared (reversed, left to right) the previous year,
and was to reappear in such works as, in 1877, *The
Question* and, in 1883, *Xanthe and Phaon* (the 'question' was
whether Xanthe should marry Phaon). Alma-Tadema's
mentor, the Egyptologist Georg Ebers, was inspired to write
a novel based on the theme of these paintings.

—— PLATE 8 ——

A HEARTY WELCOME

Opus CXC, 1878
Oil on canvas, 12 × 36½ in/30.5 × 92.7 cm
Ashmolean Museum, Oxford

Alma-Tadema aspired to feature on canvas the Pompeii that
Bulwer-Lytton had described in his 1834 novel, *The Last
Days of Pompeii*, including the minutiae of daily life. Also
known by the alternative title, *A Roman Garden*, *A Hearty
Welcome* was painted for his doctor, pupil and friend, Sir
Henry Thompson. On the surface it is a scene in a
Pompeian courtyard, showing a *larrarium*, or household
shrine, a sundial on the wall and a well-tended garden
filled with poppies – and uncharacteristically anachronistic
sunflowers, since they were unknown in Europe until
brought from the Americas. The painting is in fact a more
personal memento of the friendship between the
Alma-Tadema and Thompson families, for the woman in the
garden is Laura Alma-Tadema and the two girls her
stepdaughters, Laurence and Anna, while descending the
staircase is the painter himself. He had previously
depicted himself with his first wife and their daughters as a
Roman family, and increasingly featured them as well
as the family's friends alongside professional models.

—— PLATE 9 ——

STRIGILS AND SPONGES

Opus CXCVII, 1879
Watercolour, 12½ × 5½ in/31.8 × 14 cm
The British Museum, London

Alma-Tadema again turned to his wife as a convenient model
for this more risqué subject (she is the woman in the
foreground). It shows a cold water plunge-bath in a Roman
bath-house with an elaborate fountain depicting Eros
encircled by a dolphin, based on an original in the National
Archaeological Museum, Naples. As well as their sponges,
the women use strigils, or body scrapers, but the procedure
was perhaps not as implied by this subject. Typically,
Roman athletes would protect their bodies from the rays of
the sun by applying a barrier consisting of a layer of
oil and dust. After exercising, this was scraped off with a
strigil and the body rinsed with water. The strigil was
thus more probably a masculine object used prior to bathing,
and not the feminine bath accessory as Alma-Tadema
often featured it in this and works such as *In the Tepidarium*,
A Fountain and other bathing scenes. This watercolour,
now in the British Museum, is mounted together with his
engraver Paul Adolphe Rajon's preparatory etching
heavily annotated by Alma-Tadema, demonstrating both
what a meticulous and an exasperatingly demanding
craftsman he could be.

—— PLATE 10 ——

SAPPHO AND ALCAEUS

Opus CCXXIII, 1881
Oil on canvas, 26 × 48 in/66 × 122 cm
The Walters Art Gallery, Baltimore

Regarded in his day as one of Alma-Tadema's most successful
paintings, *Sappho and Alcaeus* depicts two famous Greek
lyric poets. Sappho lived in Mytilene on the island of Lesbos
in the 6th century BC with a company of girls dedicated
to the cult of Aphrodite and the Muses. Her love for them
gave rise to the word 'lesbian', which Alma-Tadema
hints at with the gentle show of affection of the girl beside
Sappho, who sits at a lectern of the painter's invention.
Alcaeus, an aristocratic poet, also came from Lesbos and was
a friend of Sappho who is here shown entranced by his
recital. Alcaeus sits opposite her in a Greek *klismos* chair. He
accompanies his song on a stringed instrument known
as a *kithara* painted with a scene representing Apollo, God of
Music, and his sister, Artemis, both of whose names are
inscribed. The setting is a corner of an *odeion*, a building used
for musical performances, sited by the sea, the design
of which appears to be based on a Greek vase-painting much
reproduced at the time Alma-Tadema was working,
but which is now discredited as a fabrication.

———— PLATE 11 ————

In the Tepidarium

Opus CCXXIX, 1881
Oil on panel, 9½ × 13 in/24.1 × 33 cm
The Lady Lever Art Gallery, Port Sunlight

This relatively small painting shows a woman lying
on a bearskin in a tepidarium, a chamber
between the hot and cold rooms in a Roman bath,
exemplifying Alma-Tadema's skill in depicting,
almost in miniature, textures such as fur, feathers
and flesh. Hailed as his most erotic *tour de
force*, the sultry model's pose, her parted lips, the
phallic strigil and the teasing attitude of the
ostrich-feather fan are far more 'provocative' (as the
Bishop of Carlisle commented about *A Sculptor's
Model*) than, for example, Manet's *Olympia* or
Déjeuner sur l'Herbe. The latter were attacked,
however, less because they depicted nudes than
because they were avowedly contemporary.
The very title of *In the Tepidarium*, the presence of an
oleander in a Roman bronze container, the
strigil itself and the marble, on the other hand, all
remind us that this was a classical scene which
was thus beyond reproach.

———— PLATE 12 ————

THE PARTING KISS

Opus CCXL, 1882
Oil on panel, 44½ × 29 in/113 × 73.7 cm
Private collection

According to his biographer Percy Cross Standing, *The Parting Kiss* was one of Alma-Tadema's favourite paintings. It features a woman bidding her daughter farewell as she leaves for the amphitheatre that we see in background. The Roman lady beneath the umbrella in the carriage at the door was modelled by Laura Alma-Tadema. In the street are others making their way to the same venue, one accompanied by a slave bearing cushions, a reminder by the artist that Romans, like his fellow-Victorians, loved their comfort. The word *salve*, welcome, is inscribed at the entrance – as it was at the door of Alma-Tadema's own house in St John's Wood. He revelled in packing his paintings with artefacts, but was aware of critics of his technique. 'The people of today,' he commented, 'will tell you that all this minute detail is not art! But it gives so much pleasure to paint him [sic] that I cannot help think it will give at least someone pleasure to look at him too.' Somewhat confusingly, when this painting was restored, it acquired the incorrect Opus number, 'CCXLI'. Several other Alma-Tadema paintings have suffered similar depredations at the hands of clumsy restorers.

———— PLATE 13 ————

ANTONY AND CLEOPATRA

Opus CCXLVI, 1883
Oil on panel, 25¼ × 36¼ in/65.4 × 92.1 cm
Margaret Brown Collection

In 1875 and 1877 Alma-Tadema had painted profiles
of Cleopatra, Queen of Egypt, modelled on a
bust of her mother, Berenice. From these preparatory
portraits, he developed his idealized complete
figure, depicting her as she awaits the arrival of
Mark Antony on her royal barge. She is holding
the insignia of her rank, the flail and crook, and sits
serenely on a throne flanked by figures of
baboons. Alma-Tadema follows Shakespeare, where
the vessel is vividly described by Domitius
Enobarbus, who refers to her cloth-of-gold pavilion,
the flautists and the 'strange invisible perfume' –
which Alma-Tadema explains by showing slaves
wafting incense through the canopy. Beyond, a
fleet of triremes looms into view as Antony prepares
expectantly to come aboard.

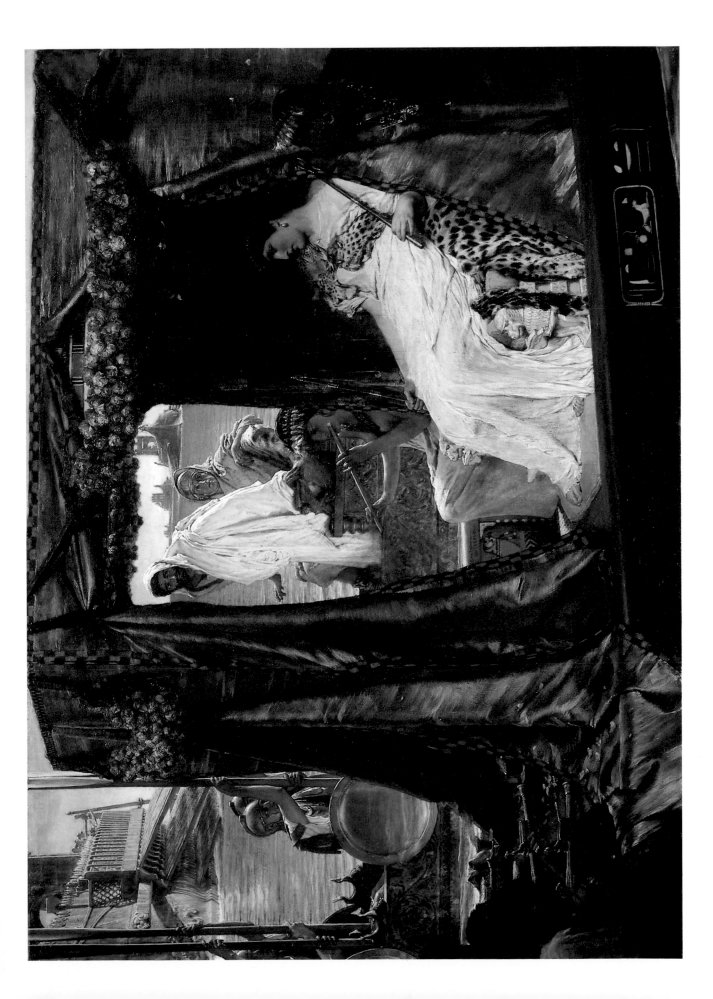

———— PLATE 14 ————

WELCOME FOOTSTEPS

Opus CCLVII, 1883
Oil on canvas, 16½ × 21½ in/41.9 × 54.6 cm
Private collection

Specific historical events and named characters became
increasingly rare in Alma-Tadema's work as timeless
anecdotal subjects took precedence. The theme of a
rendezvous of two lovers was perhaps his most dominant
single subject from the 1880s onwards. From this
period, women sit in eager expectation of the arrival of a
suitor in paintings with titles such as *Watching and
Waiting* or *Who Is It?* Perhaps, as here, his appearance is
imminent, or he has just arrived, as in *A Silent Greeting*,
in which a man finds his lover has fallen asleep while waiting
for him; in one picture we witness a lie in the telling
as an unwanted suitor is informed, '*My Sister is Not at Home*'.
Along with this development, descriptive titles gave way
to poetic quotations and memorable clichés – *A Message of Love*,
Wandering Thoughts, *Love's Jewelled Fetter*, *Fortune's Favourite*.
From this period too in many paintings the archaeological
detail is incidental and sufficient only to remind us that
we are in ancient Rome and not attending a fancy-dress party
in modern London. In *Welcome Footsteps* a statue of a
marble faun is seen from behind and there is the tiger-skin
that features in several paintings: when Alma-Tadema
was pointing it out to a visitor in his *An Audience at Agrippa's*,
he asked, 'Can't you see him wag his tail?'

———— PLATE 15 ————

EXPECTATIONS

Opus CCLXVI, 1885
Oil on panel, 8¾ × 17¾ in/22.2 × 45.1 cm
Private collection

A critic wrote of the typical Alma-Tadema painting as
consisting of 'a sapphire sea, white-crested waves, a blue sky,
sweet-smelling flowers', to which he might have added
'and a girl on a marble bench dreaming of her lover'. In a
number of pictures painted in his last quarter-century,
these were the elements to which he was repeatedly to
return. Such works were customarily painted in the
Bay of Naples, where he often used the cliff-top setting to
dispose of the middle-ground, thereby placing the
white marble in sharp contrast against the blue of the sky and
sea behind. The stark lines of the *exedra* would often
be broken by the addition of a blossom-laden tree, as here
with a Judas-tree. Beside it the girl awaits the arrival
of her lover, for whose ship she scans the sun-drenched sea.
Together with *The Women of Amphissa*, *Expectations* won
Alma-Tadema the Gold Medal at the Paris Exposition
Universelle of 1889.

—— PLATE 16 ——

A Reading from Homer

Opus CCLXVII, 1885
Oil on canvas, 36 × 72⅜ in/91.4 × 183.8 cm
Philadelphia Museum of Art: George W. Elkins Collection

After Alma-Tadema's move to his new studio with its famed
aluminium ceiling, there was a notable enhancement
in the brightness of his paintings, of which this is an early
example. Eight months' research were said to have
been devoted to this and an abandoned companion painting,
Plato, with two months' work in its painting. The theme
and composition are redolent of *Sappho and Alcaeus*, and the
kithara is present in both works. Here we see an intimate
gathering for a recital from the epics of the poet Homer,
whose name is inscribed in Greek behind. A *rhapsode*
(professional reciter) sits before an enraptured audience.
Homer was held in great esteem by the Victorians, and
this could equally have been a soirée in a Victorian drawing
room – where the rugs would at least have been more
comfortable than the cold marble floor. According to his
biographer Helen Zimmern, *A Reading from Homer*
contained the best flesh painting he had ever done.

—— PLATE 17 ——

THE WOMEN OF AMPHISSA

Opus CCLXXVIII, 1887
Oil on canvas, 48 × 72 in/121.9 × 182.9 cm
The Sterling and Francine Clark Museum, Williamstown

One of Alma-Tadema's largest and most striking paintings, it is also among the last in which he portrayed a dated historical event. Amphissa in western Locris commanded the route leading west from Mount Parnassus. It was the location of a festival held in honour of Dionysos, but in the year 350 BC, when the territory was overrun by soldiers from Phocis, it was feared that while exhausted by their religious frenzy the *mænades* or bacchantes would be vulnerable to being ravished by the soldiers. Accordingly, when they came to Amphissa after their rites, the women of the town surrounded them throughout the night in order to protect them, and the following morning, when they awoke, fed them and escorted them to safety.
Alma-Tadema portrays the Amphissan market-place at dawn, a dozen dazed bacchantes sprawled on the ground, gradually awakening. An assortment of south Italian and Athenian painted verses are combined anachronistically with a large silver *krater* from the Roman Hildesheim treasure – Alma-Tadema is known to have owned a replica, which features in several works. In the centre, beneath the roundel, perhaps intended as the leader of the women of Amphissa, is Laura Alma-Tadema.

—— PLATE 18 ——

THE ROSES OF HELIOGABALUS

Opus CCLXXXIII, 1888
Oil on canvas, 52 × 84⅛ in/132.1 × 213.7 cm
Private collection

The *Magazine of Art* wrote of this painting: 'No incident could
be more happy for the painter to exercise his skill
upon, rich and delicate colouring combining marvellously
with all the possibilities of marble painting and
archaeological accessory.' The circumstances of the incident
depicted were, however, less than happy. Marcus
Aurelius Antonius, better known by his adopted name,
Heliogabalus or Elagabalus, ruled Rome briefly from
AD 218 to 222. He attempted unsuccessfully to introduce
the cult of the oriental sun-god of Emesa to Rome, and
was notorious for his oriental-style court and its extravagant
banquets at which the menu might include the brains
of 600 ostriches, powdered glass or camel dung, such was the
Emperor's perverted sense of humour. By the time he was
eighteen, he was murdered by the Praetorian guard, his body
dragged through the streets and hurled into the Tiber.
Among his celebrated practical jokes was the releasing of a
canopy over his guests, suffocating them beneath tons
of rose petals, which Alma-Tadema depicts with the
debauched emperor and his world-weary companions
gazing at the scene in detached amusement. In the background
stands a statue (now in the Vatican) of Dionysos with
a panther at his feet and a young faun companion, a subtle
token of the 'forbidden love' that was numbered among
the emperor's excesses. In order to paint the roses precisely
during the winter, he had them sent from the French
Riviera, and for months afterwards Alma-Tadema's studio
floor was littered with rose petals.

—— PLATE 19 ——

The Favourite Poet

Opus CCXC, 1888
Oil on panel, 14½ × 19½ in/36.8 × 49.5 cm
The Lady Lever Art Gallery, Port Sunlight

One girl reads verses from a scroll while another listens
dreamily. Behind, roundels depicting the muses, including
Thalia, Urania and Polyhymnia, reiterate the literary
context, but it is inevitably incidental to the true purpose of
the work, which is to portray two beautiful women
revelling in the luxury of their leisured lifestyle. The
composition was so successful that it was repeated
with modifications in such works as *Comparisons*. The models'
poses are similar to those of his contemporary, Albert
Moore, who also depicted languid women in Greek and
Roman settings, in or out of costume – though his aims
were so much more aesthetic than antiquarian that he was
untroubled by showing an ancient Roman playing a
violin. The fundamentally Hellenic costumes worn by
Alma-Tadema's models were designed with such
attention to detail that some were copied and sold by such
firms as Liberty's and others used as stage costumes
by famous actresses of the day, including Ellen Terry.

—— PLATE 20 ——

A Dedication to Bacchus

Opus CCXCIII, 1889
Oil on canvas, 30½ × 69¾ in/77.5 × 177.2 cm
Hamburger Kunsthalle

This is the first and larger of two versions of this painting. Its
wealth of archaeological detail was so much discussed
that it became the subject of a bestselling pamphlet by
Frederick Stephens. The work focuses on a child
who, accompanied by her mother and family, is about to be
dedicated to Bacchus, the god of wine. A Dionysiac
procession bearing wine approaches an altar, behind which is
the statue known as the 'Younger Furietti Centaur',
now in the Capitoline Museum, Rome. Behind the altar there
is a relief adapted from the *centauromachy* frieze
(depicting the legendary battle between Lapiths and centaurs)
which comes from the Temple of Apollo at Bassae and is
now in the British Museum. On the far left stands a priestess
with the silver *krater* from the Hildesheim Treasure,
previously seen in such pictures as *The Women of Amphissa*.

——— PLATE 21 ———

THE FRIGIDARIUM

Opus CCCII, 1890
Oil on panel, 17¾ × 23½ in/45.1 × 59.7 cm
Private collection

'The composition is exceptionally complex, difficult
and successful,' wrote the art critic of the
Athenaeum, who was permitted to see the painting
while work was in progress. When it was
shown at the Royal Academy several months later,
Alma-Tadema had altered it yet again. Like
his other scenes of Roman baths, such as *An
Apodyterium*, which shows a changing room, it
provided a respectably academic excuse, replete
with such archaeological reconstructions as
the niches in the wall for clothes and valuables, for a
voyeuristic sortie into a world normally barred
to Victorian men. *The Frigidarium* was painted as a
commission for Sir Max Waechter, High
Sheriff of Surrey, as a companion to *A Kiss*.

—— PLATE 22 ——

PROMISE OF SPRING

Opus CCCIII, 1890
Oil on panel, 15 × 8⅞ in/38 × 22.5 cm
Bequest of Frances M. Baker
Courtesy, Museum of Fine Arts, Boston

This small picture features Alma-Tadema's stock-in-trade of
a courting couple, blossom and marble. Like many of
his later paintings its title, *Promise of Spring*, is deliberately
enigmatic – who is promising what to whom, or is it
the hopefulness of the new season and of the lovers' vows to
each other that are suggested? Such paintings thereby
became conversation-pieces, inviting the viewer to speculate
on its meaning and that of the subject. Also in common
with much of his late work, it has some of the qualities of a
snapshot, as if the woman is looking directly into the
camera's lens. It is known that Alma-Tadema was a devotee
of photography which he used to full effect in compiling
his voluminous reference albums. The Kodak camera had
been invented just two years earlier, and Alma-Tadema,
fascinated by mechanical gadgets, was one of George
Eastman's earliest customers.

—— PLATE 23 ——

AN EARTHLY PARADISE

Opus CCCVII, 1891
Oil on canvas, 34 × 65 in/86.4 × 165.1 cm
Private collection

At the time of its first showing at the Royal Academy, the
Athenaeum described *An Earthly Paradise* as 'A subtle and
refined exercise in blue and its allies . . . tints which,
severally, are most tender and delicate, and, as a
whole, combined charmingly in every respect.' Inspired by a
quotation from Algernon Swinburne, 'All the Heaven
of Heavens in one little child', the sentimentality of the
mother-and-child theme appealed to Victorian taste
and featured frequently in Alma-Tadema's work, both in
superficially 'Roman' subjects such as this and in more
conventional portraits. The Mexican onyx window seen in
the right background was one of the exotic details to
be found in Alma-Tadema's studio.

———— PLATE 24 ————

A Kiss

Opus CCCXII, 1891
Oil on panel, 18 × 24¾ in/45.7 × 62.9 cm
Private collection

Commissioned as a companion to *An Apodyterium*, *A Kiss* was
painted beside the Starnberger See near Munich
where Tadema visited Georg Ebers. We are spectators on a
Roman terrace overlooking a lake in which several
women are bathing, with a broad panoramic vista behind. A
woman carrying a towel and a triple hook from which
toilet articles were suspended ascends the stairs with a child,
who is kissed by a girl. Incidental antiquarian interest
is provided by the tripod and bas-relief and lettering so
distorted by the perspective as to be illegible. This
skilful combination of sentiment and archaeology, with a hint
of the risqué provided by the solitary nude bather,
was shown at the Royal Academy in 1891 and was one of the
213 works shown at the Alma-Tadema Memorial
Exhibition at the Royal Academy the year after his death.

——— PLATE 25 ———

COMPARISONS

Opus CCCXVI, 1892
Oil on canvas, 18 × 24 in/45.7 × 61 cm
Cincinnati Art Museum
Gift of Emile L. Heine in memory of Mr and Mrs John Hauck

In *Comparisons* Alma-Tadema revisits the composition
of his popular painting, *The Favourite Poet*, which
similarly features two elegant women in rich
costume, one of whom is reading. In this
instance her book is a codex that is bound in a
recognisable cover, the late 4th century AD
Roman ivory Symmachi leaf of the Nicomachi and
Symmachi Diptych, which Alma-Tadema would
have seen in the Victoria & Albert Museum
collection. His studio sofa is once again in
evidence, its delicate moulding contrasting with the
impressive solidity of the table's griffin
supports. They are reminders of the advice given by
Alma-Tadema's teacher, Baron Leys, who urged
his pupil to paint convincingly, demanding the sort
of table that "everyone knocks his knees to
pieces on!"

—— PLATE 26 ——

Unconscious Rivals

Opus CCCXXI, 1893
Oil on canvas, 18 × 25 in/45.7 × 63.5 cm
City of Bristol Museum and Art Gallery

Two Roman women pose beneath an impressive atrium,
apparently unaware, as the title suggests, that they
represent two points in a lover's triangle. The putto on the
pillar playing with a tragic mask is taken from one in
the Capitoline Museum, Rome. On the right, there is the
lower part of a seated figure of Dionysos, while
decorative relief of erotes and swags ornamented with
dramatic masks perhaps symbolize both the drama
and pleasures of courtship. The models indicate the two
types of women most frequently encountered in
Alma-Tadema's paintings – the dark Mediterranean,
appropriately derived from the Greek and Italian models
who flocked to London in the late nineteenth century, and
the red-haired *femme fatale* much favoured by the
Pre-Raphaelites and their followers. Alma-Tadema's models
were seldom beautiful according to classical ideals,
but their 'girl-next-door' quality further emphasized that he
was presenting scenes of everyday life, his Romans
indistinguishable from Victorians.

——— PLATE 27 ———

GOD SPEED!

Opus CCCXXII, 1893
Oil on panel, 10 × 5 in/25.4 × 12.7 cm
Reproduced by Gracious Permission of Her Majesty the Queen

In paintings such as *A Coign of Vantage*, *The Coliseum*, *At Aphrodite's Cradle* and this work, Alma-Tadema adopted an unusual perspective, looking down upon a group of people who are in turn looking down on others – in this instance some departing traveller. We do not actually see who this is, but are led to assume by the woman's enthusiastic gesture as she scatters flowers that he is her beloved. The triumphal arch is based on that at Benevento, to the north-east of Naples, erected in AD 114 in honour of the Emperor Trajan. *God Speed!* was one of several paintings that were acquired by the Prince of Wales, later King Edward VII, who was a frequent visitor to Alma-Tadema's house.

——— PLATE 28 ———

SPRING

Opus CCCXXVI, 1894
Oil on canvas, 70½ × 31½ in/179.1 × 80 cm
The J. Paul Getty Museum, Malibu

The procession is of servants of the Temple of Flora who are
celebrating the Roman festival of Cerealia. A verse
from Algernon Swinburne's poem, *Dedication*, appeared on
the original frame:

In a land of clear colours and stories,
In a region of shadowless hours,
Where earth has a garment of glories
And a murmur of musical flowers.

The setting is imaginary, bringing together architectural
details from a multiplicity of sources, including
wall-paintings from Pompeii in the roundels on the banner,
the *centauromachy* frieze from the Temple at Bassae
recycled from *A Dedication to Bacchus* on the building on the
left and a votive plaque beginning with the phrase,
Hunc Lucum Tibi Dedico – 'I dedicate this wood to you'.
Carried in the procession are two silver satyr herms,
each with an infant Dionysos on his shoulder and carrying a
liknon, or winnowing basket filled with fruit. One of
Alma-Tadema's most famous and popular works, it took him
four years to complete the extraordinary detail of its
impressive composition, during which time it was repeatedly
reworked in his quest to combine aesthetic perfection
and historical accuracy. The innumerable figures were
constantly erased or added, and the final tableau
features members of his family, friends and fellow artists,
such as the musicians Sir George and Lillian Henschel
and their daughter Helen who looks down from the balcony
on the right.

——— PLATE 29 ———

A Coign of Vantage

Opus CCCXXXIII, 1895
Oil on panel, 25⅕⁄₁₆ × 17½ in/64 × 44.5 cm
Private collection

A coign is literally a cornerstone, and the phrase 'a
coign of vantage' is a quotation from Shakespeare's
Macbeth. Alma-Tadema's unusual use of vertiginous
perspective had already featured in such works
as *God Speed!* and was later employed to great effect
in *The Coliseum* and *At Aphrodite's Cradle*, but
A Coign of Vantage was perhaps his most successful
excursion into this technically challenging
composition. Three elegantly draped women watch
the Roman fleet's arrival in a remarkable work
that combines a dizzying viewpoint and the contrast
of the sumptuous blue of the Mediterranean
and dazzling white marble (which in part has
regrettably suffered from heavy-handed restoration).

—— PLATE 30 ——

A Difference of Opinion

Opus CCCXXXIX, 1896
Oil on panel, 15 × 9 in/38.1 × 22.9 cm
Private collection

In this almost shimmeringly bright painting, Alma-Tadema
returns to a favourite theme of two lovers posed
beside a fountain or laver, like an oasis in the heat, where
they air their feelings – in this instance conflictingly,
or so the title tells us. The archaeological elements include,
on the laver, a bronze figure of a boy with a goose,
based on one found in Pompeii, and in the background a
relief showing a satyr with Pan pipes at a rustic shrine
·topped by a herm, with Alma-Tadema's signature
incorporated in the masonry and a sundial above. His
contrasting types of model, the swarthy Mediterranean male
and winsome 'English rose' are again in evidence.

—— PLATE 31 ——

The Baths of Caracalla

Opus CCCLVI, 1899
Oil on canvas, 60 × 37½ in/152.4 × 95.3 cm
Private collection

For his most spectacular Roman baths painting, Alma-Tadema
chose the Baths of Caracalla, their ruins famed as the
location where Shelley wrote *Prometheus Unbound*. Dedicated
in AD 212, they were of gigantic dimensions with three
bathing halls capable of accommodating 1,600 bathers. He
studied reports of the latest archaeological excavations,
embellishing the scene with a marble ship in the centre of
the baths, which he probably based on a Renaissance
copy of a model found in Rome. The result, according to the
Art Journal, was that 'Mr Alma-Tadema has once more
built up a fascinating picture of Roman life, wonderful in its
classical faithfulness and truth to archaeological detail.
He has restored on canvas the famous bath of Caracalla.' The
Emperor Caracalla himself enters in the background
in a vignette that was destined to become the subject of
another painting, *Caracalla*. First shown at the Royal
Academy in 1899, the year of Alma-Tadema's knighthood,
The Baths of Caracalla was bought by an American
collector, one of many who ensured that his work is as well
represented in the United States as in Europe.

—— PLATE 32 ——

VAIN COURTSHIP

Opus CCCLXII, 1900
Oil on canvas, 30½ × 16¼ in/77.5 × 41.3 cm
Private collection

By this stage in Alma-Tadema's career, the
archaeological basis of his paintings was often
relegated as the anecdotal or sentimental elements
took precedence (though, as some of his last
paintings were to prove, he retained his mastery of
the genre to the end). *Vain Courtship* was clearly
painted in his studio, with their walls of 'sea-green
marble', a silver vase of hollyhocks and his
much-painted studio sofa appearing in duplicate,
only the couple's costumes indicating that we are
not witnessing a tryst during one of the artist's
famous 'At Homes'.

—— PLATE 33 ——

Under the Roof of Blue Ionian Weather

Opus CCCLXIII, 1901
Oil on panel, 21¼ × 47½ in/55.3 × 120.7 cm
Private collection

One of Alma-Tadema's finest paintings of sunny indolence,
its title appears to derive from a line in a letter from
Shelley to Maria Gisborne, written in 1820: 'We watched the
ocean and sky together, under the roof of blue Italian
weather.' When the picture was exhibited at the Royal
Academy in 1901, the *Art Journal* noted: 'Under the
Roof of Blue Ionian Weather is concerned with lightly
draped, garlanded figures grouped about a semi-circular
tiered lounge, each vein of whose white marble, whether in
scintillating light or reposeful shadow, is scrupulously
rendered.' The painting took over two years, on and off, to
complete, but certain elements were based on other
works: the woman in the foreground and the man beside her,
for example, had appeared previously in a very similar
composition in the 1899 watercolour, *Attracted*, which is in
the Royal Collection.

—— PLATE 34 ——

SILVER FAVOURITES

Opus CCCLXXIII, 1903
Oil on panel, 27¼ × 16⅝ in/69.2 × 42.2 cm
Manchester City Art Galleries

The 'silver favourites' of the title are the carp in the pond
that one of the girls is feeding, using her tympanum as
a makeshift receptacle. To emphasize the piscatorial
reference, the frame bears the lines from Wordsworth:

Where, sensitive of every ray,
That smites this tiny sea,
Your scaly panoplies repay
The loan with usury.

The sky, brightening toward the horizon, the sea and marble
bench are represented as three serried and contrasting
bands that create an illusion of breadth that is remarkable in
so vertical a painting. The composition evidently posed
difficult problems which Alma-Tadema was still struggling to
resolve up to the date by which he had promised the
painting to its purchaser. He was forced to write to apologize
for having been '. . .unable to master all the difficulties
in the picture. . . I would have been much more ashamed of
myself if I would have let the picture go without being
thoroughly satisfied. Give me one more day for by tomorrow
night I trust your messenger will not come in vain.'

—— PLATE 35 ——

The Finding of Moses

Opus CCCLXXVII, 1904
Oil on canvas, 54⅛ × 84 in/137.5 × 213.4 cm
Private collection

Commissioned in 1902 by the engineer Sir John Aird (who
paid £5,250 for the painting), it commemorates Aird's
work on the Nile, where his company built the Aswan Dam –
the opening of which Alma-Tadema attended in the
company of Winston Churchill and other dignitaries. The
task of executing this for him unusually large painting
preoccupied him for so long that Lady Laura Alma-Tadema
joked that Moses was now 'two years old, and need no
longer be carried': It was the only painting he completed in
1904. Despite its title, Alma-Tadema has chosen to
show the scene immediately after the finding of Moses as he
is carried in his basket to Pharaoh's palace. On the
far bank there is a throng of slaves with the Pyramids behind.
The identical tables and vases are based on objects in
the British Museum. As well as replicas of such items,
Alma-Tadema's reference scrapbooks of prints,
photographs and sketches included numerous Egyptian
motifs such as the hieroglyphs seen here representing,
on the statue base on the left, 'Beloved of Ra, King of Upper
and Lower Egypt' and, on the seat, 'Life' and 'Dominion'.

——— PLATE 36 ———

A WORLD OF THEIR OWN

Opus CCCLXXVIII, 1905
Oil on panel, 5⅛ × 19¾ in/13 × 50.2 cm
Bequest of Mr and Mrs Charles Phelps Taft; the Taft Museum,
Cincinnati, Ohio

Alma-Tadema's only painting of 1905 was this small
but delicate study on the eternal subject of
lovers engrossed with each other as they lie on a
flowery clifftop. It is an unusually wide-angle
composition in which the ivory-headed stick, the
cameo brooch and the couple's costumes are
the only clues that we are in the ancient world,
reiterating that their preoccupations were
essentially identical to those of the modern one, that
human nature is the one great constant.

—— PLATE 37 ——

Ask Me No More

Opus CCCLXXIX, 1906
Oil on canvas, 31½ × 45½ in/80 × 115.6 cm
Private collection

To Alma-Tadema's only painting of this year was appended a
quotation by Tennyson:

Ask me no more: thy fate and mine are seal'd;
I strove against the stream, and all in vain;
Let the great river take me to the main:
No more, dear love, for at a touch I yield.

The somewhat melodramatic gesture and title of this work
could open it to a charge of mawkish sentimentality,
but as with so many of Alma-Tadema's later works the
overriding response is one of admiration of his ability
to convey the viewer to a timeless sun-blessed land.

CARACALLA AND GETA

Opus CCCLXXXII, 1907
Oil on panel, 48½ × 60½ in/123.2 × 153.7 cm
Private collection

As if to demonstrate that, even though he was now over seventy years old, he had lost none of his technical mastery, Alma-Tadema embarked on one of the most complex paintings he had ever undertaken. His last painting of a specific historical event depicts the gala given in the Coliseum in AD 203 by Septimus Severus on the occasion of his bestowing the title of Antoninus Caesar on his son, Bassianus, better known as Caracalla, who stands behind the seated emperor, beside whom is his second wife, Julia Domna. She is seen surreptitiously passing letters to an attendant, presumably in connection with her aspiration to gain similar honours for her son Geta (who was later murdered by Caracalla), here shown standing between his sisters. Geta's toga is emblazoned with gladiatorial scenes that we partially see enacted below, where bear-baiters are goading the animals with red cloths and avoiding attack by pole-vaulting – a practice that Alma-Tadema based on an ivory carving he had seen. He has spared no labour in his attention to such archaeologically speculative details as the inclusion of drinking fountains and altars, while on the steps can be seen hirers of cushions, drink and cake vendors, amid the 2,500 spectators he calculated would be visible. The right-hand portion in which the attendant stands, modified to show the scene before the audience arrives, became the subject of his last finished painting, *Preparations in the Coliseum*.

——— PLATE 39 ———

A Favourite Custom

Opus CCCXCI, 1909
Oil on panel, 26 × 17¾ in/66 × 45.1 cm
The Tate Gallery, London

In a recapitulation of some of his earlier paintings,
Alma-Tadema returned to the theme of
Roman baths, here locating the viewer beside the
water, with the changing room behind – a
direct reversal of the view seen in *The Frigidarium*.
Architecturally, *A Favourite Custom* is based
on Pompeian originals, the frieze above the door
being derived from one discovered in a
Pompeian bath and identified in a photograph in
Alma-Tadema's reference albums. On the left
we again find the silver *krater* from the Hildesheim
Treasure. A related drawing entitled *Splashing*
dates from the same year.

———— PLATE 40 ————

The Voice of Spring

Opus CCCXCVII, 1910
Oil on panel, 19⅛ × 45¼ in/48.6 × 114.9 cm
Private collection

This was one of Alma-Tadema's last important
works, and his sole oil painting of the year, his only
other output consisting of pencil drawings and
a watercolour address from the Royal Academy to
King George V to commemorate his accession.
In it, groups of people enjoy the coming of spring in
a flower-strewn coastal meadow, some gathering
garlands of flowers, others listening to a poet with a
lyre, while the central figure sits pensively.
The 'Cinemascope' panorama of such paintings and
the precision of Alma-Tadema's reconstructions
of Roman buildings and scenes of daily life and
Imperial drama were destined to become important
sources of reference for the coming generation
of Hollywood epic film-makers.

PAINTINGS IN PUBLIC COLLECTIONS

AUSTRALIA

Adelaide
Art Gallery of South Australia

Melbourne
National Gallery of Victoria

Sydney
Art Gallery of New South Wales

AUSTRIA

Vienna
Kunsthistorisches Museum

BELGIUM

Antwerp
Koninklijk Museum voor
Schone Kunsten

CANADA

Montreal, Quebec
Museum of Fine Arts

Sackville, New Brunswick
Owens Art Gallery, Mount
Allison University

FRANCE

Paris
Centre Georges Pompidou

GERMANY

Hamburg
Hamburger Kunsthalle

GREAT BRITAIN

Aberdeen
Aberdeen Art Gallery

Barnard Castle
Bowes Museum

Bedford
Cecil Higgins Art Gallery

Birkenhead
Williamson Art Gallery

Birmingham
Birmingham City Art Gallery

Brighton
Brighton Art Gallery

Bristol
Bristol Art Gallery

Burnley
Towneley Hall Art Gallery

Cambridge
Fitzwilliam Museum

Cardiff
National Museum of Wales

Glasgow
Glasgow Art Gallery

Kilmarnock
Dick Institute

Liverpool
Walker Art Gallery

London
British Museum
Guildhall Art Gallery
Hammersmith & Fulham Libraries
Leighton House
National Portrait Gallery
Royal Academy
Royal Institute of British Architects
Royal Society of Painters in Water-Colours
Tate Gallery
Victoria & Albert Museum
William Morris Gallery

Manchester
Manchester City Art Gallery

Newcastle-upon-Tyne
Laing Art Gallery

Oxford
Ashmolean Museum

Port Sunlight
Lady Lever Art Gallery

Preston
Harris Museum & Art Gallery

INDIA

Hyderabad
The Salar Jung Museum

ITALY

Florence
Uffizi Gallery

Rome
R. Accademia Romana di San Luca

THE NETHERLANDS

Amsterdam
Amsterdams Historisch Museum
Rijksmuseum

Arnhem
Rijksmuseum voor Volkskunde 'Het
Nederlands Openluchtmuseum'

Dordrecht
Dordrechts Museum

Groningen
Groningen Museum voor Stad en Lande

The Hague
Rijksmuseum Hendrik Willem Mesdag

Leeuwarden
Fries Museum

Soestdijk
Soestdijk Palace

NEW ZEALAND

Auckland
Auckland City Art Gallery

POLAND

Warsaw
National Museum

SOUTH AFRICA

Johannesburg
Johannesburg Art Gallery

SOVIET UNION

Leningrad
Museum of Pavlosk Palace

Moscow
Museum of Fine Arts (Pushkin Museum)

SPAIN

Madrid
Prado Museum

UNITED STATES OF AMERICA

Akron, Ohio
Akron Art Institute

Baltimore, Maryland
Walters Art Gallery

Boston, Massachusetts
Boston Museum of Fine Arts
Fogg Art Museum

Cincinnati, Ohio
Cincinnati Art Museum
Taft Museum

Hanover, New Hampshire
Dartmouth College

Madison, Wisconsin
Madison Art Center

Malibu, California
J. Paul Getty Museum

Milwaukee, Wisconsin
Milwaukee Art Center

Mineapolis, Minnesota
Mineapolis Institute of Art

Muskegon, Michigan
Hackley Art Gallery

New Haven, Connecticut
Yale University Art Gallery

New Orleans, Louisiana
New Orleans Museum of Art

Philadelphia, Pennsylvania
Philadelphia Museum of Art

Poughkeepsie, New York
Vassar College

Provo, Utah
Brigham Young University

Washington, DC
Corcoran Gallery of Art

Williamstown, Massachusetts
Sterling & Francine Clarke Art Institute

Zanesville, Ohio
Zanesville Art Center

SIR EDWARD
BURNE-JONES

Edward Burne-Jones
1833–1898

Portrait of Edward Burne-Jones by his patron, George Howard, 9th Earl of Carlisle (c.1875).

The name of Burne-Jones is synonymous with the history and achievements of the Pre-Raphaelites, yet he was a relative latecomer to the movement and in many respects transcended its aspirations, becoming regarded as the leader of the Aesthetic Movement, a precursor of Symbolism, and one of the most pivotal figures in nineteenth-century art.

Edward Coley Burne Jones was born in Birmingham on 28 August 1833. The hyphenation of his name to Burne-Jones was an affectation he adopted in later life to avoid the obscurity of being 'one of the Joneses' (his contemporary, Lawrence Alma-Tadema, had done the same thing in order to appear at the head of alphabetical catalogues). His three names came from, respectively, his father, Edward Richard Jones, a Londoner who had settled in his wife's native city, where he had established a modest business as a gilder and framer with premises on Bennett's Hill, Birmingham; Coley from his mother, Elizabeth Coley; and Burne from the married name of his aunt Keturah Jones. A previous child, Edith, had died, and Mr and Mrs Jones had every hope of restoring their happiness through their new son, but this aspiration was dashed when, on 3 September, six days after Edward's birth, Elizabeth died. This tragic sense of loss was to characterize Edward's relationship with his father, as he later considered: 'There's one thing I owe to my father, that is his sense of pathos. Oh, what a sad little home was ours and how I used to be glad to get away from it.' Edward Jones Snr was thrifty but not commercially skilled. Every penny had to be counted, and it was in this gloomy environment, in a grimy industrial city, with little in the way of artistic stimulation, that Edward Burne-Jones grew up.

Following his mother's death, Edward was cared for by a succession of largely incompetent nannies until a Miss Sampson arrived, remaining in the household for the rest of her life. Although she appears to have been considerate of his needs – he was always frail, and she took him on country visits to build up his strength – she constrained his enquiring mind and imagination (a devout Christian, she told him, for instance, that it would be sinful to call a model city he had built 'Jerusalem'). Edward grew up deeply introspective: his answer when Miss Sampson asked what he was thinking about was invariably the dismissive 'camels'. One route out of this repressive atmosphere, as many only children have discovered, was to devote himself to reading, and among his favourite books in this largely un-bookish house was *Aesop's Fables*. A family friend called Caswell encouraged his drawing ability, and he was sensitive to such images as Birmingham offered. Among his earliest memories was the pageantry associated with the city's celebrations of the coronation of Queen Victoria, on 28 June 1838, when he was not quite five years old. 'Unmothered, with a sad papa, without sister or brother, always alone,' was how he looked back on his childhood, and yet, he recalled, 'I was never unhappy because I was always drawing.'

Edward's father wanted him to pursue a career in commerce, or perhaps become an engineer, and at the age of 11 he was enrolled in the old-established King Edward's School, Birmingham. The school's neo-Gothic buildings, since demolished, had been designed 10 years earlier by Sir Charles Barry and Augustus Pugin, the architects responsible for the Houses of Parliament. It was a notoriously strict establishment, where corporal punishment and bullying were rife (on one occasion Burne-Jones was even stabbed during morning prayers), yet he not only survived but became head boy in his final year and flourished academically, invariably placed top of his class. When, later in life, he came to compare his knowledge of subjects such as Latin and history with that of his closest friend, William Morris (who had attended Marlborough, one of Britain's greatest schools, and had private tutors), he was astonished to discover that he exceeded him on all counts. With his schoolfriend Cormell Price, later a noted educationalist, Burne-Jones studied books of heroic legends and, at the age of 15, created a small museum and embarked on the grandiose and romantically unrealistic project of writing a history of the world. Meanwhile, he began attending art classes at the local School of Design, initially as an adjunct to his historical researches. Immensely widely read, he developed an extensive general knowledge and, with his enthusiasm for researching even the most trivial detail, laid the foundation for the later studies that were of direct importance in his artistic development. He became fascinated by religion, and visits to Hereford cathedral enhanced his growing interest in formal Christianity, which was further influenced by the publicity given to the High Church Oxford Movement led by Cardinal Newman. He later acknowledged how

Burne-Jones's birthplace, Bennett's Hill, Birmingham, by Frederick Griggs.

The Annunciation, The Flower of God (1862). Burne-Jones's deep religious beliefs pervaded much of his early work.

Newman's teachings had affected him during his formative years: 'When I was 15 or 16 he taught me so much I do mind – things that will never be out of me. In an age of sofas and cushions he taught me to be indifferent to comfort, and in an age of materialism he taught me to venture all on the unseen.' Until circumstances altered his life for ever, Burne-Jones seemed destined for a career in the church.

In his teens Burne-Jones visited remote places in Wales, and became passionate about medieval abbeys. Staying with his aunt Keturah in London, he saw St Paul's Cathedral and other impressive buildings and made numerous trips to the British Museum where he drew the Assyrian bas-reliefs, describing them in detailed letters home. His love affair with the Museum lasted throughout his life, and one of his most personal productions, his *Flower Book*, was donated to it on his death. In 1852 he visited the home of his school-friend Harry Macdonald and there, among the large group of Harry's sisters, first met Georgiana Macdonald who was later to become his wife and biographer. She was to recall this first meeting and provide one of the earliest descriptions of the young Burne-Jones:

'His aspect made the deepest impression upon me. Rather tall and very thin, though not especially slender, straightly built and with wide shoulders. Extremely pale he was, with the paleness that belongs to fair-haired people, and looked delicate, but not ill. His hair was perfectly straight, and of a colourless kind. His eyes were light grey (if their colour could be defined in words).'

Burne-Jones went up to Exeter College, Oxford, in January 1853. His father had to move from their Bennett's Hill home and workshop to a small house in Birmingham's

Bristol Road in order to make the necessary economies to afford to send him to university. When, the previous June, he had sat examinations, Burne-Jones first saw, but did not speak to, William Morris. Now he met him and became an immediate and close friend – to the extent that the latter, being wealthier than Burne-Jones, offered to share his income with him (which, characteristically, Burne-Jones declined). The pair were regarded as oddities among a rather raucous group of men in their college, and, with a mutual dislike of Exeter, they spent most of their time with an ex-Birmingham clique in Pembroke College. There they developed the notion of founding a brotherhood (coincidentally, since they were as yet unaware of it, in some respects an emulation of the Pre-Raphaelite Brotherhood founded during the previous decade). It had the quest for the Holy Grail and the chivalric ideals of Sir Galahad as its guiding ideals in a campaign against what they regarded as the industrial horrors and moral decline of the age. Coupled with this crusading zeal, Burne-Jones developed his interest in medieval romance literature, with its particular appeal of a mysterious, unexplained, occult world. He and his compatriots were also enthusiastic devotees of Tennyson's works, for their insights into the medieval age, and such modern writers as Edgar Alan Poe. For recreation, Burne-Jones took up fencing, and his teacher, the eccentric Archibald Maclaren, encouraged his continuing interest in drawing.

During 1854 Burne-Jones and Morris ('Ned' and 'Topsy', as they called each other – Topsy from the character in *Uncle Tom's Cabin*, first published in England in 1852) continued their varied studies and got into habit of reading aloud to each other. It was from one such session, a transcript of one of John Ruskin's lectures, that they first learned about the Pre-Raphaelites and heard the name of Dante Gabriel Rossetti, one of the founders in 1848 of the Pre-Raphaelite Brotherhood. With John Everett Millais, William Holman Hunt and other like-minded young artists, Rossetti had sought to break away from the academic subjects then in vogue, with the aim of creating a pure art founded in social realism, inspired by the poetry of Keats and Tennyson and focusing on noble medieval themes. In

The Burne-Jones and Morris families at The Grange in 1876. Left to right: Edward's father, Margaret, Edward, Phillip and Georgiana Burne-Jones, with May, William, Jane and Jenny Morris.

reality, they had worked little as a group, and by 1854 no longer existed as a coherent movement. Nonetheless, Burne-Jones and Morris became aware of their work, the first example of which they saw was Millais' *Return of the Dove to the Ark* when it was exhibited in Oxford. Burne-Jones's response was to begin working in pen and ink in a minutely detailed and increasingly Pre-Raphaelite style, illustrating a fairy book by Maclaren. He visited London and at the Royal Academy saw Holman Hunt's controversial paintings *The Awakening Conscience* and *The Light of the World*, later commenting that, 'I saw that the Pre-Raphaelites had indeed come at a time when there was need for them, and resolved after my little ability to defend and claim a patient hearing for them.' Back at Oxford, with Morris, he continued in his studies of medieval manuscripts, now with a fresh impetus and goal.

In 1855 Burne-Jones toyed with the idea of joining the army to fight in the Crimean War, but was rejected on health grounds. He visited London and went to inspect the paintings of a collector who owned Ford Madox Brown's *The Last of England* and works by Millais. He also saw paintings by Holman Hunt in an Oxford collection and read Rossetti's *Blessed Damozel*, coming increasingly to idolize him as the undisputed leader of the Pre-Raphaelites. During the long vacation in 1855 Burne-Jones visited France with Morris and two other friends, taking in Beauvais Cathedral, Paris and Chartres, as well as dozens of medieval churches en route. Almost as a culmination of their years of studies and their recent exposure to a feast of medieval architecture, it was on the quay at Le Havre that the dramatic decision was taken that was to chart the rest of their lives: Morris would train as an architect and Burne-Jones would become a painter – an ambitious venture for one who had never previously painted.

Back in Birmingham, with Morris and others, Burne-Jones planned to start a magazine (ultimately published as the short-lived *Oxford and Cambridge Magazine*) in the spirit of the Pre-Raphaelite Brotherhood's *Germ* – and largely financed by Morris – to express their ideals through selections of poetry, essays and literary criticism. At this time a copy of the poet Robert Southey's 1817 reprint of the first ever printed edition of Malory's *Morte d'Arthur*, originally published in 1485 by William Caxton, was offered for sale in Birmingham. The book exerted perhaps the greatest single influence on Burne-Jones, even though he could not afford to buy it and had to stand in the bookshop reading it (Morris eventually purchased it and loaned the volume to him). Georgiana Burne-Jones later described the

Dante Gabriel Rossetti photographed by Lewis Carroll.

Originally conceived as an embroidery design, *Pilgrim at the Gate of Idleness* (1875–93) exemplifies Burne-Jones's lifelong fascination with medieval themes.

book's importance to Morris and her husband: 'I think that the book can never have been loved as it was by those two men. With Edward it became literally a part of himself. Its strength and beauty, its mystical religion and noble chivalry of action, the world of lost history and romance in the names of people and places – it was his own birthright upon which he entered.' This, above all, was the root of Burne-Jones's fascination with the mythical Arthurian world and its visionary quest for the unattainable.

Having made his crossroads decision, Burne-Jones began to have serious doubts about continuing at Oxford. His eagerness to start work immediately as painter was tempered by his awareness that, for financial reasons, it was utterly impractical – and he was hesitant about broaching the subject with his father. Morris gained his degree and, true to his vow to become an architect, entered the office of George Edmund Street, the architect of churches and the neo-Gothic Law Courts in London. Burne-Jones left Oxford at Christmas 1855 and, although he later returned, he no longer seriously intended pursuing his degree. January 1856 found him in London where he set himself the task of meeting his hero Rossetti, whose *The Maids of Elfen-Mere* illustrations he had recently seen and had praised in the *Oxford and Cambridge Magazine*. Learning that Rossetti lectured at the Working Men's College in Great Ormond Street, he went there and saw him but did not speak to him; by chance, though, he met Vernon Lushington, who invited him to meet Rossetti at his home soon afterwards. This first encounter led to a visit to Rossetti's studio by Blackfriars Bridge, and a friendship that was to last for more than a quarter of a century. Rossetti, though only five years older than Burne-Jones, immediately adopted him as his pupil, describing him as 'one of the nicest young fellows in Dreamland', a reference to the dreamlike state of mind of most of the idealistic contributors to the *Oxford and Cambridge Magazine*.

Burne-Jones saw progressively more of Rossetti as their master/pupil relationship developed into an informal apprenticeship, although Rossetti's methods were instinctive and far removed from conventional art tuition. Coming to art late in life (Burne-Jones was now aged 24), he

The Knight's Farewell (1858), an early pen and ink drawing once owned by William Morris.

combined this instruction with attendance at life classes given by the history painter James Matthews Leigh in Newman Street – and, as if to make up for lost time, also enrolled at the same time in two further art classes. The Royal Academy exhibition of that year included *The Scapegoat*, the masterwork of Holman Hunt (who Burne-Jones was to meet in Rossetti's studio), and Arthur Hughes's *April Love* – which Burne-Jones was commissioned to purchase on Morris's behalf. In 1856 Burne-Jones became engaged to the 16-year-old Georgiana Macdonald, whose family was now living in London. According to some accounts, he proposed to her as they stood in front of Hughes's sentimental painting.

Morris moved with Street from Oxford to London (soon afterwards leaving this employment altogether) and shared

Self-caricature of Burne-Jones's Red Lion Square home and studio (1856). He is examining a chair back decorated by Rossetti.

lodgings with Burne-Jones in Bloomsbury, moving in November 1856 to rooms in Red Lion Square. Burne-Jones' art was to pass through several distinct phases, and his characteristic works from this period were his medieval drawings, such as *The Knight's Farewell*. It was also in Red Lion Square that he undertook his first decorative work, a Chaucerean design painted on a wardrobe. Having met Rossetti, Hughes and Hunt, he now met the other artists in the Pre-Raphaelite circle, Millais and Ford Madox Brown, his widening group of influential acquaintances

extending to include John Ruskin and the poet Robert Browning.

The practical and pressing requirement for Burne-Jones to earn an income, however modest, could not be ignored, and Rossetti aided him in getting early commissions, including a cartoon for *The Good Shepherd*, a stained glass for James Powell & Son, which was used several years later in a church in Maidstone; this was followed by further stained-glass commissions, such as his *St Frideswide* for Christ Church, Oxford. These were to become Burne-Jones's principal source of income until he had established his reputation and livelihood as a painter, and continued to be his principal ancillary activity throughout his life. While it is significant that this early work should follow the Ruskin and Morris ideal of being available to the public, and not hidden in a private collection, he did not neglect the latter category of work, among which were his first paintings commissioned by a patron, Thomas E. Plint, a Leeds businessman, for two watercolours on the theme of *The Blessed Damozel*. Watercolour was to become one of Burne-Jones's most important mediums: it is known that the odour of turpentine made Burne-Jones nauseous, so throughout his working life he habitually turned to watercolour in preference to, but used almost as thickly as, oil, often mixed with other materials, such as gold, to create jewel-like surfaces.

When in 1857 Rossetti received the commission to decorate the debating hall of the Oxford Union with a series of murals, it was natural that Burne-Jones should be included in the group of associates he took with him: not that it

The Wedding of Sir Tristram, a stained-glass window designed by Burne-Jones for the music room at Harden Grange, Bingley (1862).

was a lucrative commission, since only the costs of the group's materials and accommodation were to be paid, but no fees. A group of scenes from the *Morte d'Arthur* was agreed, and Burne-Jones, Morris, Arthur Hughes and others worked on them for months in a spirit of camaraderie and enthusiasm coupled with chaos and incompetence. This was compounded by the fact that none of them had the least idea of the technique of mural painting. The work, for which Burne-Jones contributed scenes depicting Merlin, was never finished (at least by Rossetti, *et al*), but the trip was not without its lasting effects: it honed Burne-Jones's painting skills and reinforced the would-be muralists' friendship, while during their stint Morris first met Jane Burden, an ostler's daughter, who was recruited as a model – becoming one of the most-painted of all Pre-Raphaelite women. During their Oxford sojourn Burne-Jones grew the beard which he retained for the rest of his life, establishing a distinctive visage that scarcely altered during the ensuing forty years.

Soon after the Oxford enterprise – and this was a common reaction to any unusual or stressful circumstances – he fell ill and was cared for by the family of society hostess Sara Prinsep who he was to describe as 'the nearest thing to a mother I ever knew'. The celebrated painter George Frederick Watts had a studio in her house, and so Burne-Jones saw him at work and was encouraged by Watts to improve his drawing beyond the often slapdash style of Rossetti (apart from these two 'tutors' and occasional attendance at classes, Burne-Jones did not study art in any sense formally, and was thus one of the greatest of all self-taught artists). Upon his recovery he moved to new accommodation near his old rooms in Red Lion Square.

In 1859 Georgiana Macdonald and her large family moved to Manchester, while Burne-Jones set off on a trip to Italy with Sara Prinsep's son Val and a friend, Charles Faulkner, falling under the spell of the paintings he saw in Florence and Venice. Morris married Jane Burden and, on Saturday 9 June 1860, after their four-year engagement, Burne-Jones at last married Georgiana in Manchester. Nervous as ever, their planned joint honeymoon in Paris with Rossetti and Elizabeth Siddal was abandoned when Burne-Jones was taken ill, and Georgiana immediately adopted the role she was to endure for almost forty years, that of Burne-Jones's nurse.

For his patron James Leathart, Burne-Jones produced the two watercolours *Sidonia von Bork* and *Clara von Bork*, but was nevertheless constantly plagued by money worries.

Georgiana Burne-Jones and Jane Morris soon became pregnant. Elizabeth Siddal gave birth to a child that died, and she herself died the following year after taking an overdose of laudanum. Rossetti buried a book containing his unpublished poems in her coffin, later macabrely arranging for her body to be exhumed to recover them. After these traumas he became increasingly reclusive and, though they continued to see each other occasionally, gradually faded from Burne-Jones's life, dying in 1882.

Morris, Marshall, Faulkner & Co, William Morris's company, was inaugurated in 1861, providing commissions for his closest associates, among them Burne-Jones, Rossetti, Brown and Philip Webb, who had designed Morris's Red House in Kent, which Burne-Jones and others of the group had had a hand in decorating. They were to devote themselves to creating decorative work in such areas as furniture, pottery, tiles, textiles and stained glass – the latter becoming increasingly Burne-Jones's special forte. Burne-Jones's son Philip was born in October 1861, and the following May he and Georgiana left the baby with her family and set off to accompany Ruskin to Italy on a conservation trip, copying paintings threatened with decay. In 1864 Burne-Jones was elected an Associate of the Old Water-Colour Society, against the better judgement of some of its venerable members to whom he represented the unacceptable face of the new. At an exhibition that followed his election, his works *The Merciful Knight* and *Annunciation* were severely criticized, yet he was not unappreciated among a select following. He steadily acquired further patrons, among them Frederick Leyland, a shipowner, who became the owner of a number of his works (and for whom Burne-Jones eventually designed his 'Arts and Crafts' tomb in Brompton Cemetery, London), William Graham, Liberal MP for Glasgow, and George Howard, later Earl of Carlisle, himself an accomplished artist.

Burne-Jones painted his first version of *Green Summer* at Morris's Red House in Kent, which became the country retreat of members of his circle. Morris proposed to extend the house to enable the Burne-Jones family to live there and to open a guild workshop on the premises, but, unable to meet the cost of the conversion, the plan was abandoned. Edward and Georgiana's second child, Christopher, was born but died soon afterwards, and the family moved to a rented house in Kensington Square, furnishing their new home with Morris fabrics and furniture. Morris's

St Martin, a design for stained glass, one of Burne-Jones's preoccupations throughout his working life.

Burne-Jones's sensitive pencil portrait of Maria Zambaco (1871).

firm received a series of important commissions, including the dining room at the Victoria & Albert (then South Kensington) Museum for which Burne-Jones executed the windows and panels depicting the signs of the zodiac. He also began a series of illustrations for Morris's epic poem, *The Earthly Paradise*, Morris himself undertaking the woodcuts. A long-term project, it was many years before the final result was achieved.

A daughter, Margaret, was born in June 1866, and the following August Georgiana's sister Aggie married the painter Edward Poynter in a double wedding with her sister Louie, who married Alfred Baldwin (their son, Stanley Baldwin, became prime minister in 1923); another sister, Alice, and her husband John Lockwood Kipling were the parents of Rudyard Kipling.

Burne-Jones made the acquaintance of the wealthy expatriate Greek family, the Ionides. They became important patrons and through them he was introduced to Mary Zambaco, *née* Cassavetti. A beautiful 'stunner' (in the jargon of the Pre-Raphaelite circle) for whom the cliché 'flame-haired temptress' might have been invented, she had married a Dr Demetrius Zambaco by whom she had two children, but left him in Paris and moved to London. Her relationship with Burne-Jones began when her family commissioned her portrait, and she soon became his favourite model. Although he made extensive use of the professional Italian and Greek models resident in London and shared certain models with other Pre-Raphaelites, among them Rossetti's Fanny Cornforth, he also painted many friends and members of his family: Georgiana appears in a number of works, as, later, do his children, including Margaret in the *Briar Rose* paintings, and members of the Morris family. Maria Zambaco, however, became more than a sitter and more than a model; she

became his ultimate muse and inspiration as he rapidly became obsessed with her and an intense affair began.

He and Georgiana spent the summer of 1867 near Oxford with friends, but while they were away their Kensington Square house was sold. They duly moved to Fulham, now a western suburb of London but at the time virtually in the countryside. The Grange, the house they now occupied, was the large but run-down mansion where, in the 1740s, Samuel Richardson had written *Pamela* and *Clarissa*. Within hours of their housewarming party, the ceiling collapsed, showering Burne-Jones's studio with plaster and ruining the work he had on display.

His liaison with Maria Zambaco blossomed, but was ultimately disastrous: she threatened suicide and his marriage almost broke up. Burne-Jones was horrified by the powerful emotions released by his affair: 'Lust' (as he was later to comment in connection with the images depicted in Aubrey Beardsley's drawings) 'does frighten me. I say it looks like such despair – despair of any happiness and search for it in new degradation.' After it was finally over, he continued to maintain close relationships with many women friends, particularly Frances Horner, *née* Graham, the daughter of his patron William Graham, to whom he wrote many passionate letters. Meanwhile, Georgiana became friendly with the novelist George Eliot and sought her company as a sympathetic confidante. It seems likely that Edward's subsequent affairs were platonic, but his domestic life was never again as happy as it had been: he and Georgiana had no more children and increasingly led separate lives and pursued their own interests, she devoting herself to charitable causes and community activities.

Yet out of his tormented affair great works had emerged: *Evening Star*, *Night* and *Phyllis and Demophöon*,

Study for *Hope*, one of Burne-Jones's 'Venetian' paintings of the 1860s.

three works shown at the Old Water-Colour Society in April 1870, are typical of many superb subjects featuring Maria Zambaco that date from this troubled period, the last among them leading to controversy. His affair with Maria Zambaco was an open secret in the artistic community, but here she was being flaunted naked to public gaze. Whether for this reason, or simply because the nudity of the figures depicted in it had resulted in public complaints, as it was alleged, he was asked to remove the picture from the Society's walls. While he calmly acceded to this

The nudity of *Phyllis and Demophöon* (1870) led to its withdrawal from exhibition.

request, he was untactfully requested to choose an innocuous picture by another artist in its place. In response, he refused and resigned from the Society.

In the same year as this scandal took place, Burne-Jones's portrait was painted by Watts, and he fell under the older artist's influence, to the extent that their works of this period have close affinities. In 1871, the year in which William Morris began renting Kelmscott Manor, Burne-Jones travelled to Italy, visiting the country again with Morris in 1873. Increasingly, the paintings of the great Italian masters began to exert their influence in his works.

Burne-Jones's wide network of friends included actresses Ellen Terry and Mrs Patrick Campbell, writers Oscar Wilde, Robert Louis Stevenson and Henry James, who was to describe Burne-Jones's work as the 'art of culture, of reflection, of intellectual luxury'. He was also close to fellow artists such as Leighton and Alma-Tadema, whose work, perhaps surprisingly, he greatly admired, and who introduced him to Jules Bastien-Lepage (who painted Burne-Jones's portrait), and he was also familiar with and an admirer of James Tissot. It was at The Grange that the young illustrator Aubrey Beardsley first met Oscar Wilde, later illustrating his celebrated *Salome*. His circle also extended into the political arena, to Mary Gladstone, the daughter of prime minister William Gladstone, and Arthur Balfour (later prime minister), who ordered paintings for his music room, which resulted in the *Perseus* series (the unfinished oil set in Stuttgart, with full-sized studies in Southampton).

Evening Star (1870), an ethereal image modelled by Maria Zambaco.

Appreciative patrons such as Balfour generally gave him full rein and the lack of importance he attached to public approbation meant that he could afford to be uncompromising in his choice of subjects. Certain themes continued to obsess Burne-Jones throughout his working life; a recent biographer, Penelope Fitzgerald, comprehensively summarized them as: 'The enchantment of the willing victim, sleep, waiting, imprisonment, loneliness, guiding, rescue, the quest, losing and finding, tending the helpless, flying, sea-crossing, clinging together, the ritual procession and dance, love dominant and without pity, the haunting angel, the entry into life.' He returned to these motifs time and time again, painting the same subjects repeatedly, often producing an oil version of a watercolour or vice versa, or painting versions of subjects that he had originally designed as tapestries or stained glass.

Despite his disinterest in public shows of his work, he was persuaded in 1877 to exhibit at the newly-opened Grosvenor Gallery alongside works by Alma-Tadema, Millais, Leighton and Whistler, representatives of the varied schools that co-existed at the time. Ruskin's criticisms of Whistler's displayed work resulted in a celebrated libel case (which Whistler won, but was bankrupted as a result). Much to his chagrin and embarrassment, Burne-Jones was called as a witness on Ruskin's side in the case. His work was considered characteristic of the first stirrings of the Aesthetic Movement, and publicity from

John Ruskin's support of Burne-Jones was reciprocated when he acted as a witness in the Whistler *v* Ruskin libel case.

The Adoration of the Magi, a tapestry version of Burne-Jones's large watercolour, *The Star of Bethlehem*.

this supposed association, coupled with the wider exhibition of his works and reproductions through engravings, led to an almost overnight surge in Burne-Jones's popularity. His work became much copied and emulated, and his *Golden Stairs* was satirized in Gilbert and Sullivan's comic opera *Patience*.

Burne-Jones appears to have been genuinely disinterested in criticism of his work, and retained his sense of humour: when the potter William de Morgan asked if he was starting a new painting, he answered in the style of a critic, 'Yes, I am going to cover that canvas with flagrant violations of perspective and drawing and crude inharmonious colour.' Despite his disregard for the opinion of others, his shunning of the established routes followed by many of his contemporaries (such as exhibiting at the Royal Academy), and determined pursuit of his own distinctive style of painting during the 1880s and 1890s, Burne-Jones's

of a tennis court. Many of his paintings were conceived on a colossal scale (unlike those of his friend Alma-Tadema, whose works, though crowded with detail, often surprise by their small scale). Their size and his prolific output, with numerous works in progress at any one time, meant that he was compelled to employ studio assistants, among them Charles Fairfax Murray and Thomas Rooke. The range of Burne-Jones's work is also impressive. As well as paintings and designs for stained glass, he created numerous portraits, book illustrations, decorative work such as the famous Graham piano, the mosaic for the American Episcopal church in Rome, completed after his death, and theatre sets for a production of *King Arthur* at London's Lyceum Theatre.

In 1885 – and much to his surprise – he was elected an Associate of the Royal Academy. As with his earlier membership of the Old Water-Colour Society, he was ill at

Houses at Rottingdean, the Burne-Jones family's country home from 1880 onwards.

renown steadily grew until, in his last years, he was widely regarded as Britain's greatest living artist.

The final years of Burne-Jones's life were occupied by his ongoing paintings – and one in particular. As a retreat from London, the Burne-Joneses bought Prospect House in Rottingdean, on the Sussex coast, later purchasing next-door North End House and connecting them. There, after it was transported from a studio in Campden Hill Road, London, he devoted many years to *The Last Sleep of Arthur in Avalon*, originally commissioned by George Howard. It measured a vast 21 feet (6.5 metres) long – half the size

Edward Burne-Jones and his granddaughter Angela, later Angela Thirkell, (c.1893).

Detail from *The Last Sleep of Arthur in Avalon* (1881–98), the gigantic painting that he intended as the culmination of his life's work.

ease with the organization and resigned a few years later, having only once exhibited at the Academy. With Watts and Alma-Tadema he became one of the principal exhibitors at the New Gallery, opened in 1888. In the same year, to commemorate the marriage of his much-loved daughter Margaret to the classical scholar John W. Mackail in, appropriately, St Margaret's church, Rottingdean, Burne-Jones created a three-light stained-glass window depicting the archangels Gabriel, Michael and Raphael. In 1890 Margaret had a daughter who grew up to become the novelist Angela Thirkell.

The Paris Exposition Universelle of 1889 had led to Burne-Jones's discovery by French Symbolists and a wave of public interest in France. He devoted himself to his work on Kelmscott Press illustrations with Morris, starting with *Chaucer*, the resulting book containing 87 illustrations by Burne-Jones. In 1894 he was offered a baronetcy by Gladstone 'in recognition of the high position which you have obtained by your achievement in your noble art.' When he died, suddenly, on 17 June 1898, such was his fame that his was the first ever memorial service for an artist held in Westminster Abbey. His ashes were buried at Rottingdean, in a niche in the wall in sight of North End House, to

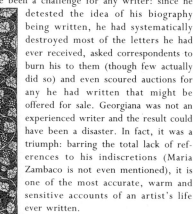

where Georgiana retired, with her nephew Rudyard Kipling living in the house opposite.

Burne-Jones was fortunate indeed to have had the enduring support of his wife Georgiana, who tolerated his moods and behaviour as he embarked on one infatuation after another. In fact, her love for him extended beyond their life together. After his death, she diligently assembled the materials to compile a substantial two-volume biography of her husband, *Memorials of Edward Burne-Jones* (1904). It would have been a challenge for any writer: since he detested the idea of his biography being written, he had systematically destroyed most of the letters he had ever received, asked correspondents to burn his to them (though few actually did so) and even scoured auctions for any he had written that might be offered for sale. Georgiana was not an experienced writer and the result could have been a disaster. In fact, it was a triumph: barring the total lack of references to his indiscretions (Maria Zambaco is not even mentioned), it is one of the most accurate, warm and sensitive accounts of an artist's life ever written.

Many of his contemporaries also thought fit to include reminiscences of Burne-Jones in their autobiographies,

The first page of the magnificent Kelmscott *Chaucer* (1896), one of the finest results of the collaboration between Burne-Jones and William Morris.

Portrait of Katie Lewis (1882). She is shown reading the story of St George and the Dragon.

while the studio diary kept by his assistant Thomas Rooke has even preserved virtually verbatim conversations with the 'master'. From such accounts have emerged an impression of Burne-Jones the man. His customary greeting, which endeared him to his friends, was, 'Are you happy?' Mostly, he was not. His was a withdrawn, introspective and in many ways depressive personality. Highly strung and sensitive, there are many descriptions of his collapse under stress, and of a life wracked with anxieties, hypochondria and pessimism. Yet for all his gloom, he could, as all who knew him testified, emerge to become the most charming company. He evidently enjoyed bohemian male companionship, dining, smoking old clay pipes and playing practical jokes with his cronies. His sense of humour was legendary. One of his favourite devices was massive exaggeration for dramatic effect: in a letter he told of visiting 2,845 houses in the search for his Chelsea flat, and once told Gladstone that precisely 801,926 birds nested in a particular tree in his garden. He took to calculating his age according to how he felt, thus in 1888 he reckoned he was 97, and in 1893 variously 175 and 485. He was an eloquent and witty speaker and a writer with a true artist's sense of imagery, for example describing the black-draped coffin borne aloft by six pall-bearers at Browning's funeral as resembling a beetle. Throughout his life he produced comic sketches and caricatures, and he was famed for his ability to entertain children: his letter-writing, art and humour all coalesced in his *Letters to Katie*, a collection of his illustrated letters to Katie Lewis, the daughter of his

friend and lawyer, George Lewis, written in 1883 and later published. Intolerant of bores and frivolous time-wasters and shy in unfamiliar company, he often hid when visitors came to see his paintings. Although quiet in his manners, he had occasional flares of violent temper: once, using a red-hot poker, he burned a hole through a book to which he had taken exception. His generosity was widely noted: once he was able to afford to do so he supported his father and old nanny Mrs Sampson, and loaned money to Constance Wilde when Oscar Wilde was jailed. He was also actively involved in encouraging the nation to acquire and preserve art treasures.

Burne-Jones's paintings, especially those from the later phase of his 40-year career, possess an irresistibly dream-like and often mysterious and detached quality, while he displayed a technical virtuosity unmatched by his rivals and the many followers he influenced. Cumulatively, these attributes meant that Burne-Jones was one of the most admired painters both in his own century and in our own. His art was a highly personal interpretation of Pre-Raphaelitism, and it is perhaps the uniqueness of his own imagination that makes his paintings so significantly different from those of his contemporaries. His artistic life was a continual pursuit of beauty, an obsession with battles fought and choices made between good and evil, with chivalry and courtly love, all intricately interwoven with High Victorian ideals, yet rejecting Victorian materialism. His sense of beauty was one that was never diluted with ugliness, once writing, 'Only this is true, that beauty is very beautiful, and softens, and comforts, and inspires, and rouses, and lifts up, and never fails.' Lord David Cecil saw him as 'A highly civilized aesthete, born in an uncongenial period of material progress, philistine taste and religious doubt. He lived for beauty, but saw it as something alien, remote, out of reach' as he confronted the problem of being 'a poetic artist in a prosaic age' – a *fin de siècle* mentality that is not without its echoes as we ourselves approach the end of another century.

Burne-Jones's letters to Katie Lewis contain this sequence of caricatures in which he tries unsuccessfully to enter the imaginary world of his *Briar Rose* paintings, signing himself with a pictorial 'Mr Beak', Katie's nickname for him.

THE PLATES

1. SIDONIA VON BORK
2. ASTROLOGIA
3. THE PRINCESS SABRA LED TO THE DRAGON
4. GREEN SUMMER
5. SPRING *AND* AUTUMN
6. DAY *AND* NIGHT
7. PORTRAIT OF MARIA ZAMBACO
8. TEMPERANTIA
9. PAN AND PSYCHE
10. THE BEGUILING OF MERLIN
11. THE LAST JUDGEMENT
12. THE DAYS OF CREATION – THE FIFTH *AND* SIXTH DAYS
13. LE CHANT D'AMOUR
14. THE MIRROR OF VENUS
15. PYGMALION AND THE IMAGE – THE GODHEAD FIRES
16. PYGMALION AND THE IMAGE – THE SOUL ATTAINS
17. LAUS VENERIS
18. THE ANNUNCIATION
19. THE GOLDEN STAIRS
20. THE MILL
21. THE HOURS
22. TREE OF FORGIVENESS
23. THE WHEEL OF FORTUNE
24. KING COPHETUA AND THE BEGGAR MAID
25. SIBYLLA DELPHICA
26. THE DEPTHS OF THE SEA
27. THE ARMING OF PERSEUS
28. THE ROCK OF DOOM
29. THE BALEFUL HEAD
30. DANAE AND THE BRAZEN TOWER
31. THE BRIAR ROSE – THE PRINCE ENTERS THE BRIAR WOOD
32. THE BRIAR ROSE – THE SLEEPING PRINCESS
33. THE STAR OF BETHLEHEM
34. SPONSA DE LIBANO
35. VESPERTINA QUIES
36. LOVE AMONG THE RUINS
37. ANGELI LAUDANTES
38. THE WEDDING OF PSYCHE
39. LOVE LEADING THE PILGRIM
40. THE PRIORESS'S TALE

NOTES
Burne-Jones frequently worked on his paintings over very long periods, sometimes spanning many years.
Both the commencement and completion years are given where known, and the plates are arranged
in chronological order of completion.
Oil: oil on canvas.
Watercolour/gouache: watercolour/gouache on paper, unless otherwise stated.

PLATE 1

SIDONIA VON BORK

———— 1860 ————

Gouache, 13.0 x 6.7 in / 33 x 17 cm
Tate Gallery, London

Completed just prior to Burne-Jones's marriage to Georgiana, this painting and its companion, *Clara von Bork*, are derived from the story of *Sidonia the Sorceress* by the German author Johann Wilhelm Meinhold. Translated into English in 1849 by Oscar Wilde's mother, Lady Jane Wilde (known as 'Speranza'), it is a chronicle of a noblewoman who in 1620, at the age of 80, was put to death for witchcraft. Her evil combined with her beauty and the mysterious occult element appealed to the Pre-Raphaelite imagination; *Sidonia* was a favourite book of Rossetti's and William Morris issued a reprint of it under his Kelmscott Press imprint in 1893. In the painting the Duchess of Wolgast appears in the background, while Sidonia herself is seen plotting some new crime.

The inscription 'Sidonia von Bork 1560' appears on the mount, thus indicating that Burne-Jones considered her to be aged 20 in the picture. It was one of his earliest watercolours and was possibly modelled by Rossetti's mistress Fanny Cornforth. The marvellously intricate design of the dress is said to have been based on a portrait of Isabella d'Este at Hampton Court where the royal galleries had been opened to the public in 1830 and were customarily visited by groups from art schools; Burne-Jones is known to have gone there to see the Raphael cartoons. The elaborate hairstyle comes from Meinhold's own description of a fictitious portrait of Sidonia by Lucas Cranach. The work and the accompanying *Clara*, which deals with Sidonia's virtuous cousin by marriage, were framed by Burne-Jones's father before being sent at Christmas 1860 to James Leathart of Newcastle. A replica of *Sidonia* (now in a private collection) was produced for Thomas E. Plint, another important patron of his early years.

Astrologia
——— 1865 ———
Gouache, 21.5 x 18.3 in / 54.5 x 46.5 cm
Private collection

In 1862 Edward and Georgiana Burne-Jones visited Italy, where he was employed by Ruskin in copying crumbling works by Venetian masters, including Paolo Veronese and Jacopo Tintoretto. Ruskin clearly selected the paintings as important not only as visual records but in aiding Burne-Jones's own development as an artist, and the trip undoubtedly had a considerable influence. *Hope* (collection of the Duke of Wellington), a 'Venetian half-length' portrait, dating from 1862, was the first obvious result, and, like *Astrologia*, also contains an image of globe, while the sphere motif reappears in further works, such as the *Days of Creation* series (Plate 12) and even became a studio prop that featured in portraits, such as that of the Baronne Deslandes (1898).

Astrologia was modelled by Augusta Jones, who appears in *The King's Daughter* (1865–66; Musée d'Orsay, Paris). The esoteric symbols in the ancient manuscript that the subject examines hark back to Burne-Jones's own studies of medieval literature during his years at Oxford University. The picture was exhibited at the Old Water-Colour Society in 1865, at the New Gallery in 1892, and again in the memorial exhibition of 1898.

The characteristic richness of Burne-Jones's watercolours is often surprising, and is partly explained by his use of techniques that were opposed to those of the medium with which he was working. As the portrait painter and illustrator W. Graham Robertson (1867–1948), a young admirer and friend of Burne-Jones, later explained: 'In water-colour he would take no advantage of its transparency, but load on body colour and paint thickly in gouache; when he turned to oil he would shun the richness of impasto, drawing thin glazes of colour over careful drawings in raw umber heightened with white.'

THE PRINCESS SABRA LED TO
THE DRAGON
———————————— 1866 ————————————
Oil, 42.5 x 38 in / 108 x 96.6 cm
Private collection

The artist Myles Birket Foster commissioned Burne-Jones to produce seven pictures on the theme of St George and the Dragon, of which this is one. It represents the legend of St George, a Roman tribune from Cappadocia, who went to Silene in Libya where a dragon was terrorizing the town, demanding young women be sent to it as sacrifices. When it was the turn of the king's daughter, Princess Sabra, to be sacrificed, she was rescued by St George who agreed to slay the dragon if the king and his subjects would convert to Christianity. Foster ordered the paintings for the dining room of his Tudor-style house, The Hill, at Whitley in Surrey, which he had designed himself in 1863 and had decorated by the newly-established firm of Morris, Marshall, Faulkner & Co. These were among the first pictures on which Burne-Jones's talented studio assistant Charles Fairfax Murray was employed. After Foster left the house, the St George paintings came up for sale in 1894. The following year Burne-Jones undertook some restoration work to the set and it was exhibited in 1897, winning the gold medal at the Munich International Exhibition, and again at his memorial exhibition. The series, which has since been widely dispersed, includes *The Return of the Princess* (Bristol City Art Gallery), *The King's Daughter* (Musée d'Orsay, Paris) and *St George Kills the Dragon* (Art Gallery of New South Wales, Sydney), with studies in Birmingham City Art Gallery and the British Museum.

GREEN SUMMER

———— 1868 ————

Oil, 25.5 x 41.8 in / 64.7 x 106.1 cm
Private collection

Burne-Jones began his first version of this work in watercolour in May 1864 at William Morris's Red House at Upton in Kent. It features eight young women, with Georgiana in black reading to the others, and her sister Louie and Jane Morris (holding peacock feathers, a symbol of the month of May) in the centre. The work, studies of which exist in Birmingham City Art Gallery and in the Ashmolean Museum, Oxford, was undertaken in the Red House studio – not, as might be supposed, in the garden itself. Burne-Jones was opposed to the Impressionist technique of painting from nature and seldom worked out of doors except for sketching occasional backgrounds to be incorporated into studio works. Also, according to W. Graham Robertson, he never expressed 'pleasure at a natural effect except when it reminded him of a picture or a story.'

Green Summer was exhibited in 1865 at the Old Water-Colour Society, the body to which he had been elected the previous year. The *Art Journal* critic was perplexed by this 'harmony in green', querying, 'Why is it that he has woven the robes of the picnic party of the green grass whereon they sit, thus bidding defiance to known laws of chromatic art, which are now established with the certainty of scientific axioms?' This later oil dates from 1868 when it was acquired by Burne-Jones's patron William Graham. For Burne-Jones it is an unusual scene, bearing comparison with works by Giorgione, but with affinities to such contemporary paintings as Millais' *Apple Blossoms* of 1859 (Lady Lever Art Gallery, Port Sunlight), which similarly features eight girls, and Tissot's *Le Printemps* of 1865 (private collection). It may be viewed simply as a memoir of a happy summer in the country, lacking any obvious literary origin. However, two possible sources of inspiration have been suggested: Burne-Jones was on close terms with Algernon Swinburne, whose 'In the Orchard', published in his *Poems and Ballads*, 1860, contains the lines:

> The grass is thick and cool, it lets us lie.
> Kissed upon either cheek and either eye,
> I turned to thee as some green afternoon
> Turns toward sunset, and is loth to die.

Perhaps more significantly, Burne-Jones's beloved *Morte d'Arthur* observes how winter 'doth always erase and deface green summer', which it compares with the transient nature of the love between man and woman. In 1979 this work was sold for the then record price of £48,000, marking the beginning of the sharp escalation in the value of Burne-Jones's paintings that continued during the 1980s.

PLATE 5

SPRING *AND* AUTUMN
———————— 1869–70 ————————
Gouache, 48.2 x 17.7 in / 122.5 x 45 cm
Private collection

Burne-Jones's 'Four Seasons' were painted as part of a commission for the dining room of the house at 49 Prince's Gate, London, of his patron the Liverpool shipowner Frederick Leyland. In a letter Burne-Jones told Leyland, 'I hope you will eat and drink with friends in their company for fifty years to come,' but his wish was thwarted when as part of the Aesthetic interior design Whistler's famed 'Peacock Room' was created in the house (1876–77) and the *Seasons* were moved to another location, eventually being sold at Leyland's death in 1892.

The paintings, with *Day* and *Night*, are similar in many respects to the Aesthetic compositions on the same subjects by Albert Moore, another artist whose work Leyland collected. The colours chosen were deemed appropriate for each season, as the critic for the *Athenaeum* wrote: '*Spring* is represented by a damsel in fresh green robes . . . *Autumn*, the third member of the group of painted allegories, is of graver character than her sisters, standing before us and clad in a robe of deep crimson, the colour of the vintage season, lined with blue, the colour of the declining year.' Maria Zambaco, whose affair with Burne-Jones was waning, was the model for *Summer*. Poems by William Morris were added beneath each painting:

> Spring am I, too soft of heart
> Much to speak ere I depart;
> Ask the Summer-tide to prove
> The abundance of my love.
>
> Laden Autumn here I stand,
> Worn of heart, and weak of hand,
> Nought but rest seems good to me,
> Speak the word that sets me free!

The series was sold as recently as 1965 for only £65 – although it fetched $37,800 when it was re-sold in 1973.

DAY AND NIGHT

———— 1870 ————

Watercolour and gouache, 47.5 x 17.5 in / 120.7 x 44.4 cm
The Fogg Art Museum, Harvard University, Cambridge, Massachusetts
Bequest of Grenville L. Winthrop

Produced as companion paintings to his 'Four Seasons' for Frederick
Leyland's dining room, the blazing torch of *Day* and welcoming open
door is contrasted with *Night* – modelled by a blue-clad Maria
Zambaco – extinguishing her torch as she closes the door. The latter
painting was one of five Burne-Jones exhibited at the Old Water-
Colour Society in 1870. The accompanying poems by William
Morris were:

> I am Day, I bring again
> Life and glory, love and pain,
> Awake, arise from death to death,
> From me the world's tale quickeneth.
>
> I am Night and bring again
> Hope of pleasure, rest from pain,
> Thoughts unsaid 'twixt life and death,
> My fruitful silence quickeneth.

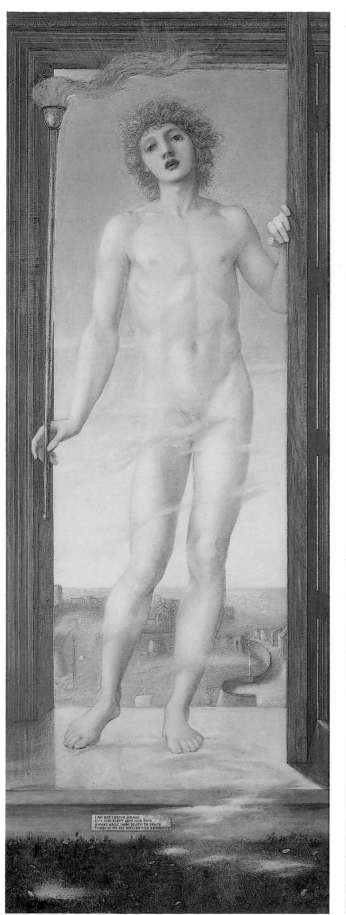

PORTRAIT OF MARIA ZAMBACO
———— 1870 ————

Gouache, 30 x 21.7 in / 76.3 x 55 cm
Clemens-Sels-Museum, Neuss

Maria Theresa Zambaco, *née* Cassavetti, a cousin of Constantine Alexander Ionides, one of Burne-Jones's important patrons, began her affair with Burne-Jones in 1867. It proved stormy and by 23 January 1869 Rossetti was writing to Ford Madox Brown to inform him, 'poor old Ned's affairs have come to a smash all together'. The reference is to a series of incidents: following her attempted suicide in the Regent's Canal, Maria and Burne-Jones ran off together, but he was taken ill at Dover, en route for France (just as had befallen him on his honeymoon), after which he returned to Georgiana. Despite this crisis, the affair continued during the next few years, until Maria finally accepted that he was never going to leave his wife.

This very personal portrait shows Maria with Cupid and his arrow, the message attached to which reads, '*Mary Aetat XXVI* [aged 26] *August 7th 1870 EBJ pinxit*'. She holds a medieval manuscript which contains a miniature painting of his *Chant d'Amour* (Plate 13), emphasizing the ambiguity of the pleasure and pain of his relationship with the sitter. Following its sale by the Cassavetti family, the portrait was acquired by the Clemens-Sels-Museum, Neuss, Germany (the only German public collection other than Stuttgart containing Burne-Jones paintings), which additionally owns a pastel portrait of Maria by Rossetti, also dating from 1870.

PLATE 8

TEMPERANTIA
—— 1872 ——
Watercolour, 60 x 23 in / 152.4 x 58.4 cm
Private collection

The year 1872, in which Burne-Jones finished this allegorical representation of Temperance, was particularly prolific. *Temperantia*, a companion painting to *Fides* and *Spes* (Faith and Hope) from the same year, was described by Malcolm Bell as depicting 'a stately woman pouring water from a large jar upon the flames, on which she also tramples with unharmed feet, in which the artist for the first time made use of those elaborately folded and wrinkled draperies which are so characteristic of much of his later work.'

Temperantia is one of Burne-Jones's typical elongated subjects that clearly derive from his designs for stained-glass windows, the output of which increased steadily in response to the expansion of church building and restoration in Victorian England. It was commissioned with other works by Frederick Startridge Ellis, a bookseller and author. Ellis, a leading authority on Percy Bysshe Shelley, edited Kelmscott Press books for William Morris and himself published works by both Morris and Rossetti. Burne-Jones wrote to Ellis to inform him, '*Temperance* is nearly finished, and has taken much longer than *Faith* – God who rules these matters knows why.' All three were shown with five others at the inaugural exhibition of the Grosvenor Gallery in 1877.

One of his last identifiable pictures of Maria Zambaco, it can be read symbolically as an image of Maria finally extinguishing the flames of their passion. Her subsequent life remains mysterious. She appears elusively in other work, including stained-glass designs, and it is known that after living in Paris she returned to London where she became a sculptress, at one time occupying a studio next door to Burne-Jones.

PAN AND PSYCHE
──────── 1872 – 74 ────────
Oil, 25.6 x 21.4 in / 65.1 x 54.3 cm
The Fogg Art Museum, Harvard University, Cambridge, Massachusetts
Bequest of Grenville L. Winthrop

In a letter Burne-Jones presented a personal view of his work: 'I mean by a picture a beautiful, romantic dream of something that never was, never will be – in a light better than any lights that ever shone – in a land no one can define or remember, only desire – and the forms divinely beautiful – and then I wake up.' *Pan and Psyche* belongs to his developing obsession with legendary incidents occurring in dream-like landscapes, in this instance the story of Psyche and Cupid as told in Apuleius's *The Golden Ass* and elsewhere in classical literature. Burne-Jones embarked on the theme in 1864 in illustrations for Morris's *The Earthly Paradise*, but the oil painting was originally conceived in 1869. This was around the time that Maria Zambaco threatened to commit suicide by drowning herself, and there are obvious parallels as Psyche, in despair at being abandoned by Cupid, fails to drown herself and is consoled by Pan. The figure of Pan, half man, half goat, is closely based on a mythological subject by Piero di Cosimo that is traditionally identified as *The Death of Procris* (National Gallery, London).

PLATE 10

THE BEGUILING OF MERLIN
—————— 1874 ——————
Oil, 73.3 x 43.5 in / 186.2 x 110.5 cm
National Museums and Galleries on Merseyside
(Lady Lever Art Gallery, Port Sunlight)

Commissioned by the shipowner Frederick Leyland during the late 1860s, Burne-Jones commenced work on the painting in 1872. This proved a false start, however, due to a fault with new painting materials with which he was experimenting, and he began afresh in 1873. Although the picture is dated 1874, he was still making alterations to the head of Merlin during 1875 and 1876. Merlin was modelled by the American journalist William J. Stillman, a friend of Rossetti and husband of Marie Spartali, one of Rossetti's models and herself an accomplished artist. Burne-Jones had been aware of the legends of King Arthur, particularly since Morris acquired a copy of the *Morte d'Arthur* a decade earlier, and had tackled Merlin's fate in the Oxford Union murals and in *Merlin and Nimuë* (Victoria & Albert Museum, London). He now turned to an alternative version of the subject, probably deriving the hawthorn bush motif from a French medieval *Romance of Merlin*. In this Nimuë (also known by various other names, including Vivien), trades her love for lessons in enchantment from Merlin, but finally turns on him, using one of his own spells to ensnare him in a hawthorn bush and transport him to a tower as an eternal prisoner. Burne-Jones clearly had the subject in mind as early as 1858, for in that year he persuaded Tennyson not to use the name Nimuë in one of his *Idylls* (Tennyson helpfully changed it to Vivien). Nimuë, with her sinuous body and snake-entwined hair, shown consulting her book of spells, was one of Burne-Jones's first images of a *femme fatale*, a woman depicted as a seductress with a man as her helpless victim. The image was to recur repeatedly in his work, and was clearly how he viewed his own recently terminated relationship with Maria Zambaco. He later wrote to Helen Mary Gaskell, one of his several female confidantes:

'The head of Nimuë in the picture called *The Enchanting of Merlin* was painted from the same poor traitor, and was very like – all the action is like – the name of her was Mary. Now isn't that very funny as she was born at the foot of Olympus and looked and was primaeval and that's the head and the way of standing and turning... and I was being turned into a hawthorn bush in the forest of Broceliande – every year when the hawthorn buds it is the soul of Merlin trying to live again in the world and speak – for he left so much unsaid.'

Burne-Jones poured so much emotional energy into the work that after completing it he collapsed and was bed-ridden for many weeks. It was shown at the Grosvenor Gallery in 1877, where it was dramatically displayed on a red silk wall. It was variously ridiculed and praised, Henry James considering it 'a brilliant piece of simple rendering demanding a vast amount of looking on the painter's part', while William Michael Rossetti (Dante Gabriel's brother) writing in the *Athenaeum*, referred to 'the grand figure of Nimuë dark and lovely with a loveliness that looks ominous and subtle without being exactly sinister and the exquisite painting of the lavish white hawthorn bush.' One of Oscar Wilde's favourite paintings, he called it 'brilliantly suggestive' and had a photographic reproduction of it in his rooms at Oxford University. The work was shown at the 1878 Paris Exposition Universelle, making it the first of Burne-Jones's works to be shown abroad, but it failed to create the sensation that was anticipated. At the Leyland sale on 29 May 1892 it fetched £3,780 (when Whistler's *Princesse du Pays de Porcelaine* made just 420 guineas) and later entered the collection of Lord Lever. A watercolour study for the head of Maria – which Burne-Jones claimed to prefer to the finished version – came up in the studio sale of Burne-Jones's work after his death in 1898 and is now in the Bancroft Collection, Delaware Art Museum. This and further sketches in the Fitzwilliam Museum, Cambridge, and the Tate Gallery, London, indicate something of Burne-Jones's debt to classical sculpture in devising the figure of Nimuë.

PLATE 11

THE LAST JUDGEMENT
------ 1874 – 75 ------
Stained glass
St Michael and All Angels Church, Easthampstead, Berkshire

The Last Judgement, the east window of St Michael and All Angels Church, Easthampstead, was one of Burne-Jones's most ambitious stained-glass commissions to date, a large and complex subject executed by Morris and Company. Describing the window as 'one of the painter's finest efforts in this direction,' his biographer Malcolm Bell analyzed the work:

'In the centre light of this magnificent piece of decoration the stately figure of St Michael stands on a cloud, the banner of Christ in one hand, the folds of it forming a background for his head, the great scales for the weighing of good and evil in the other. Beneath him, giving solidity to the group, three winged angels are seated, the middle one of whom, with a stern expression, reads from the wide open book of doom. The angel on his right, symbolic of the sheep that shall be set on the right hand of the throne as signs of their salvation, looks on with fearless clam, while he on the left, the side of the goats that are condemned, shrinks back in horror from the dreadful sights to come. The curved line of the lower part of this mass is carried up in a graceful sweep through the lights to the right and left by cloudlets supporting angels, two on either side, blowing the great trumpets that summon the souls to judgement.'

The cartoon for the design was later coloured and exhibited at the Grosvenor Gallery in 1881. The same theme was developed in other locations, especially in the west window of St Philip's Cathedral in Burne-Jones's native Birmingham, which he produced 20 years later.

PLATE 12

THE DAYS OF CREATION—
THE FIFTH *AND* SIXTH DAYS
————— 1870–76 —————

Watercolour, gouache and shell gold on linen, 40.1 x 14 in / 101.9 x 35.6 cm
Watercolour, gouache and shell gold and platinum paint on linen,
40.1 x 14 in / 101.9 x 35.6 cm
The Fogg Art Museum, Harvard University, Cambridge, Massachusetts
Bequest of Grenville L. Winthrop

The series of six 'Days of Creation' watercolours originated as designs for a stained-glass commission for a church in Tamworth, Staffordshire. Each successive 'day' consists of a number of angels corresponding to that day – thus the fifth day has five angels. In each, the angel in the foreground holds a sphere in which the events of the day are presented as related in the bible, so that the progressive creation of the universe is seen as a sequence in which the previous angels withdraw into the background: 'The fifth,' as described by Malcolm Bell, 'stands upon the wet sea-margin strewn with fragile shells, and supports a globe containing a swift whirl of white-winged sea-birds sweeping up from the stormy waters,' while behind and to the left is the fourth day, on which the sun and moon were created.

The last in the six *Days of Creation* series actually represents both the sixth and seventh days, as explained by Malcolm Bell: 'The sixth and last shows Adam and Eve new met in the Garden of Eden beside the forbidden tree, behind which the great coils of the threatening serpent are faintly shadowed forth. At the feet of the Angel of this sixth day sits the seventh, the Angel of the day of rest, flower-garlanded among roses, playing upon a many-stringed instrument.'

Variously called *The Days of Creation* and *The Angels of Creation*, their completion totally occupied Burne-Jones during the first five months of 1876, with Jenny Morris, William's daughter, posing for some of the angels. The entire set of six was originally owned by William Graham and was sold after his death in 1885 for £1,732, eventually finding its way to the Fogg Art Museum.

PLATE 13

LE CHANT D'AMOUR
―――――― 1868 – 77 ――――――
Oil, 44.9 x 61.4 in / 114 x 156 cm
The Metropolitan Museum of Art, New York,
The Alfred N. Punnett Endowment Fund, 1947

The theme of music and musical instruments recurs constantly in Burne-Jones's work. Georgiana Burne-Jones was an accomplished musician and she and her husband numbered many notable musicians among their friends. Here an ancient Breton song that was probably known to Georgiana provides the subject and title for the painting: *Hélas! je sais un chant d'amour/Triste ou gai, tour à tour* (Alas, I know a love song/Sad or merry, each in turn). The work depicts an organist with a figure representing Love operating the bellows. The figure of Love is sightless ('Love is blind'), while Burne-Jones's abiding interest in the language of flowers is manifest in the painting, where tulips (symbolizing 'ardent love') and wallflowers ('bitterness') jointly represent the contradictory emotions expressed in the song.

The subject was originally painted in about 1864 on the inside of the lid of the upright piano (now in the Victoria & Albert Museum) that Edward and Georgiana had received as a wedding gift four years earlier, and it was from this, over a number of years, that he developed the full-sized painting. Also, ironically, in view of its origin within the Burne-Jones family, the same subject appears as an illustration within the illuminated medieval manuscript in his *Portrait of Maria Zambaco* of 1870 (Plate 7). In the intervening years, Burne-Jones developed the theme, adding the figure of the knight in a watercolour version (1865; Museum of Fine Arts, Boston – one of the first Burne-Jones pictures to arrive in the United States) that was acquired by his patron William Graham, who then commissioned this large replica. The oil version of *Le Chant d'Amour* was shown publicly in 1878 at the second Grosvenor Gallery exhibition. Henry James, a visitor to the Gallery, remarked that 'we should hardly know where to look for a more delicate rendering of a lovesick swain', considering the colour 'like some mellow Giorgione or some richly-glowing Titian.' At the sale following Graham's death in 1885, it fetched the highest price of £3,307, sustaining its price when it was re-sold in the year of Burne-Jones's death.

THE MIRROR OF VENUS
——————— 1870–76 ———————
Oil, 47.2 x 78.7 in / 120 x 200 cm
Calouste Gulbenkian Foundation, Lisbon

Produced as an avowedly aesthetic image with no specific reference
to any legend, this is the large version of a painting dating from
1866–77, in which Venus and her handmaidens gaze at their own
reflections in a pool in a rocky landscape that could have come from
Botticelli or Leonardo da Vinci. Commissioned by Leyland, Burne-
Jones devoted three months to the work in 1874 alone. In her *Memorials of Edward Burne-Jones* Georgiana notes that when Ruskin saw the
oil in progress he was convinced that it was a watercolour. It was
eventually shown at the first Grosvenor Gallery exhibition in 1877,
sold after Leyland's death for 3,570 guineas, and again in May 1898
for 5,450 guineas, finally entering the collection of the Calouste
Gulbenkian Foundation, Lisbon. There are studies of the work in the
Fitzwilliam Museum, Cambridge, and the Tate Gallery, London.

PLATE 15

PYGMALION AND THE IMAGE— THE GODHEAD FIRES

——————————— 1868–78 ———————————

Oil, 38.4 x 29.5 in / 97.5 x 74.9 cm
Birmingham Museums and Art Gallery

As told in Ovid's *Metamorphoses*, the legend relates how Pygmalion, a misanthropic king of Cyprus, having built an ivory statue, fell in love with it. Answering his prayers, the goddess Venus gave life to the statue, who, naming her Galatea, he married. In 1867 Burne-Jones executed 12 illustrations based on the story for William Morris's *The Earthly Paradise*, subsequently developing a sequence of four paintings on the identical theme: *The Heart Desires*, *The Hand Refrains*, *The Godhead Fires* and *The Soul Attains*. His first series of four oils was painted in 1868–70 for Euphrosyne Cassavetti, the mother of Maria Zambaco, while the more detailed set from which this subject and the next come, spanning a longer period of execution, was shown at the Grosvenor Gallery in 1879 and purchased by Frederick Craven.

PYGMALION AND THE IMAGE—
THE SOUL ATTAINS

——————— 1868–78 ———————

Oil, 38.4 x 29.5 in / 97.5 x 74.9 cm

Birmingham Museums and Art Gallery

For his *Pygmalion and the Image* series Burne-Jones modelled Pygmalion's head on W. A. S. Benson, appropriately a craftsman himself, and later the architect responsible for the conversion of the Burne-Jones's Rottingdean property. Coincidentally, in 1871, while Burne-Jones was at work on the paintings, W. S. Gilbert's comedy *Pygmalion and Galatea* was first performed on the London stage.

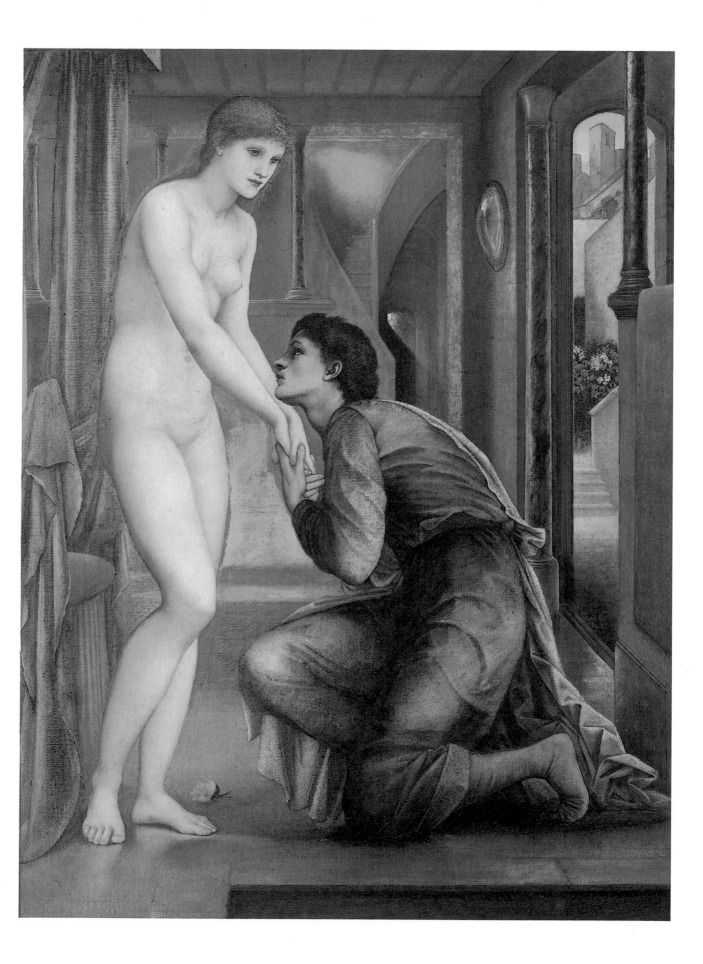

PLATE 17

LAUS VENERIS
—— 1868 ——
Oil and gold paint, 48 x 72 in / 122 x 183 cm
Laing Art Gallery, Newcastle upon Tyne

A German legend relates how Tannhäuser, the poet and wandering knight, discovered the Venusberg, the subterranean home of Venus, goddess of love, and spent a year there with her. Released and filled with remorse for his sinful behaviour, he travelled to Rome to seek absolution from Pope Urban, who told him that forgiveness would be as impossible as that his papal staff should blossom. Tannhäuser returned to Venus, and three days' later the Pope's staff miraculously flowered. During the Romantic period, numerous German writers produced versions of the Tannhäuser story, many of which were translated into English, the best-known appearing in Thomas Carlyle's *German Romance* of 1827. Later, William Morris retold the legend as 'The Hill of Venus' in his *The Earthly Paradise* (1868–70). Two other versions had appeared in 1861 when Burne-Jones himself first tackled the subject as a watercolour that was acquired by his patron, William Graham, who was to commission the larger oil painting. This was started in 1873, finished five years later and shown at the second Grosvenor Gallery exhibition. The critical response was generally favourable, F. G. Stephens in the *Athenaeum* declaring it 'the finest work he has achieved' and a source of 'unending pleasure' – but it was also attacked as an example of all that was held by some to be despised in the Aesthetic Movement: the peacock feathers on the floor alone would have been sufficient to identify its dubious 'aesthetic tendencies'. Algernon Swinburne produced a poem with the same title, which similarly explored the theme of the destructive power of love, publishing it in *Poems and Ballads*, which he dedicated to Burne-Jones, in 1866. A mutual influence has been suggested: Swinburne probably saw the watercolour version before writing the poem, while Burne-Jones, having read the poem, incorporated many of its images into his painting. Certain phrases in it replicate poetically the mood Burne-Jones conjures up on canvas, including its almost claustrophobic atmosphere and the predominant use of red tones: 'Her little chambers drip with flower-like red', in Swinburne's verse. Further contemporary influences that have been proposed include Charles Baudelaire's *Les Fleurs du Mal* (1857) and Wagner's *Tannhäuser*, performed in Paris in March 1861 and at the Royal Opera House in 1876. Both Swinburne and Burne-Jones were admirers of Wagner, and in 1863 Baudelaire sent Swinburne his pamphlet, *Richard Wagner et Tannhäuser à Paris*.

W. Graham Robertson saw *Laus Veneris* as resembling 'clusters of many-coloured gems or stained windows through which shone the evening sun', and in a letter describing the Burne-Jones centenary exhibition of 1933 asked a friend, 'I wonder which you consider his best picture? I should vote for *Laus Veneris*…a lovely, glowing thing -- as fresh and brilliant as ever after all the years.' Robertson's opinion is widely shared, and the work is regarded as the finest example of Burne-Jones's skill in composition and use of surface pattern. It resembles a tapestry with exceptionally rich textures, that of the dress of Venus being achieved by stippling with a circular punch in the underpaint before the colour was added. The vivid contrast the painting must have made against the green walls of the Grosvenor Gallery, where it was first exhibited, can only be imagined. The actual tapestry on the right of the painting depicts Venus in a chariot and was created in 1861 as a design for tiles and in 1898 adapted as a tapestry made by William Morris's company.

PLATE 18

THE ANNUNCIATION
——— 1879 ———
Oil, 98.5 x 41 in / 250.1 x 104.1 cm
National Museums and Galleries on Merseyside
(Lady Lever Art Gallery, Port Sunlight)

Annunciations became something of a stock-in-trade for Burne-Jones:
the same subject, along with a *Nativity*, had been commissioned from
him in 1862 for a bible produced by the Dalziel brothers, and on
numerous subsequent occasions for stained glass. In this version, the
expulsion from Eden frieze on the wall was derived directly from a
stained-glass design. Sketches for the composition are in the
Fitzwilliam Museum, Cambridge, and the original cartoon re-worked
in watercolour in the Castle Museum, Norwich. The oil, which was
originally in the George Howard collection, was modelled by Sara
Prinsep's niece Julia. In 1878 she had become the wife of the writer
Leslie Stephen, and was appropriately painted while pregnant with
her first child, Vanessa Stephen, later Bell (herself destined to
become an artist, and the elder sister of Virginia Woolf), who was
born on 3 May 1879. Having decided against a career in the church,
the myth and mystery of his art became a substitute for religion in
Burne-Jones's life. He created a highly personal adaptation of the
Christian view of life, in Lord David Cecil's words, making it 'a
search for spiritual salvation to be achieved with the help of the
specifically Christian virtues of charity, humility and mercy', yet
despite the gravity of his religious subjects, and especially his church
stained-glass work, Burne-Jones's mythological works are invariably
more deeply felt and convincing.

PLATE 19

THE GOLDEN STAIRS
———— 1872 – 80 ————
Oil, 109 x 46 in / 277 x 117 cm
Tate Gallery, London

Burne-Jones often worked for several years on his paintings, many of which were created to the large scale of this work, which stands some nine feet tall. The picture was designed in 1872, but not begun until 1876, and was completed just in time to be shown at the Grosvenor Gallery in 1880. Georgiana Burne-Jones noted in her diary on 22 April 1880, 'The picture is finished, and so is the painter almost. He has never been so pushed for time in his life.' Burne-Jones himself wrote that 'I have drawn so many toes lately that when I shut my eyes I see a perfect shower of them.' F.G. Stephens, reviewing the Grosvenor exhibition in the *Athenaeum* on 8 May, remarked that the figures 'troop past like spirits in an enchanted dream, each moving gracefully, freely, and in unison with her neighbours... What is the place they have left, why they pass before us thus, whither they go, who they are, there is nothing to tell.' Victorian critics and the public alike invariably sought the 'meaning' or story behind every painting, but were frequently thwarted by Burne-Jones. Letters to the publication *Notes and Queries* asking for an explanation of this work evinced contradictory replies, and like several of his paintings, its subject is without specific literary or historical reference (he considered several alternatives including *The King's Wedding* and *Music on the Stairs*), although the title is derived from a passage by Dante. In many Aesthetic and Symbolist works, such as Whistler's 'Symphonies' and 'Nocturnes', connections are often drawn between art and music. Burne-Jones and his family were noted for their love of music, and here, as in many of his most successful paintings, the figures carry or are playing musical instruments, but neither the final title nor the painting itself offers us any clues as to the circumstances of this musical procession, and we must conclude that it possesses no 'subject' beyond being an exercise in Aesthetic composition.

This painting belongs to a group of works of this period which are pale, almost monochromatic and highly classical, contrasting with the richly coloured *Laus Veneris*. F. G. Stephens had evidently seen the work in progress and commented: 'Since we first saw this picture it has lost much of that Greek quality we then admired... It has been modified, and now resembles in many points the art of Piero della Francesca. The pale golden carnations, the broad foreheads, the deep-set, narrow eyes and their fixed look, even the general contours and the poising of the heads on the shoulders, plainly tell of the influence of that lovely painter and poetic designer.' Many studies for the work are known – those for the hands and feet, for example, are in the Fitzwilliam Museum, Cambridge. A well-known Italian professional model, Antonia Caiva, modelled nude for all the bodies, which accounts for the chorus-line equality of their proportions, while the heads of the eighteen women were mostly members of Burne-Jones's family and his friends: they perhaps include his daughter Margaret at the bottom of the stairs with arm and waist wreaths, Edith Gellibrand, an actress, bending on the staircase, Laura Lyttleton and May Morris, facing, right centre, Frances Graham, the daughter of his patron William Graham, holding cymbals in the bottom left, and Mary Stewart Wortley, the second of the two entering the doorway. *The Golden Stairs* entered the collection of Cyril Flower, later Lord Battersea, and his wife Constance, a member of the Rothschild family, but it became widely known through popular engravings. It was said to have become an important inspiration for W.S. Gilbert in writing his operetta *Patience*, first produced in 1881, which satirized the Aesthetic Movement.

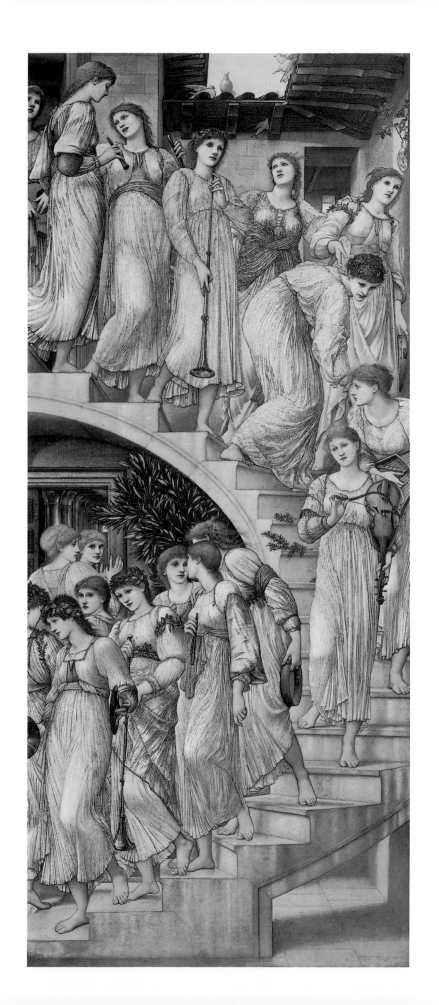

PLATE 20

THE MILL
—— 1872 – 80 ——
Oil, 35.8 x 77.8 in / 90.9 x 197.6 cm
Victoria & Albert Museum, London

Constantine Ionides, the wealthy Greek businessman patron of Burne-Jones, commissioned this work which Burne-Jones begun in 1870. It was shown at the Grosvenor Gallery in 1882 and ultimately entered the Victoria & Albert Museum through the Ionides Bequest. Modelled by Maria Zambaco, Aglaia Coronio (Constantine Ionides' sister) and Marie Spartali (whose husband was Merlin in *The Beguiling of Merlin*), The Three Graces – as the three models, who were also cousins, were known in the artistic community – dance to the music of Love. The naked men in the pool behind perturbed Henry James in his review, and when the Royal School of Art Needlework created an embroidered version, this detail was deliberately omitted. The mill from which the title is derived is almost a minor element, with minute punting millers and grain sacks in the background, but there is the implied symbolism of the water mill as a natural (in modern jargon, 'green') source of energy, and the harmony between work and play. The work has affinities to Botticelli 's *Primavera*, which similarly depicts Three Graces dancing, and other Italian masters, and was also influenced by Rossetti's illustrations for *The Maids of Elfen-Mere*, which Burne-Jones is known to have admired. Marie Spartali also appears in Rossetti's *The Bower Meadow* of 1872 (Manchester City Art Gallery), which, like *The Mill*, depicts girls dancing in a field.

THE HOURS
—— 1870–82 ——
Oil, 34 x 72.7 in / 86.5 x 183.5 cm
Sheffield City Art Galleries

This row of draped figures has close affinities to the Aesthetic works of Albert Moore, the pre-eminent exponent of the genre, who in the same year, 1882, produced a similar subject depicting a seated group of women in various states of repose (*Dreamers*, Birmingham City Art Gallery). Although dated 1882, Burne-Jones was clearly still putting the finishing touches to the painting the following year, since he then wrote a letter to Lady Leighton, telling her, 'I have been working hard in spite of all things, and hope to finish the *Wheel of Fortune* and the *Hours*. I think you never saw the last – not a big picture, about five feet long – a row of six little women that typify the hours of day from waking to sleep. Their little knees look so funny in a row that wit descended on from above, and I called them the "laps of time". Every little lady besides the colour of her own frock wears a lining of the colour of the hour before her and a sleeve of the hour coming after – so that Mr Whistler could, if he liked, call it a fugue.'

TREE OF FORGIVENESS
──────── 1881–82 ────────
Oil, 75 x 42 in / 190.5 x 106.7 cm
National Museums and Galleries on Merseyside
(Lady Lever Art Gallery, Port Sunlight)

Various versions of the Greek legend, related in both Ovid's *Heroides* and Chaucer's *Legend of Good Women*, tell how Phyllis, queen of Thrace, falls in love with Demophoön, king of Melos, the son of Theseus and Phaedra, who visits her court en route for Athens after the Trojan War (where he had hidden inside the Trojan Horse). He left the court, but when he failed to keep his promise to return within a month, she committed suicide, whereupon Athena, taking pity on her, turned her into an almond tree. Eventually, Demophoön returned to Thrace and, discovering what had happened, embraced the tree, which immediately burst into blossom.

Burne-Jones's first version of the subject, *Phyllis and Demophoön*, was the cause of his rift with the Old Water-Colour Society in 1870. In Great Britain, the 1870s was a sensitive decade on the issue of nudity in art, even if it was made respectable by classical references (Alma-Tadema, later a master of the genre, did not risk presenting a nude to public scrutiny until 1875 and was attacked for his 1877 work, *A Sculptor's Model*). Burne-Jones's work went too far, presenting both a male and female nude clasped together. The *Times* critic observed that the 'idea of a love-chase, with a woman follower, is not pleasant.' There was a further underlying cause for complaint among those in the know, for the figure of Phyllis was modelled on Burne-Jones' mistress, Maria Zambaco, while Demophoön, representing Burne-Jones himself, struggles to free himself from his forgiving former lover. As if to add emphasis to his turbulent affair, he took from Ovid the phrase, 'Tell me what I have done, except to love unwisely', and appended it to the picture.

Tree of Forgiveness, which was originally owned by William Morris, is a later oil version of the *Phyllis and Demophoön* gouache, shown at the Grosvenor Gallery in 1882, which reverses the subjects' nudity: the formerly partly draped Phyllis is now totally naked, while the previously totally nude Demophoön, clutched in her erotic embrace, is barely disguised by an improbably convenient wisp of fabric. The sturdier male figure in the second version indicates Burne-Jones's debt to Michelangelo.

PLATE 23

THE WHEEL OF FORTUNE
——————— 1875 – 83 ———————
Oil, 78.35 x 39.4 in / 199 x 100 cm
Musée d'Orsay, Paris

The Wheel of Fortune is part of an ambitious (and never completed) series of paintings for a triptych on the Fall of Troy, a theme planned as an epic poem by William Morris (and also never finished) in which four sections were designed to represent Fortune, Fame, Oblivion and Love. The work is known from an unfinished oil representing the whole grand conception (Birmingham City Art Gallery), and paintings derived from sections of it, such as versions of the *Feast of Peleus* (Birmingham; Victoria & Albert Museum) and *Venus Discordia* (National Museum of Wales, Cardiff). In this work, the allegorical figure of Fortune turns her wheel to which are bound, at the top, a slave, in the centre, a king, and at the bottom a poet. The composition is derived from the Mantegna altarpiece in San Zeno, Verona, which Burne-Jones saw in 1862, while the unusually robust male figures show the influence of Michelangelo, as does the figure of Fortune which resembles a Sibyl in the Sistine Chapel (Burne-Jones had studied them in detail in 1871, reportedly by lying on his back with a pair of opera glasses). Several versions of this subject are in the collections of the National Museum of Wales, Hammersmith Public Libraries, the National Gallery of Victoria, Melbourne, and the Watts Gallery, Compton, but this was his personal favourite among his entire oeuvre. In 1893 Burne-Jones wrote to Helen Mary Gaskell, telling her, 'my Fortune's Wheel is a true image, and we take our turn at it, and are broken upon it.' Fortune's head-dress was created by Alice Comyns Carr, the wife of the Grosvenor Gallery director Joseph Comyns Carr, who designed stage costumes for the actress Ellen Terry. The scale of the figures is somewhat bizarre, but the disproportion was perhaps a deliberate reflection of the technique found in ancient art whereby important characters are represented in sizes in proportion to their status. Burne-Jones is recorded as having worked round the clock to complete this picture for the Grosvenor Gallery exhibition of 1883, where it was warmly praised and acquired by Arthur Balfour, for whom Burne-Jones was already commissioned to produce the *Perseus* series. Acquired by a French collector after Balfour's death, (the Luxembourg had already acquired related drawings), it entered the French national collection as recently as 1980.

PLATE 24

KING COPHETUA AND THE BEGGAR MAID

—— 1884 ——

Oil, 114.2 x 53.5 in / 290 x 136 cm
Tate Gallery, London

The subject of the work is an Elizabethan ballad, retold in Tennyson's poem *The Beggar Maid*, in which a king searches for a pure wife. After finding her, the king offers his crown in return for the love of the ragged beggar girl, who in Burne-Jones's painting sits as if enthroned while he sits beneath her in homage. The anemones in the girl's hand symbolize rejected love, while the characters represents Burne-Jones himself and his wife Georgiana; it is said that the head of the king had to be modified to make its model's identity less obvious. Starting with a small oil version in about 1861, Burne-Jones progressively developed the theme with an extensive series of pencil studies of the various elements (now in the Birmingham City Art Gallery, Manchester City Art Gallery, the Ashmolean Museum, Oxford, and the Fitzwilliam Museum, Cambridge). Certain details were derived from actual objects – the crown, for example, was specially made by W. A. S. Benson. Burne-Jones commented in a letter, 'I work daily at *Cophetua and his Maid*. I torment myself every day – I never learn a bit how to paint. No former work ever helps me – every new picture is a new puzzle and I lose myself and am bewildered – and it's all as it was at the beginning years ago. But I will kill myself or Cophetua shall look like a King and the beggar like a Queen, such as Kings and Queens ought to be.' He had worked on it for so long that he had grown '...very tired of it – I can see nothing any more in it, I have stared out of all countenance and it has no word for me. It is like a child that one watches without ceasing until it grows up, and lo! it is a stranger.'

The resultant somewhat laboured and overworked quality of the painting has attracted a degree of criticism, yet it remains one of Burne-Jones's most impressive and best-known images. When the huge painting was exhibited at the Grosvenor Gallery in 1884, the art critic of *The Times*, which had previously been only moderate in its praise of Burne-Jones, described it as 'not only the finest work that Mr Burne-Jones has ever painted, but one of the finest pictures ever painted by an Englishman.' It also received acclaim when it was shown in Paris at the Exposition Universelle in 1889 (at which the centre of attraction was the newly-completed Eiffel Tower). Burne-Jones was duly awarded the Croix de Legion d'Honneur. The painting was shown in England at the New Gallery in 1892 and again at the memorial exhibition after Burne-Jones's death. Following this last showing, Georgiana hoped that it would go to the National Gallery, but it was acquired by the Tate Gallery.

PLATE 25

SIBYLLA DELPHICA

—— 1868 ——

Oil, 60.2 x 23.7 in / 152.8 x 60.3 cm
Manchester City Art Galleries

Described by Malcolm Bell as 'a figure in a gorgeous orange robe standing in a doorway beside a burning tripod and reading the mystic messages,' Sibylla Delphica, or the Delphic Sibyl, was the priestess of Apollo who presided over the Oracle at Delphi, where she wrote her prophecies on bay leaves. Burne-Jones painted classical subjects and draped figures in wet, clinging robes, this vivid one resembling the pale girls previously seen processing in *The Golden Stairs*.

THE DEPTHS OF THE SEA
——— 1887 ———

Watercolour and gouache, 66.7 x 29.8 in / 169.4 x 75.8 cm
The Fogg Art Museum, Harvard University, Cambridge, Massachusetts
Bequest of Grenville L. Winthrop

Burne-Jones was elected an Associate of the Royal Academy in 1885, but resigned eight years later, having only ever exhibited a single work, an oil of *The Depths of the Sea* (private collection). This is a watercolour version of the same subject, painted after experiments with the effects of underwater light in a water tank loaned to him by the painter Henry Holiday. The shoal of fishes was added after encouragement by Lord Leighton, who saw the work in progress to check its suitability for exhibition at the Academy. Like *The Beguiling of Merlin* and *Phyllis and Demophoön/Tree of Forgiveness*, the image is one of man and woman engaged in a struggle. The mermaid, with her siren-like beauty and potential of menace (as here, where she has dragged a drowned sailor to the bottom of the sea) was a popular nineteenth-century *femme fatale* image among a number of Pre-Raphaelite followers, such as John William Waterhouse, and to Symbolists including Gustave Klimt.

The artist's interest in mermaids developed particularly after his acquisition of his seaside home in Rottingdean. There he created a 'tavern' which he called 'The Merry Mermaid', and turned frequently to the motif in various sketches and watercolours, one of which, formerly owned by Burne-Jones's young friend Katie Lewis, is now in the Tate Gallery, and produced a mermaid drawing (Victoria & Albert Museum) that was made into an apparently unrealized wallpaper design (William Morris Gallery, Walthamstow). There are reasons to believe that the head of the mermaid was modelled by Laura Tennant (one the subjects in *The Golden Stairs*), the wife of Alfred Lyttleton, who died in 1886 while the oil was being painted, Burne-Jones telling Alfred, 'I am painting a scene in Laura's previous existence.' Gerard Manley Hopkins saw *The Depths of the Sea* at the Royal Academy and wrote to a friend, 'You speak of powerful drawing. I recognize it in that mermaid's face and in the treatment of her fishnets and fishermanship, the tailfin turning short and flattening to save striking the ground – the stroke of truly artistic genius.'

PLATE 27

THE ARMING OF PERSEUS

──────── 1885 – 88 ────────

Oil (unfinished), 60.2 x 50 in / 153.x 127 cm
Private collection

Perseus was a series of paintings commissioned in 1875 by Arthur
Balfour, a wealthy politician (and later British Prime Minister) who
had previously acquired his *Wheel of Fortune*, for display in the music
room of his London house at 4 Carlton Gardens. Burne-Jones
selected the subjects from his earlier treatment of the legends associated with Perseus, the offspring of Danaë and Zeus, as illustrations
for Morris's *The Earthly Paradise*. The subjects were modified as work
progressed slowly over many years, with eight large paintings and a
range of extra decorative details indicated in his drawings of the
entire room (now in the Tate Gallery). Burne-Jones worked on a set
of full-sized cartoons (Southampton City Art Gallery) until 1885,
when he turned his attention to the oil versions, but the ambitious
series was never completed. W. Graham Robertson, on his first visit
to The Grange, described seeing them in progress, scattered
throughout his studio. The paintings were acquired by Huntington
Hartford and in 1972 sold to the Staatsgalerie, Stuttgart. In this, the
third work from the cycle, Perseus meets the Nereides or sea
nymphs who arm him with the winged sandals of Hermes, a helmet
to make him invisible and a bag in which to place the head of the
gorgon Medusa. The nymph on the far right is has been identified as
modelled by Frances Graham, the daughter of his patron William
Graham, and one of his many close female friends.

THE ROCK OF DOOM
———— 1885–88 ————
Oil, 61 x 51.2 in / 155 x 130 cm
Staatsgalerie, Stuttgart

In the Perseus legend, after vanquishing and escaping with the head
of Medusa, Perseus journeys to Joppa where he finds, rescues and
marries Andromeda, who had been chained to a rock as a sacrifice to
a sea monster after her mother Cassiopeia had offended the gods.
This work was exhibited in 1888 at the New Gallery, London, a
newly-established venture that had been set up following a schism
among the directors of the Grosvenor Gallery.

THE BALEFUL HEAD
———— 1886 – 87 ————
Oil, 61.4 x 50.4 in / 156 x 128 cm
Staatsgalerie, Stuttgart

Although chronologically later in the Perseus cycle, *The Baleful Head* was one of the first to be finished – if any of them can be described as finished, since Burne-Jones continued to tinker with them until his death, and Balfour's patience over the 23 years on which Burne-Jones worked on his commission is to be admired. The work, which was exhibited at the Grosvenor Gallery in 1887, shows Perseus with his wife Andromeda viewing the reflection of Medusa's head in a well, as a way of avoiding the direct gaze of the gorgon whose glance would otherwise have turned them to stone. The head of Medusa was based on a portrait of the daughter of Burne-Jones's friend W.A.S. Benson.

DANAE AND THE BRAZEN TOWER
——————————— 1887–88 – ———————————
Oil, 91 x 44.5 in / 231.1 x 113 cm
Glasgow Museums: Art Gallery and Museum, Kelvingrove

The painting recounts a scene from the legend of King Acrisius of Argos, who was warned by an oracle that he would be slain by the son of his daughter Danaë. So that she could not have children, he incarcerated her in a brazen tower, but there she produced a son, Perseus, fathered by Zeus who visited her in a shower of gold. Acrisius hurled the baby into the sea in a wooden chest, but Perseus was rescued, returned as an adult and, during games, accidentally killed his grandfather with a discus, thus fulfilling the prophecy. The story is told in Morris's *Earthly Paradise*, while the painting portrays Danaë watching as the tower is constructed. The head of Danaë, with the typical nervous, hesitant hand to her face, was modelled by Marie Spartali, Maria Zambaco's cousin, who Burne-Jones considered the most beautiful model of all, and who also sat for several other works, including *The Mill* (Plate 20). Other versions exist in the Ashmolean Museum, Oxford, and the Fogg Art Museum, Harvard University.

THE BRIAR ROSE—THE PRINCE
ENTERS THE BRIAR WOOD

───────── 1870–90 ─────────

Oil, 48 x 98 in / 121.9 x 249 cm
Faringdon Collection, Buscot Park, Berkshire

In the 1860s Burne-Jones created designs for a series of tiles based on
the story of Sleeping Beauty, as told by Charles Perrault. From these
in 1870–73 he developed a series of three small paintings for William
Graham (now in the Museo de Arte, Ponce, Puerto Rico), and four
larger works which occupied him intermittently from 1870 to 1890.
The figure of Sleeping Beauty was modelled by Margaret Burne-
Jones, and several writers have observed the psychological link
between the story and Burne-Jones's own aspirations, as one of
arrested ageing and protecting his virginal daughter from being
violated. In an attempt to make the briar wood as threatening as
possible, he had prickly thorns sent to his studio from the garden of
his friend Lady Leighton, requesting an example as 'thick as a wrist
and with long, horrible spikes on it.'

PLATE 32

THE BRIAR ROSE—THE SLEEPING PRINCESS

─── 1870–90 ───

Oil, 48 x 90 in / 121.9 x 228.6 cm
Faringdon Collection, Buscot Park, Berkshire

The series, embellished with descriptive verses by William Morris beneath each painting, entered the collection of the financier Alexander Henderson, later Lord Faringdon, who paid £15,000 for it, making it one of the most valuable commissions of the era. When the *Briar Rose* paintings were exhibited at Agnews in 1890, the *Times* critic was enthusiastic: 'We are accustomed to this evidence of loving care in Mr Burne-Jones's pictures, but it has never been shown before on so large a scale and with such exuberance of fancy as in these four pictures. The world of dreams and fairies has surely never been so prodigally illustrated.' After this show, and as a gesture to the poor of East London, the works were displayed free of charge at Toynbee Hall in Whitechapel before being installed at Buscot Park, which Henderson had recently bought. Burne-Jones later added intervening scenes to create a decorative frieze. Numerous studies are dispersed in various private and public collections with full-sized versions in Bristol, Dublin and elsewhere.

PLATE 33

The Star of Bethlehem
———————— 1888–91 ————————
Watercolour, oil, tempera and gouache on paper, laid onto canvas,
101 x 152 in / 256.5 x 386 cm
Birmingham Museums and Art Gallery

The nativity was a subject to which Burne-Jones turned on a number of occasions for stained-glass commissions. After Morris opened his tapestry-weaving workshops at Merton Abbey in 1881, several such designs had a further life as textiles, and this subject, created in 1887 (the cartoon for which is in the Victoria & Albert Museum), was supplied as a tapestry to such locations as the chapel of Exeter College, Oxford (which Burne-Jones and Morris had attended in the 1850s), Eton College Chapel and Norwich Castle. In this instance, however, the process was also reversed when, commissioned by Birmingham Corporation, the tapestry design was re-worked as an unusually large-scale watercolour. It was so tall that it required Burne-Jones to work on the upper parts of it on a mobile ladder, as recorded in a photograph by Barbara Leighton. Aptly, while he was working on the subject his own daughter Margaret gave birth to Angela Mackail (known in later life as the novelist Angela Thirkell).

SPONSA DE LIBANO
——— 1891 ———
Watercolour, tempera and gouache, 130.9 x 61.22 in / 332.5 x 155.5 cm
National Museums and Galleries on Merseyside
(Walker Art Gallery, Liverpool)

Sponsa de Libano, 'The Bride of Lebanon', is an illustration of passages from the biblical *Song of Solomon*: 'Come with me from Lebanon, my spouse' and 'Awake, O north wind, and come, thou south.' Burne-Jones originally created it in the 1870s for embroidery designs, in which winds urge the bride onward, with swaying lilies beside the stream. He then developed it into this watercolour, using an unnamed girl from Houndsditch to blow out her cheeks as a model for the wind – with clear echoes of the winds in Botticelli's *The Birth of Venus*.

VESPERTINA QUIES
——————— 1893 ———————
Oil, 42.5 x 24.5 in / 108 x 62.2 cm
Tate Gallery, London

The model for this portrait, the title of which means 'Evening Repose', was Bessie Keene, a young woman whose mother had previously sat for Burne-Jones. The enigmatic expression, reminiscent of that in *The Depths of the Sea*, and the landscape background, are obviously homages to Leonardo da Vinci's *Mona Lisa*.

Maud Beddington, one of the many young female artists whom Burne-Jones advised, watched him at work on *Vespertina Quies* and described his technique: 'He began by drawing the figure in raw umber...then he modelled the face in white and raw umber, lightly putting a little red on the lips, nostril and eyes – the blue of the frock and all the strong colours were painted in sweeping strokes of full colour. He used a mixture of spike [lavender] oil and turpentine as a medium. He used flat brushes to keep his canvas smooth.'

PLATE 36

LOVE AMONG THE RUINS
———— 1894 ————
Oil, 37.5 x 63 in / 95.3 x 160 cm
National Trust: Wightwick Manor near Wolverhampton

Although Browning wrote a poem of the same title, the work does not represent any specific literary incident. Many observers have noted the sadness that pervades most of Burne-Jones's work, and his figures are invariably either melancholy or expressionless. He himself commented, 'The moment you give what people call expression, you destroy the typical character of heads and degrade them into portraits which stand for nothing.' One of only two works exhibited in the seven years following the Old Water-Colour Society incident of 1870, it was shown, with *The Hesperides*, at the Dudley Gallery. An earlier gouache version (1870–73) was painted after his parting from Maria Zambaco, who appears as the woman, while the model Gaetano Meo sat for the lover. This was sent to Boussod & Valadon (the Paris company for which Theo and Vincent van Gogh had worked) in 1893. When it was being photographed there, mistaking the thick water-based paint for oil, egg white was brushed onto it to enhance the highlights, which had the effect of dissolving the surface. Burne-Jones was anguished by the damage, but immediately started work on this oil replica. In the last months of his life he discovered that by cleaning with ox gall and repainting he was able to restore the original gouache, which is now in a private collection.

PLATE 37

ANGELI LAUDANTES
——— 1894 ———

Tapestry, 93 x 72.8 in / 236.2 x 185 cm
Victoria & Albert Museum, London

In the 1880s and early 1890s, William Morris's Merton Abbey work-shops produced several tapestries based on designs derived from pictures by Burne-Jones, especially for ecclesiastical commissions. These were usually reproduced photographically from smaller cartoons, some of which had previously been produced for stained glass. *Angeli Laudantes* was originally created in 1878 as a coloured chalk cartoon (once owned by Arthur Balfour and now in the Fitzwilliam Museum) for one of two windows in the south choir aisle of Salisbury Cathedral. The other, *Angeli Ministrantes*, also became a tapestry. Even thus distanced from Burne-Jones's original design, it retains his characteristic style and much of its power.

The Wedding of Psyche
1894 – 95
Oil, 48 x 84 in / 122 x 213.4 cm
Musées royeaux des Beaux-Arts de Belgique

Like *Pan and Psyche* (Plate 9), *The Wedding of Psyche* originated with illustrations for *The Earthly Paradise*. The scattering of roses in the wedding procession recalls his own daughter Margaret's wedding at St Margaret's church, Rottingdean, in 1888, when, as Georgiana recalled, 'the way to the church door was thronged with people out of whom came four damsels in white with big baskets of rose-leaves, which they shed over the pathway.'

PLATE 39

LOVE LEADING THE PILGRIM
——————— 1896–97 ———————
Oil, 61.8 x 119.7 in / 157 x 304 cm
Tate Gallery, London

Once again Chaucer provided the literary inspiration for a painting, in this instance a scene from his *Romaunt of the Rose*, which Burne-Jones had formerly used for one of the panels of a needlework frieze which he designed in collaboration with William Morris. Embroidered in 1880 by Margaret Bell, the wife of Sir Lowthian Bell, and her daughter Florence Johnson for the dining room at Rounton Grange, Northallerton, it is now in the William Morris Gallery, London. In common with a number of Burne-Jones's major compositions, it progressed slowly: the design dates from the early 1870s, with the painting beginning in 1877, but he continued to work on it during the next twenty years, completing it only in the year before his death and dedicating it to Swinburne, exhibiting it at the New Gallery in that year. In response to a comment by his son Philip Burne-Jones that the work appeared 'cold and miserable', he lightened it. An Italian model called Giacinto sat for the Pilgrim; he was originally bearded, but this too was later altered. Thomas Rooke's studio diary of the years 1895 98 makes frequent reference to Burne-Jones's continuous work, adding details to the work over the last years of its development, anguishing over every element of the design. Even then he did not want to finish it and spoke of wanting to take 'a great big bottle of benzene and go over it and wash it all away', but a comment to Rooke was also recorded by Georgiana: 'It's nice to finish an old thing. What Mr Morris said the other day was very true; he said, "The best way of lengthening out the rest of our days now, old chap, is to finish off our old things."' Originally sold for £5,775, the painting was later acquired by the Duchess of Sutherland. However, in subsequent years Burne-Jones's star faded so much that when the National Art Collections Fund bought it in 1943 (presenting it to the Tate), they paid just £94 10s.

THE PRIORESS'S TALE

———————— 1865–98 ————————

Gouache on paper, 40.9 x 24.8 in / 104 x 63 cm
Samuel and Mary Bancroft Collection, Delaware Art Museum, Wilmington

Exhibited at the New Gallery in the last show before his death in 1898, this work depicts the story of a seven-year-old boy whose throat was cut for singing a Christian song in a Jewish city in Asia, but miraculously continued to sing when the Virgin Mary placed grain in his mouth. He died soon afterwards and was buried as a martyr. The flower symbolism of the white lily represents purity, that of the red poppy consolation, the dwarf sunflower adoration and the wallflower fidelity in adversity. A variation on the theme appears in the Kelmscott *Chaucer*, but in this work Burne-Jones's painting has come full-circle, the subject of his first oil painting becoming almost one of his last. It is also one of the best examples of how doggedly he clung to his compositions, since although this work spanned the period from 1865 to 1898, the original conception dates from even earlier, from 1858, when he created it in oil on a cabinet (now in the Victoria & Albert Museum) designed by Philip Webb the previous year and given in 1860 to William and Jane Morris as a wedding present. Georgiana, writing during Burne-Jones's final year of life, has the last word:

'The picture from Chaucer's *Prioress's Tale* which Edward completed this spring was the one designed in Red Lion Square forty years before, and the compositions of the Virgin and the little Christian boy remains exactly as he drew them – his vision had not changed. The background, however, is altered, a city replacing the landscape. As he was fitting in the poppies that grow up in front of and around the figures, some one remarked upon the importance of first lines in a composition. "Yes," he said, "they come straight from the heart."'

PRINCIPAL PUBLIC COLLECTIONS CONTAINING WORKS BY BURNE-JONES

AUSTRALIA

Adelaide
National Gallery of South Australia

Brisbane
Queensland Art Gallery

Melbourne
National Gallery of Victoria

Sydney
Art Gallery of New South Wales

BELGIUM

Brussels
Le Musée d'Art Moderne

FRANCE

Paris
Musée d'Orsay

GERMANY

Neuss
Clemens-Sels-Museum

Stuttgart
Staatsgalerie

GREAT BRITAIN

Bedford
Cecil Higgins Art Gallery

Birmingham
Birmingham City Art Gallery

Bristol
City Art Gallery

Cambridge
Fitzwilliam Museum

Cardiff
National Museum of Wales

Carlisle
Museum and Art Gallery

Compton
Watts Gallery

Faringdon
Buscot Park

Glasgow
Art Gallery

Liverpool
Walker Art Gallery

London
British Museum
Hammersmith Public Libraries
William Morris Gallery
Tate Gallery
Victoria & Albert Museum

Manchester
City Art Gallery
Whitworth Art Gallery

Newcastle upon Tyne
Laing Art Gallery

Norwich
Castle Museum

Oxford
Ashmolean Museum

Port Sunlight
Lady Lever Art Gallery

Sheffield
City Art Gallery

Southampton
Southampton Art Gallery

Wolverhampton
Wightwick Manor

IRELAND

Dublin
National Gallery of Ireland

PORTUGAL

Lisbon
Calouste Gulbenkian Foundation

PUERTO RICO

Ponce
Museo de Arte

SOUTH AFRICA

Cape Town
National Gallery of South Africa

UNITED STATES OF AMERICA

Boston, Massachusetts
Museum of Fine Arts

Cambridge, Massachusetts
Fogg Art Museum, Harvard University

Chicago, Illinois
Art Institute of Chicago

New York
Metropolitan Museum of Art

Wilmington, Delaware
Delaware Art Museum

LORD LEIGHTON

LORD LEIGHTON
1830–96

rederic Leighton was born on 31 December 1830 at Scarborough, Yorkshire, the second child of Frederic Septimus Leighton (1799–1892) and Augusta Susan Nash. His grandfather, Sir James Boniface Leighton (1769–1843), was court physician to two Tsars of Russia, Alexander I and Nicholas I, and while in their service amassed a substantial fortune. After attending school in England, Leighton's father studied medicine in St Petersburg. He was an exceptionally talented man, a polymath who had learned Russian in six months and was well versed in the classics and science. Frederic's two sisters were Alexandra (named after and the godchild of the Tsarina Alexandra of Russia), who was to become the biographer of Robert Browning, and Augusta, or 'Gussy'. Two other children, James and Fanny, died in infancy. Frederic Septimus grew increasingly deaf and was compelled to retire from medical practice, but after the death of Sir James, his inheritance meant that the family had sufficient wealth to live wherever they wished, without the need of his gainful employment. This was fortunate since Leighton's mother suffered from ill health, and the family travelled extensively abroad in search of good climates and cures. Thus the young Frederic grew up as a member of a household that was permanently on the move.

Frederic learned Latin and Greek from his father, and after moving via Bath to London attended University College School. In 1839 the Leightons visited Paris, then travelled on to Germany and Italy where they settled – for a typically brief period – in Rome. There Frederic Leighton was exposed to diverse cultural and artistic influences which he was able to absorb with great facility, not least because he was blessed with the ability to learn foreign languages: he spoke French, German and Italian with equal fluency, and later learned Spanish, as well as certain more obscure tongues such as Romanian and the less familiar dialects of some languages. At an early age he showed talent as a draughtsman which, according to some accounts, he first took up seriously while confined to bed with scarlet fever. His father, hoping that his only son would add another generation to the family's medical tradition, taught him anatomy – which he was to turn to his advantage in figure drawing.

In 1842 – after lying about his age – Frederic enrolled in the Berlin Academy of Art, and the following year attended an art school in Frankfurt. In 1845 the Leighton family moved to Florence, where Frederic joined the Academia delle Belle Arti under the teachers Guiseppe Bezzuoli and Benedetto Servolini. He was also taught by the Italian drawing master Francesco Meli and by the distinguished expatriate American sculptor Hiram Powers, who was so impressed with Frederic's ability that he not only encouraged him but, importantly, also encouraged Leighton's father to sanction his artistic training. Powers

reportedly answered Leighton's father's enquiry about whether he should permit his son to become an artist with the comment, 'Sir, you cannot help yourself; Nature has made him one already.'

When Frederic was 16, the family made Frankfurt its base, buying No. 23 Bockenheimerlandstrasse. Its location offered proximity to spas such as Wiesbaden which were popular among visitors from all over Europe (it was the town that Leighton's friend and soul-mate Sir Lawrence Alma-Tadema was to visit for his health and where, ironically, he died). In Frankfurt Frederic studied at the Städelsches Kunstinstitut where his work developed considerably. An official report noted that he 'made excellent progress and moved into his own atelier [studio] and completed a picture which was spoken of as having great painterly talent'. Fellow students painted scenes from popular German legends, influencing Leighton's own interest in mythological subjects. During political disturbances in 1848 the Leightons temporarily left Frankfurt and moved to Brussels where Frederic worked under the tutelage of the somewhat macabre painter Antoine Wiertz; there too he studied the work of Belgian masters including the history painter Louis Gallait, from whom he gained the notion of impressing through vast scale, a technique he was to emulate.

Leighton was in Paris in 1849 where he studied under Alexandre Dupuis, a history painter of mediocre reputation. While in Paris Leighton took the opportunity to visit the Louvre and, as was traditional at that time, make copies of masterpieces there. The next year, the upheavals in Frankfurt at an end, he returned to the city and worked under the newly-appointed Professor Jacob Edward von Steinle, a history painter belonging to the Nazarene School, a group sharing many of the aspirations and some stylistic characteristics of the English Pre-Raphaelites. Leighton also worked in the open air with a group of landscape painters known as the Cronberg School. Fellow student Otto Donner von Richter later recalled the impression Leighton had made on him:

He stands before me: a picture of a youthful, handsome man, full of zest for life, vigour, industriousness, health, and with an outstanding artistic talent.

The early 1850s found Leighton painting scenes from the lives of Italian Renaissance painters including, in 1852, his first major history painting, *The Death of Brunelleschi*. This was a competent but rather immature composition reminiscent of an altar piece, with Renaissance prototypes in scenes of the Virgin's or of saints' deaths, and featured both Leighton's sister Augusta and their father, who posed for the head of Donatello. At this time Leighton developed an interest in the historical aspects of Roman Catholicism and, like Rossetti and the Pre-Raphaelites in this period, in medieval themes.

He also painted a few portraits in Frankfurt, including those of other émigré Britons and members of the local aristocracy, circles in which he moved with equal ease. He was a popular guest at social gatherings and was noted for his musical talents; he studied singing and piano, and was later acquainted with notable musicians, including Rossini.

In 1851 Leighton returned to London where he visited family members, painting the portrait of his maternal great-uncle Edward I'Anson, and making contact with several English artists who found him an agreeable outsider. He also visited the Great Exhibition, the vast show of arts and sciences centred on the Crystal Palace which attracted some six million visitors.

After 20 years of unsettled but culturally stimulating travel, the Leighton family finally established a home in Bath, but Frederic decided to return to Italy. As he journeyed there he wrote, 'I have opened the introductory chapter of the second volume of my life, a volume on the title-page of which is written "Artist".' He was fully aware that Italy was to provide an enormous stimulus to his artistic imagination, and as he neared his destination he noted: 'Italy rises before my mind. Sunny Italy! I am about again to tread the soil of that beloved country, the day-dream of long years is to become a reality.'

He made architectural studies of medieval buildings in Verona, Venice and Florence before moving on to Rome, arriving there on 19 November 1852. Almost immediately, he experienced a sense of disappointment with the artistic atmosphere, and during his first months in Rome suffered

The Death of Brunelleschi (1852). Leighton's early excursion into history painting was partly modelled by members of his family.

from bouts of depression. Equally alarming, his eyesight deteriorated, perhaps a psychosomatic symptom, but one that was unrelieved by the homeopathic remedies he tried. His spirit improved with the coming of spring, though his eyesight problem continued to concern him.

In Rome, Leighton met such expatriates as the British sculptor John Gibson and formed a lifelong and firm friendship with Adelaide Sartoris. The wife of Edward Sartoris and a member of the Kemble theatrical family (her sister was the celebrated actress Fanny Kemble) she was herself an opera singer. Leighton met her early in 1853 and through her *salon* he was introduced to other members of Rome society, most especially, in 1854, Robert and Elizabeth Barrett Browning who remained close friends for many years. Leighton's relationship with Mrs Sartoris has been considered by some prurient observers as scandalous, but it seems highly unlikely that it ever went beyond that of an admiring young artist and a middle-aged woman who was delighted with his company.

Leighton's influential mentor Adelaide Sartoris (1860), by French society photographer Camille Silvy.

Leighton was clearly attractive to women: all who met him considered him handsome, with a distinctive aquiline nose and a bearing that was dignified and far removed from the casual Bohemianism of many contemporary painters. Leighton himself was to remain unmarried in an age that, at least publicly, placed great store in the institution of marriage and the family. 'I would not insult a girl I did not love by asking her to tie her existence to mine, and I have not yet found one that I felt the slightest wish to marry: it is no doubt ludicrous to place this ideal so high, but it is not my fault – theoretically I should like to be married very well,' he wrote in a letter to his mother.

At this time he spent a good deal of time in the company of Isabel Laing, the daughter of friends of his family, whose portrait he painted and whom he escorted around Rome; however, she later married Joseph Nias, a sailor and Arctic explorer. Suggestions that Leighton was latently or actually homosexual or, since he apparently painted beautiful women and handsome men with equal enthusiasm, bisexual, do not stand up to scrutiny. He was, however, emotionally insecure, and in the many records of his life there exists virtually no evidence of any emotional attachments at any stage. He was at his most relaxed with children, but with adults with whom he came into conflict, he barely kept his volatile temper under control, the Prince of Wales once commenting in a letter '…you know how touchy he is'. His outward self-confidence hid a nervous temperament, and he was prone to self-induced imaginary disorders.

To his apparent remoteness, reinforced by his somewhat austere habits – he never smoke or drank, conducted his business affairs efficiently, and was never in debt – was

Leighton based a number of works on Shakespearean scenes, including *The Reconciliation of the Montagues and Capulets over the Dead Bodies of Romeo and Juliet* (1853–55).

same venue as the celebrated dwarf known as Tom Thumb and 120,000 visited the latter and only 133 Haydon's exhibition, he shot himself in despair. What might have been a salutary lesson to Leighton in the folly of pursuing an artistic career actually made him all the more determined to do so – but to do so more successfully than any of his predecessors.

In the same year Leighton visited Germany to obtain treatment for his eyesight, visiting his parents in Frankfurt before returning to Rome by way of Venice. He resumed work on his two paintings, taking a break during the summer in Bagni di Lucca. Months of work had gone into his painting of *Cimabue's Madonna*. It had become one of the sights of Rome among fashionable visitors, one of whom criticized its static rigid composition, whereupon Leighton completely revised it. This painting and *The Reconciliation* were finally completed to his satisfaction and he packed them off to London in a crate, feeling 'a kind of strange sorrow at seeing them nailed up in their narrow boxes; it was so painfully like shrouding and stowing away a corpse.'

His intention was to have one or both paintings accepted by the Royal Academy for exhibition in its summer show. In fact, only *Cimabue's Madonna* was accepted. The painting's full title was *Cimabue's Celebrated Madonna is Carried in Procession through the Streets of Florence; in front of the Madonna, and crowned with laurels, walks Cimabue himself, with his pupil Giotto; behind it Arnolfo Di Lapo, Gaddo Gaddi, Andrea Tafi, Niccola Pisano, Buffalmacco, and Simone Memmi; in the corner Dante*. Not only was its title excessively long, but it was also a huge painting, measuring more than seven feet high and 17 feet long. 'One thing is certain,' Leighton pointed out, 'they can't hang it out of sight – it's too large for that.' Just as Cimabue's painting of the Madonna is carried in triumph in the painting and the artist showered with praise for his consummate skill, so Leighton himself, it must be acknowledged, sought the same adulation. And, indeed, he was to receive it when the painting was accepted by the Royal Academy (despite reservations about its size), exhibited and, the crowning glory, immediately purchased by Queen Victoria for 600 guineas (£630). There can be few comparable instances in artistic history: the bestselling first novel, or in modern times the box-office smash of a director's or an actor's début film are the closest parallels, but it was without precedent for an almost unknown young artist to unveil such a monumental and remarkable work as his first publicly exhibited painting – and, what is more, to so captivate the reigning monarch that on the first day of the exhibition it was purchased for the Royal Collection. The work also received critical acclaim, the *Art Journal* observing:

There has been no production of modern times more entirely excellent than this. It is of the truest order of

added the charge of some that Leighton was self-seeking and snobbish, the artist and novelist George Du Maurier considering that he would not make himself 'agreeable to anything under a duchess'. However, there is ample evidence that he was widely popular, a good friend to many, thoughtful and charitable. When he had himself become famous and successful, he gave both financial support and practical assistance to struggling young artists, even those whose work was aesthetically opposed to his own, among them Aubrey Beardsley.

Leighton's circle of friends in Rome included the architects William Burges, Alfred Waterhouse and George Aitchison, the last of whom was later to design Leighton's famous London house. He also met the landscape painters George Heming Mason and Giovanni Costa, who were to remain friends (and often financial dependants) for the rest of his life. And he numbered among his acquaintances such diverse characters as Jean Jacques Ampère, the son of the man after whom the unit of electrical current is named and an historian of Rome, and the novelist William Makepeace Thackeray, the author of *Barry Lyndon* and *The Virginians*. Clive Newcome in Thackeray's *The Newcomes* (1853–55) was in all probability based on the young Leighton. He is described in the novel as '…the young swell of the artists of that year, and adored by the whole of the jolly company. His sketches were pronounced on all hands to be admirable; it was agreed that if he chose he might do anything.' On returning to London Thackeray prophetically joked with the Pre-Raphaelite painter John Everett Millais that Leighton might well challenge him one day for the Presidency of the Royal Academy.

As his confidence returned, Leighton began work on two major paintings, *Cimabue's Madonna* and *The Reconciliation of the Montagues and Capulets over the Dead Bodies of Romeo and Juliet*. At his second studio in Rome, to which he moved in 1853, George Aitchison read aloud the *Autobiography and Journals* of Benjamin Haydon. Haydon had aspired to be a classical painter, but when his works were shown at the worth: no 'slap-dash' for effect, no 'niggling' labour in vain; it is faithful to a high purpose: the conception is worthy of the theme, and that theme is of the loftiest, for it elevates and honours and perpetuates the glory of the artist and the Art.

The influential critic John Ruskin began his annual *Academy Notes* that year, describing *Cimabue's Madonna* as 'a very important and very beautiful picture'. Dante Gabriel Rossetti was also conscious of the influence Leighton's work might have in the battle between the Royal Academy and the Pre-Raphaelites, remarking in a letter to William Allingham, 'The RAs have been gasping for years for someone to back against Hunt and Millais and here they have him.'

When news of his triumph reached him in Rome, Leighton immediately used some of his payment to buy works from fellow, less successful artists. He was aware, though, of the pressure such instant fame imposed upon him, in an untypically candid letter telling his mentor Steinle that his success, which 'for a beginner, has been extraordinarily great, fills me with anxiety and apprehension; I am always thinking, "What can you exhibit next year that will fulfil the expectations of the public?"'

Leighton left Rome, telling Steinle, 'My stay in Italy will always remain a charming memory to me; a beautiful, irrecoverable time; the young, careless, independent time! I have also made some friends here who will always be dear to me.' He travelled to London, meeting such influential figures as Ruskin, Rossetti and George Frederick Watts but, continuing his nomadic existence, journeyed on to Paris where he took a studio in the rue Pigalle and exhibited his second major picture, *The Reconciliation*, at the Exposition Universelle. In Paris he met the French artists Jean Ingres and Jean Léon Gérôme; the latter's painting *The Cock Fight* (1847) is seen as pivotal in the new movement towards academic classicism. Leighton again met George Frederic Watts, who was to become a friend, neighbour and ally, and who was similarly influential in Leighton's progressive move towards classical subjects, noted by Robert Browning as 'a sudden taste that has possessed him'. He also associated with the English painter Edward Poynter, whose work shares a stylistic affinity and Leighton is known to have admired such artists as Jean-Baptiste Corot and Jean François Millet, regarded as precursors of Impressionism. As a result of meeting certain artists, including Henri Robert-Fleury, at this point in his career, Leighton adopted the brighter palette that is evident in works from this period onward.

As Leighton had feared, *Cimabue's Madonna* was a hard act to follow. *The Triumph of Music*, shown at the Royal Academy in 1856, received a savage response ('one of the worst pictures of the Exhibition', declared the *Athenaeum*),

and he was criticized too for the anachronism of Orpheus shown playing a violin rather than a classical lyre.

In London in 1856 Leighton used Watts's studio and met the Pre-Raphaelite William Holman Hunt. His contact and friendship with members of the Pre-Raphaelite Brotherhood was especially remarkable since he was broadly opposed to their artistic ideals. But he remained on amicable terms with most of them, in particular Millais, while F. G. Stephens, one of the founders of the Movement who had become art critic of the influential journal the *Athenaeum*, became a vigorous supporter of Leighton's work.

After his failure at the Academy, Leighton did not exhibit in 1857, but worked on a literary painting, *Count Paris, accompanied by Friar Laurence and a band of musicians, comes to the house of the Capulets to claim his bride: he finds Juliet stretched apparently lifeless on her bed*, as well as *The Fisherman and the Syren – from a Ballad by Goethe*, both of which were exhibited at the Royal Academy in 1858, to a lukewarm reception. In *The Fisherman and the Syren*, later retitled *The Mermaid*, Leighton explores the *femme fatale* theme that became popular in later nineteenth-century art, especially in the work of the Symbolists.

Continuing his travels, Leighton spent the winter of 1857–58 in Algiers, where he became fascinated by the colour, architecture and costumes he encountered. Many of these were later used as motifs in his paintings, and even became decorative features in his own house. Leighton then spent his last winter in Rome where he executed paintings of Italian models, including several of the model Nanna Risi ('La Nanna'). One painting of her, *Pavonia*, had already been sold but was reluctantly copied when the young Prince of Wales, then on a tour of Italy in the company of the sculptor John Gibson, asked to purchase it. This marked the beginning of a friendship between the Prince and Leighton that was to last almost forty years.

Leighton returned to London, taking a studio in Orme Square in Bayswater. This he made his permanent base — or as permanent as any of his homes were. Chroniclers of Leighton's life have been perplexed by the almost frenetic pace with which he conducted it. More than any of his contemporaries, he took full advantage of the newly-opened European railway networks and burgeoning steamship business. For years observers noted his seemingly tireless energy as he apparently worked on half a dozen canvases simultaneously while forever dashing off to Italy, Greece, Germany, Ireland, North Africa or the Holy Land in search of new motifs and inspiration. While on these trips abroad he produced oil sketches that he would later use as backgrounds to his studio paintings, as well as fine landscapes such as his 1859 *Garden of an Inn, Capri*.

Portrait of Leighton (1881), one of several by his friend G. F. Watts.

Lieder Ohne Worte
(c.1860–61).
Leighton's exercise in
depicting a musical
theme on canvas was
originally titled
The Listener.

providing drawings, for example, for George Eliot's *Romola* (1863). A warm rapport developed between Eliot and Leighton, with Leighton advising her on historical points in her work. In *A Week in a French Country House* (1867), a novel by Adelaide Sartoris, he not only contributed two illustrations, but also features in the novel as the character Mr Kioski, just as Thackeray had used him as a the model for Clive Newcombe. Lightly disguised portraits of Leighton can also be discerned in Gaston Phoebus in *Lothair* (1870), a novel by the Prime Minister Benjamin Disraeli, and, less flatteringly, as Lord Mellifont in Henry James's *The Private Life* (1892).

When war with France was threatened, Leighton joined a volunteer brigade known as the Artists' Rifles Corps to which fellow artists such as Hunt and Rossetti belonged; he designed the Corps' cap with Millais. Leighton rose to a high rank and demonstrated natural qualities of leadership that were to stand him in good stead with his later official appointments.

On the death in 1861 of Elizabeth Barrett Browning, Robert Browning asked Leighton to design her classically-inspired tomb at the Protestant Cemetery in Florence, a poignant commission that reinforced their friendship that had been established in Rome. Decorative work of this kind was mirrored in the decorative subjects that began to emerge in paintings such as *Lieder Ohne Worte* ('Songs without Words') and other works of the period. In a letter to William Allingham dated 10 May 1861, Dante Gabriel Rossetti complained that *Lieder Ohne Worte* was unfairly ill-placed at the Royal Academy, despite being the largest and most important of six canvases Leighton showed that year. Originally intended to be entitled *The Listener*, a friend of Leighton's suggested the new title for the painting, deriving it from Mendelssohn's collection of piano compositions of the same name. *Sisters*, *Eucharis – A Girl with a Basket of Fruit*, which was praised by Ruskin, and *Girl Feeding Peacocks* date from this period, of which William Michael Rossetti wrote:

These belong to that class of art in which Leighton shines — the art of luxurious exquisiteness, beauty for beauty's sake, colour, light, form, and choice details for their own sakes, or for beauty's.

The subject of *Girl Feeding Peacocks* was chosen for its aesthetic value. The sensuous textures of a variety of materials were painted with meticulous accuracy and great technical ability. The girl's dress combines pink silk, red velvet and green-blue sleeves which pick up tones in the peacocks' feathers. To some extent Leighton's exclusion of narrative, as well as his concentration on harmonies of colour and form to affect the viewer, anticipate the Aesthetic Movement.

In 1862 Leighton began one of his few religious compositions, a fresco depicting *The Wise and Foolish Virgins* at the neo-Gothic church at Lyndhurst, Hampshire. Other biblical subjects are found in his work of the 1860s, before his characteristic classical style emerged. These include contributions, along with Hunt and other artists, to the *Dalziel*

During the 1860s, as Leighton sought to consolidate his reputation in England, he became increasingly successful financially. By the early 1860s, when the average labourer's annual income in the United Kingdom was less than £30, Leighton was earning around £4,000 a year, or more than 130 times as much. Besides, he built up substantial holdings of stocks and shares (when he received 1,000 guineas for his *Dante in Exile*, he reputedly invested it in railway shares). Dividends from his investments meant that he did not need to earn anything more professionally. Late in his life he was making around £20,000 a year, with paintings frequently selling for more than £1,000, and notable prices paid for certain important works – £3,937 10s. for *The Daphnephoria*, and *Captive Andromache* fetching a personal lifetime record of £6,000. He became established as a 'gentleman painter', a frequent visitor to many country houses and the recipient of portrait commissions from the many society figures whom he numbered among his friends. Though lucrative, Leighton eventually felt that portraiture distracted him from his true artistic intentions. Rejecting a commission, he once wrote: 'What little leisure I have for portraits (which I own to painting unwillingly) is already given away and I have had to refuse even old friends.'

He persisted with medieval subjects, among them *Paolo and Francesca*, and also began to work as an illustrator,

Bible, and subjects derived from biblical themes, such as *Salomé Dancing*, which he began in 1857 but did not complete until 1863. Despite being described by George Du Maurier as one of Leighton's best paintings, it was rejected by the Royal Academy. As a result Leighton began to fear that certain hanging committee members were secretly opposed to him.

The years since the phenomenal success of *Cimabue's Madonna* were kind but not over-generous to Leighton. The victory he had achieved at the age of 25 had not been repeated, but his reputation was steadily enhanced. Gradually his works had become popular and he was recognized for his qualities not only as an artist but also as a man. It was only a matter of time before this was publicly acknowledged through his elevation to the Royal Academy, which came in 1864 when he was elected as an Associate. Leighton's organizational skills and attributes – not least his widely noted obsession with efficiency and punctuality – immediately came to the fore, as he became increasingly active on committees and in promulgating the educational aspects of the Academy's work.

Now that he was confirmed as an establishment figure, Leighton felt the need to proclaim his status by commissioning his friend George Aitchison (later President of Royal Society of British Architects) to design a house for him. Most of the leading artists of the day built magnificent homes for themselves: Alma-Tadema, a painter whose subject matter and technical virtuosity bear comparison with Leighton's, converted Tissot's modest St John's Wood town house into a sumptuous palace with a vast domed studio. Artists' houses were often featured in the periodical press of the day, the public awed by the near-regal splendour of some of these domiciles. Leighton chose a site in Holland Park Road, London, near Little Holland House, the residence of G. F. Watts. He approached the

Study for *A Girl Feeding Peacocks* (c.1863). The subject was later developed into a rich classical composition.

design and financing of the entire operation with his characteristic thoroughness, personally supervising all stages of building and decoration in a highly businesslike manner. He furnished the house with the many treasures he had accumulated on his travels, as well as paintings purchased from contemporary artists. Leighton House — today open to the public and displaying works associated with the artist — also became a stage on which the famous men and women of the age performed, as Leighton, ever the genial host, regularly organized lavish soirées and musical evenings. James Tissot's 1872 caricature of Leighton for *Vanity Fair* aptly depicts him at such an event, languid and elegant in evening dress. A story, possibly apocryphal, recalls that when the artist and renowned wit James McNeil Whistler heard a woman praising Leighton's multifarious accomplishments, his linguistic, social and musical skills, he remarked, 'Yes – paints a little too, I believe.'

Leighton's most typical works – those of his classical period – commenced in earnest with *Orpheus and Eurydice*, his first important classical picture of the 1860s. Among other notable works of the 1860s may be numbered *Dante in Exile*, *The Painter's Honeymoon* and *Mother and Child,* the latter work refuting the occasional assertion that Leighton was incapable of portraying sentimental scenes. *The Syracusan Bride* was both a critical and a commercial success, sold to the London dealers Agnew's for £1,200 in 1866 and eight years later to the shipping magnate Frank Leyland for £2,677 10s.

In 1867 Leighton travelled to Asia Minor and Greece, producing several paintings of coastal scenes that he used

The exotic tiled Arab Hall at Leighton House, the repository of treasures from the artist's extensive travels.

as backgrounds for later works such as *Daedalus and Icarus*. In the legend of Icarus Leighton saw in the potent sun the profound power of spiritual inspiration, writing: 'Sunlight can never be an accessory – its glory is paramount where it appears everything except water is tributary to its song of splendour.' This painting shows Leighton's new-found passion for depicting landscapes bathed in sunlight, in this case based on sketches made in Rhodes in 1867. We see the town, at the head of one of the bays formed by the coastline, below from a dramatic height appropriate to the subject. The painting was acclaimed by the *Art Journal* and likened to a Greek cameo.

Venus Disrobing for the Bath, a large nude subject, shocked some despite its classical allusions. This was Leighton's first major classical nude, and one in which he challenged prevailing notions of propriety and the mistrust of the treatment of the female nude by neo-classical artists. The painting was a deliberate and salacious affront to Victorian conservatism. The vulnerable, unaware frontal nude is watched by the intrusive voyeuristic spectator. F. G. Stephens defended the controversial painting in the *Athenaeum* and the *Art Journal*, declaring that:

A figure like this, which braves prevailing prejudices, not to say principles, can only be justified by success. That Mr Leighton's *Venus* holds its ground that the bold attempt has been treated with respect, amount to a tacit admission that the artist has at any rate not failed. His picture is eminently chaste.

The work was bought by Leighton's close friend, Mrs Eustace Smith, who claimed to have modelled for Venus' feet, as hers, unlike those of the woman who posed for the figure, were so 'unspoilt'.

From this period on, nudes, mythological subjects and other motifs in classical settings dominated Leighton's work. He undertook research and compiled a summary of ideas for such themes that were to serve him for the rest of his creative life. Meanwhile, his wanderlust was unabated, and 1868 saw him in Egypt, travelling up the Nile and visiting Aswan, keeping a detailed diary of his impressions. In the same year he was elected a full member of the Royal Academy, and produced paintings that included *Jonathan's Token to David* and *Actaea, the Nymph of the Shore*.

In 1869 he went to the spa of Vichy in France, accompanying Mrs Sartoris who had been advised to go there for her health. There he met two notable Englishmen, the poet Algernon Swinburne, who was later to commemorate

the meeting in his poem 'An Evening at Vichy', and the explorer Richard Burton, whose portrait Leighton was to paint a few years later. In December Leighton's own health was poor, and he suffered from rheumatism that was to trouble him in later life; ironically, he began work on *Hercules Wrestling with Death*.

Leighton's paintings of the early 1870s include *Greek Girls Picking up Pebbles by the Sea*, which contains echoes of the work of the contemporary artists Whistler and Albert Moore, who painted similar aesthetic exercises in classical drapery with no reference to a specific legend. His *The Daphnephoria* represents his finest decorative work from this phase of his career.

Leighton visited Damascus during the autumn of 1873, producing paintings including *Old Damascus: Jews' Quarter*, and assimilating Oriental influences that were to appear in his *Study* and *Music Lesson*. He also purchased artefacts that were later used in the decorative scheme for Leighton House, in particular Arab tiles, as a result of which Aitchison designed for him an Arab Hall in which to display his finds. This exotic room, with its fountain, became the focal point of the house – even though visitors occasionally fell into it. Vernon Lee, a visitor to Leighton House in 1883, described the Arab Hall as 'quite the 8th wonder of the world'.

Mrs Sartoris (whose son Algernon married Ellen, the daughter of US President Ulysses Simpson Grant, in 1874) continued to feature prominently in Leighton's life, and he travelled to Italy with her on more than one occasion in the 1870s. Richard Burton, whom he had met on their Vichy trip, sat for his portrait in 1875. Many critics have regarded it as Leighton's finest portrait, and the most revealing of the subject's powerful personality. It had a great impact when shown at the 1878 Exposition Universelle in Paris, where it was acclaimed by the Impressionist supporter Louis Duranty. As a gesture in return, in 1876 Burton secured an important consignment of tiles for Leighton's house, taken from the tomb of Sakhar on the Indus.

Sculpture was a subject that fascinated Leighton. His wide circle of friends always included many sculptors – he was one of first British collectors of work by French sculptor Auguste Rodin – and he himself often made clay models as an aid in planning a painted composition. He produced only two full-sized works, *Athlete Wrestling with a Python*, inspired by the Laocoön that he had seen in Rome, and *The Sluggard*, both bronzes owned by the Tate Gallery and on loan to Leighton House.

Venus Disrobing for the Bath (1866-67) was considered one of the more risqué of Leighton's many nudes.

Works from the late 1870s include *Study: at a Reading Desk*, *Music Lesson* and *Winding the Skein*, the first two with nominally Oriental and the third with classical references, but all three genre pieces showing everyday life. Such works were popular with Victorian audiences: just as Alma-Tadema has been described as the painter of 'Victorians in togas', so Leighton must have been aware of the sentimental frisson that Victorians felt when they observed their own familiar daily activities translated to ancient settings, emphasizing the affinity of their own culture with that of an Imperial predecessor. Other works by Leighton in the same vogue include paintings with sentimental titles such as *Farewell!* in which a lover's departure is witnessed. Such titles and their subjects, often showing the middle classes in repose, were interchangeable with those of Alma-Tadema.

At the end of the 1870s Leighton worked on long-planned frescoes in the South Kensington (Victoria and Albert) Museum, *The Arts of Industry Applied to War and Peace*. These were not his only fresco commissions – his *Phoenicians Bartering with Ancient Britons* at London's Royal Exchange, executed in 1894–95, is, unusually (and not very successfully), a fresco executed on canvas which was then mounted on the wall.

as Academicians, and urging the nation to purchase important works of art. He was also active on the boards of national museums including the British Museum and National Portrait Gallery and used his considerable influence to enable Sir Henry Tate to establish the Tate Gallery. He was ahead of his time too in promoting environmental causes such as restricting the erection of buildings on open public spaces, in smoke abatement and the conservation of ancient buildings.

Like Burton's portrait of five years earlier, Leighton's self-portrait of 1880, painted for the Uffizi Gallery's collection of artists' self-portraits, is revealing. A simple likeness would have been inadequate for this honourable commission, so the artist chose to refer to his important office. He wears academic robes which slightly obscure the gold seal of the Royal Academy President that he wears around his neck. Leighton set himself against a background of the Parthenon frieze at the British Museum, a replica of which he had constructed in his studio.

Leighton's perceptive portrait of the traveller Richard Burton (1875).

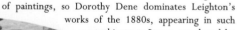

Psamathe (c.1880), an unusual and haunting image of the sister of Actaea, whom Leighton had previously depicted in Actaea, the Nymph of the Shore.

Just as Thackeray had teased Millais, hearing him speak at a dinner in London when Leighton was just 21, the painter Frederick Goodall had prophesied to a fellow guest that Leighton would one day become President of the Royal Academy. Goodall's prediction came true in 1878 when, on the death of Sir Francis Grant, who had been President since 1866, and with wide popular support – not least from his friend the Prince of Wales – Leighton was elected to this important office. Soon afterwards he was knighted at Windsor Castle.

Leighton applied his superb organizing skills to his new role, to which he was ideally suited, his popularity and linguistic ability making him the perfect ambassador of British art. He introduced various long-overdue reforms to the administration of the Academy, encouraging the election of artists who might previously not have been admitted

The year after his election, Adelaide Sartoris, Leighton's closest friend, died, and he experienced a deep sense of loss. A consolation of sorts arrived in the person of Dorothy Dene, who became his model and muse during his final years. Dorothy Dene (1859–99) was the professional pseudonym of Ada Alice Pullan, a girl from a large family that she was attempting to support through modelling; her sisters also occasionally sat for Leighton. Dorothy could have been the prototype for Eliza Doolittle to Leighton's Professor Higgins in G. B. Shaw's *Pygmalion* (and, indeed, Shaw knew them both), so much did the besotted Leighton attempt to educate her and mould her career. He aided her in her ambition to become an actress, and she had a brief but unspectacular stage career. Rumours inevitably circulated about the nature of her relationship with Leighton, but it is almost certain that it was one without impropriety. However, just as Tissot's mistress Kathleen Newton can be identified in a long series of paintings, so Dorothy Dene dominates Leighton's works of the 1880s, appearing in such subjects as *Bianca*, purchased by

The Arts of Industry Applied to War (1878–80), one of a pair of large frescoes executed for the Victoria and Albert Museum.

The Private View of the Old Masters, Royal Academy, 1888 (detail) by Henry James Brooks. Ten years after his appointment as President of the Royal Academy, Leighton holds centre stage with distinguished visitors.

encapsulate the artistic currents of the age. In 1885 he was instrumental in ensuring that Burne-Jones received the honour of being elected as an Associate of the Royal Academy, even though he was to resign five years later. Leighton himself received innumerable honours that ranged from honorary doctorates of many universities to European knighthoods and membership of leading art academies.

By the late 1880s he was suffering increasingly from ill-health – angina was diagnosed – but he kept up his relentless European travels and demanding work schedule. Friends died: he was a pall-bearer at Browning's funeral in 1889, and his father died at a great age in 1892. The following year he undertook a hectic tour of Germany, and in 1894 was suffering from exhaustion, despite which, in 1895, he travelled to North Africa and Italy. In the 1896 New Year Honours List he was created Baron Leighton of Stretton but, uniquely, was a peer for a single day. The Letters Patent confirming his Baronetage were signed on 24 January, and he died the next day at his home in London with his sisters and friends beside him. Without heirs, his peerage became void upon his death. On 3 February he was buried in St Paul's Cathedral. In his last hours he had written a will leaving a sum of money for Dorothy Dene and setting up the Dene Trust, for the benefit of her and her sisters. His last publicly reported words were 'Give my love to all at the Academy'.

the Prince of Wales, and in some of Leighton's best-known and most spectacular late paintings, including *Captive Andromache*, *The Bath of Psyche*, *Flaming June* and *The Garden of the Hesperides*.

Leighton conducted his office as President of the Royal Academy with great diligence. From 1879 to 1893 he delivered biennial addresses in which he attempted to

Leighton, surrounded by the results of his work, photographed for F. G. Stephens' *Artists at Home* (1884).

THE PLATES

1 CIMABUE'S CELEBRATED MADONNA

2 PAVONIA

3 GARDEN OF AN INN, CAPRI

4 MAY SARTORIS

5 SISTERS

6 EUCHARIS – A GIRL WITH A BASKET OF FRUIT

7 DANTE IN EXILE

8 THE PAINTER'S HONEYMOON

9 MRS JAMES GUTHRIE

10 MOTHER AND CHILD

11 THE SYRACUSAN BRIDE

12 JONATHAN'S TOKEN TO DAVID

13 ACTAEA, THE NYMPH OF THE SHORE

14 HERCULES WRESTLING WITH DEATH FOR THE BODY OF ALCESTIS

15 GREEK GIRLS PICKING UP PEBBLES BY THE SEA

16 OLD DAMASCUS: JEWS' QUARTER

17 THE DAPHNEPHORIA

18 STUDY: AT A READING DESK

19 MUSIC LESSON

20 WINDING THE SKEIN

21 ELIJAH IN THE WILDERNESS

22 BIONDINA

23 LIGHT OF THE HAREM

24 IDYLL

25 WEDDED

26 MEMORIES

27 CYMON AND IPHIGENIA

28 CAPTIVE ANDROMACHE

29 GREEK GIRLS PLAYING AT BALL

30 THE BATH OF PSYCHE

31 'AND THE SEA GAVE UP THE DEAD WHICH WERE IN IT...'

32 PERSEUS AND ANDROMEDA

33 RETURN OF PERSEPHONE

34 THE GARDEN OF THE HESPERIDES

35 AT THE FOUNTAIN

36 FATICIDA

37 THE SPIRIT OF THE SUMMIT

38 FLAMING JUNE

39 LACHRYMAE

40 PERSEUS ON PEGASUS HASTENING TO
THE RESCUE OF ANDROMEDA

PLATE 1

CIMABUE'S CELEBRATED MADONNA
────── 1853–55 ──────
Oil on canvas, 87¹/₂ × 205 in / 222.2 × 520.5 cm
HM The Queen

Leighton's second history painting, begun in late 1853, was executed in the artist's studio on the Via San Felice, Rome. His first processional painting, it is a scene of medieval Italian life, for which Leighton made studies of models wearing authentic costumes from the Middle Ages. It is a celebration of Florentine art, and was inspired by Vasari's description of the procession of the Rucellai Madonna to the church of Santa Maria Novella in Florence, the striped marble walls of which can be seen behind the figures. The location can also be identified by the inclusion of another Florentine landmark, the church of San Miniato. Cimabue, the central figure, walks before his masterpiece (now known in fact to be the work of Duccio). Cimabue is accompanied by his pupil Giotto and is observed by Dante on the right. Cimabue and Giotto are separated from the other characters, both physically and it seems psychologically, a feature that is enhanced by the comparatively simple background behind them. Symmetry has been employed here on a large scale, the composition balanced on either side of a vertical dividing line through Cimabue, with the Madonna mirrored by a Gothic niche in the wall. The figures are arranged in balanced flanking groups with a slightly raised figure to the far right and left of the painting. *Cimabue's Madonna* is an exposition of the artist's remarkable talent of composition and his skill in representing linearity and spatial relations, its uniformity broken at intervals only to prevent monotony. The canvas was the culmination of laborious and meticulous preparatory study. As well as seeking advice from several painters in Italy, Leighton corresponded with his former tutor Steinle in Frankfurt about the treatment of this subject, writing in 1854: 'I therefore took a canvas of 17¹/₂ feet (English measure), in consequence of which my figures have become half life size...and do not look at all ill.'

On seeing early designs for the composition of the painting, the artist Cornelius advised Leighton to direct the nearest group towards the spectator to prevent a frieze-like effect; however Leighton set the figures too low and failed to create a naturalistic effect of perspective. The painting had an eclectic range of influences, not simply Florentine. Leighton was inspired by the processional paintings of Bellini and Carpaccio that he had seen in Venice, as well as the rich use of colour in Venetian art generally. He was also influenced by early nineteenth-century German painters who had painted the same subject, particularly the large-scale works of Moritz von Schwind. The relationship between the human and architectonic elements in the composition reveals the influence of Raphael and Leonardo da Vinci. The painting is classical in its symmetrical form and balanced areas of colour. It is embellished with Gothic motifs, rather like the contemporary architecture of Barry and Pugin's Palace of Westminster. The painting earned Leighton much attention, Ruskin admiring it for its fulfilment of what he saw as true Pre-Raphaelite principles. The subject-matter is highly appropriate to the success of the work and the artistic prestige it brought to Leighton. Sent to the Royal Academy in early 1855, this large painting was accepted, albeit with concern about its size. It was bought on the opening day of the exhibition by Queen Victoria for 600 guineas (£630), the Queen noting:

There was a very big picture by a young man, called Leighton...it is a beautiful painting quite reminding one of a Paul Veronese, so bright and full of lights. Albert was enchanted with it, so much that he made me buy it.

PAVONIA
————— 1859 —————
Oil on canvas, 21 × 16½ in / 53.3 × 41.9 cm
Private collection

In a letter to his mother, Leighton wrote, 'I am just about to despatch to the Royal Academy some studies from a handsome model, "La Nanna". I have shown them to a good many people, artists and "Philistines", and they seem to be universally admired.' Bearing various titles, this was a series of portraits of the model Nanna Risi, known as 'La Nanna', later the mistress of the German painter Anselm Fuerbach, an artist whose career closely paralleled Leighton's. Various titles were given to paintings in the series, including the model's nickname, *A Roman Lady*, and this subject, *Pavonia*, a reference to the peacock-feather fan that frames her head. The portraits were well received at the Royal Academy, the *Athenaeum* critic commenting:

> Mr Leighton, after a temporary eclipse, again struggles to light. His heads of Italian women this year are worthy of a young old master — so rapt, anything more feeling, commanding or coldly beautiful we have not seen for many a day.

GARDEN OF AN INN, CAPRI
———————— 1859 ————————
Oil on canvas, 19¼ × 26¼ in / 48.9 × 66.7 cm
Birmingham Museums and Art Gallery

A companion piece to *Capri: Sunrise* of the same year, this painting
was executed during a five-week working visit to southern Italy.
Leighton painted as series of small urban studies of Capri to remind
him of the effect of sunlight falling on the clustered houses. The
whitewashed buildings absorb the bright light that is strongly
contrasted by the dark green, lush foliage. Pre-Raphaelite in its level
of detail, the still and claustrophobic atmosphere of the
Mediterranean climate has been effectively captured. Painted for
personal pleasure rather than public criticism, *Garden of an Inn, Capri*
is on a slightly larger scale than the other studies Leighton made of
Capri. It was painted in the garden of an inexpensive hotel, run by
Pagano and frequented by artists seeking cheap accommodation. The
painting was bought for 200 guineas (£240) by Benjamin Godfrey
Windus, a retired coachmaker from Tottenham, London, who
collected works by Turner and was a patron of the Pre-Raphaelites.

MAY SARTORIS
———————— c.1860 ————————
Oil on canvas, 59⅞ × 35½ in / 152.1 × 90.2 cm
Kimbell Art Museum, Fort Worth, Texas

Leighton was extremely grateful to Adelaide Sartoris, who helped to launch him into society in Rome. After moving around Europe with almost as much frequency as the Leightons, the Sartoris family settled at Westbury House in Hampshire in 1859. Leighton spent a lot of time, including several Christmases, with the Sartorises at their country home, where this portrait of May (Mary Theodosia, born 1845) was executed. The self-assured young woman, then aged 16 though she appears younger, strides towards the spectator through her family's estate. It was something of a rarity for Leighton to paint such an evocative English landscape. He has constructed spatial relations in the composition by means of placing a felled tree across the path to obscure the junction of the foreground and background. May holds up her heavy blue skirt, away from the chalky ground, and her solemn riding attire is brightened by a vibrant red scarf. This painting has a certain vivacity that is lacking in Leighton's other portraits, perhaps because Leighton was especially fond of the attractive young woman. The artist painted a very distinctive portrait of May later in life when she was Mrs Henry Evans Gordon.

SISTERS

———— c.1862 ————

Oil on canvas, 30 × 15 in / 76.2 × 38.1 cm
Private collection

One of six canvases accepted (out of eight submitted) by the Royal
Academy in 1862, the good hanging position of *Sisters* was some
compensation for the rejected and badly hung canvases that Leighton
had previously submitted to the Academy. It is a charming depiction
of two female figures in a lush garden. The young woman bends
down lovingly towards the little girl; their relationship is unclear,
appearing more maternal than sisterly, but was possibly a loving tribute to Leighton's own two sisters Alexandra and Augusta. The
evocation of affection and delight was later captured by Leighton in
Music Lesson. The young woman's dress is a luxuriant masterpiece in
voluminous yellow drapery, cascading from her narrow waist and
contrasting with the lustrous texture of the marble pavement. Sisters
was very well received and according to Leighton was particularly
admired by the Pre-Raphaelite painter John Everett Millais. The
atmosphere of the painting can be likened to that of Arthur Hughes's
simpler single figure composition, *April Love* of 1855. The purchase
of *Sisters* by Stewart Hodgson, a wealthy solicitor whose daughters
were painted by Leighton and who later commissioned *The
Daphnephoria*, gave the artist a needed boost of confidence after a lull
in acclaim since the success of *Cimabue's Madonna*. The painting was
sold at auction in London in 1990 for £480,000.

EUCHARIS – A GIRL WITH A BASKET OF FRUIT

———— c.1863 ————

Oil on canvas, 33 × 22 ¾ in / 83.8 × 57.8 cm
Private collection

Exhibited at the Royal Academy in 1863 together with *A Girl Feeding Peacocks*, this painting was first owned by a collector called Albert Levy. The concentration on the girl's neck and the treatment of her upraised arm is reminiscent of Mannerist art. The lighting from the front, which recalls Caravaggio, illuminates the model's back and shoulder rather than her face, and silhouettes the nape of her neck against the sombre background. This flamboyant use of lighting and the painting's dramatic form were considered by some critics as a challenge by the artist to the traditional propriety of representation. The figure has none of the qualities customarily associated with her caryatid pose, the reference to antiquity merely having a decorative function. John Ruskin recognized a source in Venetian art, but criticized the painting for what he considered incorrect perspective in the treatment of the basket.

DANTE IN EXILE

———————— c.1864 ————————

Oil on canvas, 60 × 100 in / 152.5 × 254.0 cm
Private collection

Also known as *Dante at Verona*, this large and complex painting was exhibited at the Royal Academy in 1864. It illustrates verses in Dante's *Paradiso*:

> Thou shalt prove
> How salt the savour is of others' bread;
> How hard the passage, to descend and climb
> By others' stairs. But that shall gall thee most
> Will be the worthless and vile company
> With whom thou must be thrown into the straits,
> For all ungrateful, impious all and mad
> Shall turn against thee.

Dante is ridiculed by an antagonistic crowd, having been forced to leave Florence for Verona. Once again, Leighton has used the device of distancing figures from the central character to represent psychological isolation, as previously seen in *Cimabue's Madonna* and later in *Captive Andromache*. The drama is heightened by the aristocratic woman in green, to Dante's left, who gazes upon him with pity and, to his right, the mocking jester, while other groups of activity fade into the background. This painting is considered the culmination of Leighton's early work as well as a precursor to his later decorative works. The success of the painting helped Leighton to establish his reputation at home and was instrumental in securing his election as an Associate of the Royal Academy in the summer of 1864. It was even praised by the *Art Journal*. Previously critical of the lack of concrete subject matter in Leighton's paintings, it stated that '...powers which have previously been scattered, strivings that have hitherto fallen short of the ends at which they have aimed, are in the present exhibition gathered together, and have now in great degree found their fulfilment.' In the year of its exhibition, *Dante in Exile* was purchased for £1,000 by Ernest Gambart, the shrewdest and most successful European art dealer who had bought much of Dante Gabriel Rossetti's work. In 1990 this painting was sold at auction in London for £1,000,000, establishing a new world record price for a work by Leighton.

THE PAINTER'S HONEYMOON
———— c.1864 ————

Oil on canvas, 33 × 30½ in / 83.8 × 77.5 cm
Charles H. Bayley Picture and Painting Fund, Courtesy Museum of Fine Arts,
Boston

The provenance of this painting cannot be traced from 1870. Bought by a Mr Moreby in 1864, *The Painter's Honeymoon* was not exhibited at the Royal Academy until 1866. The cause of this is unknown but perhaps the painting had too many personal connotations for the introverted and solitary Leighton. In contrast to the viraginous women in his classical paintings, here Leighton has captured the intimacy, affection and serenity of companionship. The mood recalls some Pre-Raphaelite paintings, such as Michael Frederick Halliday's *The Measure for the Wedding Ring* and John Everett Millais' *The Huguenot*. The figures are captivated by their love for each other, and this is emphasized by the lack of accessories or background detail. The same models appeared in Leighton's painting *Golden Hours*, also executed and exhibited in 1864.

MRS JAMES GUTHRIE

c.1864–66

Oil on canvas, 83 × 54 ½ in / 210.7 × 138.5 cm
Yale Center for British Art, Connecticut

Exhibited at the Royal Academy in 1866, the early ownership of this painting past that of the sitter cannot be traced. The canvas is richly decorative with meticulous attention to detail and ornament. The chair, inlaid with ebony and mother-of-pearl, is balanced by two contrasting vases of roses and lilies. Leighton's precocious depiction of texture was unrivalled in this period. The sombre background is created by the fading tapestry of a pastoral scene, with the artificial lighting enhancing the sitter's pallid fragility; many sittings were cancelled as a result of her poor health. The painting is reminiscent of Venetian portraits of the sixteenth century, which Leighton had seen on his visit to Venice in the autumn of 1865. The colour scheme is low key and balanced, the model's dress forming a black pyramid broken by minimal ornamental elements and flanked by areas of red from the tablecloth and seat cover. There is little indication of the sitter's personality, Leighton using beauty for its own sake in his portraits of women as well as in idealized narrative compositions.

MOTHER AND CHILD
—————— c.1865 ——————
Oil on canvas, 19 x 32¼ in / 48.2 x 82.0 cm
Blackburn Museum and Art Gallery

Mother and Child, one of five paintings exhibited at the Royal Academy in 1865, is a theme steeped in Victorian sentimentality, a celebration of family life in a climate of high infant mortality and questionable morals. F. G. Stephens wrote of the painting:

> Another picture, a very charming one indeed, illustrates what is the most popular side of Mr. Leighton's art... A young mother lies sidelong upon the floor of a room; her head is raised upon her elbow, and, in the hollow of her bent form, nestles a little child, her own, who playfully, daintily, and with exquisite childish grace, presses to her lips a full blooded cherry.

The reclining pose of the woman anticipates Leighton's *Actaea, the Nymph of the Shore*. The artist was concerned about avoiding prettiness when representing sentimental themes: 'By the by, if you think my picture pretty, please don't say so: it's the only form of abuse which I resent.' There is a close focus on the figures, the mother's sleeve and shirt cropped by the edge of the painting and her draped hips at the centre of the composition. The Oriental carpet in the foreground, the gilded decorative screen in the background and the vase of lilies to the left of the composition reveal Leighton's preoccupation and delight in detail and ornament, while the rich colouring once again recalls Venetian art.

PLATE 11

THE SYRACUSAN BRIDE
— 1865–66 —
Oil on canvas, 53 × 167 in / 134.7 × 424.3 cm
Private collection

Leighton was anxious about the reception of *The Syracusan Bride*, the full title of which is *The Syracusan Bride leading Wild Beasts in Procession to the Temple of Diana*. However, the painting became the sensation of the Royal Academy in 1866 and was sold to Agnew's for £1,200. Considered a key work in the development of Leighton's classical style, it is his largest painting since the mannered *Cimabue's Madonna*, executed a decade earlier, and until *The Daphnephoria* of a decade later which marks Leighton's High Renaissance. The processional painting has an unremitting symmetrical composition, the figures moving uniformly across the canvas, broken at intervals by others who have turned. Once again, the painting has no concrete subject, but was suggested by a passage in the second *Idyll* of Theocritus. Leighton linked this scenario to the Syracusan tradition of sending betrothed girls to the temple of Artemis to appease the virgin goddess. Theocritus's description of the procession is somewhat incidental to the main theme of his poem, and thus the link between image and text is rather tenuous. The main source of inspiration was probably the aesthetic potential of a procession of graceful young women, a theme also exploited by contemporary painters such as Alma-Tadema, although here the statuesque brides-to-be are decidedly reserved. As in *Cimabue's Madonna*, the main figure is isolated at the centre of the composition, flanked by symmetrical groups of figures. The rather static left side of the painting is contrasted by the animated contrapposto dynamics of the animals and their attendants on the right. The cropped figures in the foreground enhance the movement in the composition. The white platform, a common compositional device used by Leighton, is echoed by the clouds, framing the shadowed figures of the procession to give a bas-relief effect. The cropped statue is a reference to the antique sculpture *Diane de Versailles* in the Louvre.

PLATE 12

JONATHAN'S TOKEN TO DAVID
c.1868

Oil on canvas, 67 1/2 x 49 in / 171.5 x 124.5 cm
The Minneapolis Institute of Arts, Van Derlip Fund

The subject of this painting, exhibited in 1868, was taken from chapter 20 of the *First Book of Samuel*. Jonathan is depicted looking out into the field as he prepares to fire three arrows. He is accompanied by Ezel who waits to retrieve them. David, not seen, is hiding somewhere in the landscape nearby and waits for Jonathan's sign that he is safe to come out of hiding from King Saul. Leighton used this story as an allegory of mutual loyalty, the subject lacking narrative but preempting the conclusion. The treatment of the subject has a certain ruggedness appropriate to the Old Testament. Jonathan's contrapposto pose was perhaps influenced by Michelangelo's *David*, evident in the angle of his shoulders and his statuesque scale. The upraised arm also suggests antique statues of Diana while the relaxed nature of the figure recalls Greek sculptures of Apollo. The picture is thus a fusion of Leighton's meticulous study of the art of antiquity coupled with his well-rehearsed and precise life studies.

ACTAEA, THE NYMPH OF THE SHORE
——————— c.1868 ———————

Oil on canvas, 22 1/2 × 40 1/4 in / 57.2 × 102.2 cm
National Gallery of Canada, Ottawa

Exhibited in 1868, this painting was inspired by the ancient works of art and the dramatic landscape Leighton saw on his visit to Greece in 1867. Concluding that the Ancient Greeks had executed classical art in its true spirit and purest form, particularly in the sculpture and architecture of the fifth century BC, Leighton denounced Renaissance art, which had previously been a great source of influence to him, as artificial and less refined. This, Leighton's second attempt at painting a nude, depicts a Nereid, a mythic guardian of the sea. The Nereids were the 50 daughters of Nereus and Doris, the daughter of the ocean. The classically posed reclining figure, a configuration usually associated with Venus, has anatomical discrepancies: Actaea's top half is disproportionate to her lower body, a mistake that occurred in Leighton's previous work *Venus Disrobing for the Bath*, exhibited in 1867. This, coupled with her disdainful expression, gives the figure an awkwardness and a lack of sensuality. Swinburne reviewed the painting critically, feeling that it: '...has the charm that a well-trained draughtsman can give to a naked fair figure; this charm it has, and no other.' The painting's importance lies in its commitment to classicism and knowledge of the art historical canon. Executed at the same time as work by the French Neo-Classical school of painters, such as Alexandre Cabanel, it was probably also influenced by Leighton's recent acquisition of a study by Ingres, *The Odalisque and the Slave*. The timeless seascape behind the nude, taken from sketches made in Rhodes, provides a flat background. The composition is divided by the horizon line, parallel to the broad shoulders of the reclining woman. Leighton praised the effect of this increasingly popular background to the female nude: '...the calm of the ocean is the grandest of all.' The same Rhodian coastline appears later in *Daedalus and Icarus*.

HERCULES WRESTLING WITH DEATH FOR THE BODY OF ALCESTIS
——————————— 1869–71 ———————————

Oil on canvas, 52 1/8 × 104 1/2 in / 132.4 × 265.4 cm
Wadsworth Atheneum, Hartford: The Ella Gallop Sumner and Mary Catlin
Sumner Collection Fund

Through an intermediary of Apollo, Admetus, King of Pherae, had
been assured by the Fates that he would not die if someone
consented to die in his place, which his wife Alcestis agreed to do.
Just before her burial, Hercules passed by and wrestled with
Thanatos (Death), succeeded in rescuing her from Death's clutches
and returned her to her husband. These events were described in
Alcestis, a tragedy by Euripides, and later in poems by both Robert
Browning and William Morris. Leighton included the violent
vignette, enacted off-stage in Euripides's play, in this, one of his
most elaborate and theatrical compositions. The combination of the
vigorous action and the mourning figures creates a tense atmosphere,
with the flanking groups of activity on each side connected by the
recumbent woman. A sombre eclipse shape towards the top of the
painting encloses a shimmering visionary seascape at dusk and the
illuminated figure of Alcestis, who is draped in white, symbolizing
her purity, like Juliet in Leighton's *The Reconciliation of the Montagues
and Capulets over the Dead Bodies of Romeo and Juliet*. The movement of
the wrestling figures anticipated Leighton's sculpture *Athlete Wrestling
with a Python*, executed in the mid-1870s, and is reminiscent of
imagery traditionally used for Jacob and the angel. Hercules's pose
recalls the *Burghese Warrior*. It was the sight of this painting that
inspired Browning to include Leighton in his poem *Balaustion's
Adventure*:

> I know too, a great Kaunian painter, strong
> As Hercules, though rosy with a robe
> Of grace that softens down the sinewy strength:
> And he has made a picture of it all.

PLATE 15

GREEK GIRLS PICKING UP PEBBLES BY THE SEA

————— c.1871 —————

Oil on canvas, 33 × 51 in / 84.0 × 129.5 cm
Private collection

This canvas is an aesthetic scheme without narrative or didactic purpose. In the timeless seascape setting, the four women, bending or standing, are components of an undulating abstract rhythm of colour and form. The graded warm colours and the folds of the drapery unify these four separate entities. F. G. Stephens, a frequent supporter of Leighton's work, applauded him for his choice of subject and its affinity to the artist's style:

> Never was Mr. Leighton happier in choosing a subject which, in itself, is nothing, but is charming in his hands, than in *Greek Girls Picking up Pebbles by the Sea*: a delightful composition, comprising figures of almost exhaustless grace, and wealth of beauty in design and colour, besides what loveliness it shows in the stooping forms of the damsels, whose draperies a boisterous wind tosses without betraying.

Leighton was additionally commended for representing the female form without impropriety or titillation.

PLATE 16

OLD DAMASCUS: JEWS' QUARTER
c.1873–74

Oil on canvas, 53 × 42 ½ in / 134 × 108 cm
Private collection

Leighton travelled to Damascus in autumn 1873, part of his journey spent uncomfortably aboard a Russian ship bound for Beirut. As he headed overland he gained his first glimpse of the city, a sight that impressed him as he noted: 'It is a great and rare thing for an old traveller not to be disappointed, and I am grateful that it has been so with me this time.' He explored the city and sketched some of the more interesting houses, including that owned by Richard Burton, the former British Consul. He developed one of his studies of a courtyard into this painting of girls engaged in picking lemons, which was exhibited at the Royal Academy in 1874. Leighton's fascination with Middle Eastern scenes and his magpie-like habit of collecting objets d'art wherever he visited provided him with the props for such later paintings as *Study: at a Reading Desk* and *Music Lesson*, and the furnishings and decoration for his exotic house in London. The painting made £350,000 when it was sold at auction in London in 1983, setting a new record for the artist; it was re-sold 10 years later, when it fetched £400,000.

PLATE 17

THE DAPHNEPHORIA
——————— c.1874–6 ———————
Oil on canvas, 89 × 204 in / 226.0 × 518.0 cm
Board of the Trustees of the National Museums and Galleries on Merseyside
(Lady Lever Art Gallery)

Having taken two years to complete, and exhibited in 1876, *The Daphnephoria* was Leighton's largest and most ambitious painting to date, lavishly described by Holman Hunt as: '...the finest, the most beautiful picture in the world.' Commissioned in 1874 for the Surrey home of Stewart Hodgson, who had bought Leighton's decorative painting *Sisters* in 1862, the painting was purchased for £3,937 10s. in 1893.

Daphne was the daughter of Ladon, the river god. Apollo attempted to seduce, then ravish her, but she was saved by Gaea, who opened up the earth. Daphne disappeared into the ground and a laurel tree sprang up, whereupon Apollo made the plant sacred. Here we witness the people of Thebes, seen in the distant left, in a tribute to Apollo in celebration of their victory over the Aeolians. Held every nine years, the procession was described by Proclus:

> They adorn a staff of olive wood with garlands of laurel and various flowers. On the top of it a brazen globe is placed, from which smaller globes are hung. Purple garlands, less than those on the top, are attached to the middle of the staff, and the lowest part is covered with a saffron-coloured veil.

The priest, known as the Daphnephoro or laurel-bearer, in the white and gold toga and the multi-pointed diadem and carrying a laurel branch, leads the procession to Apollo's temple. Before him is a distinguished-looking semi-nude youth who holds a standard symbolizing the sun, moon and stars. At the rear of the procession, five boys carry symbols of Apollo in the form of golden tripods. The figures in the procession are entranced by the power of Apollo. The male figure with the pronounced musculature and his back to the spectator is Choragos, representing Polykleitos's perfect man, the typical Olympian strong man. The iconography in *The Daphnephoria* is not historically or archaeologically correct, but it embodies the classical ideals of harmony, completeness and beauty and contains many references to classical sculpture. This painting combines aesthetics and music in the vibrant drapery and rhythmic movement of the chorus of young women, all of whom were modelled by the young Connie Gilchrist. With *The Daphnephoria*, Leighton moved away from the horizontal format of the procession used in his previous works. The L-shaped pavement, upon which more than thirty figures march, is seen in perspective and the merging groups of figures in an oblique line is more naturalistic. Leighton made preparatory sketches from both nude and draped models as well as making clay models that could be rearranged to work out the interrelation of the characters. The *Art Journal* praised how with the '...precision of drawing and such suavity of modelling, the poet is merged in the painter'.

PLATE 18

STUDY: AT A READING DESK
1877

Oil on canvas, 24⁷/₈ × 25⁵/₈ in / 63.2 × 65.1 cm
Board of the Trustees of the National Museums and Galleries on Merseyside
(Sudley House, Mossley Hill, Liverpool)

This was one of several canvases inspired by Leighton's Middle Eastern travels. Like *Music Lesson*, this painting features Connie Gilchrist who also posed for Lewis Carroll, and modelled for Whistler in *Harmony in Yellow and Gold*. She featured in several of Leighton's works of this period before pursuing a music-hall career as a novelty skipping-rope dancer at the Westminster Aquarium, and later married Lord Orkney. Here she appears in an Arabic setting with costumes the artist had brought back from Damascus. Every surface is lavishly ornamented. Leighton was part of a wider group of artists interested in all aspects of exotic and Eastern art that was particularly fashionable in Europe in the 1870s. The painting was purchased by a Miss Augusta Smith.

M U S I C   L E S S O N
—————————— c.1877 ——————————
Oil on canvas, 36 ¹/₂ × 37 ¹/₂ in / 92.8 × 118.1 cm
Guildhall Art Gallery, London

Musical themes had proven very successful for Leighton in the 1860s and he returned to them in the 1870s as a result of his growing preference for physically passive scenarios. This intimate variation on the theme, sold in 1891 for £2,400, depicts a woman physically helping a girl, modelled by Connie Gilchrist, to play an instrument while tuning the instrument with her left hand and holding the child's finger on the strings with her right. The figures have intent expressions and delicately modelled hands and feet. The work is similar in atmosphere to *Cleobulous Instructing his Daughter Cleoboline*, exhibited in 1871, but placed in an exotic rather than classical setting. The Arabic costumes and setting were inspired by Leighton's travels in the Middle East earlier in that decade. The models are surrounded by and dressed in souvenirs from Damascus. The painting displays Leighton's talent at depicting textures, from the variegated marble of the bench to the silk clothes. The *Art Journal* praised the painting's 'sensuousness of finish'. In this luxuriant setting the two figures form a central pyramid accentuated by their luxuriant robes. The elaborate architecture in the background has a decorative rather than narrative function. The black and white bands of cold tonality are broken by vivid touches of colour in the drapery and by the flowering pomegranate branch on the floor.

WINDING THE SKEIN

——————— c.1878 ———————

Oil on canvas, 39 1/2 x 63 1/2 in / 100.3 x 161.3 cm
Art Gallery of New South Wales, Sydney

Leighton's deliberate attempt at populism, with picturesque classical nuances, is closely linked to Jean-Louis Hamon's *Skeinwinder*. Hamon was the leader of the French Neo-Greek school who painted simple genre scenes. Such scenes were also popular with the Victorian audience in England, as the *Magazine of Art* explained:

> Mr. Leighton paints trivial subjects for his admirers, and great ones for the love of art. The public accepts him purely as a decorative painter, yet we detect far loftier aims than the ends of decoration in some...works of noble interest which he has given to the world.

In 1884 the Fine Art Society produced an engraving of this painting that was very widely distributed. The two models, seen previously in his *Music Lesson*, are engaged in the familiar task of winding wool. The relaxed postures of the fair, barefooted girls were the result of careful life studies. Leighton was criticized for his highly-finished paint surface which was not only becoming dated, but gave the models' flesh a waxy, lifeless appearance. The very ordered composition is divided into three clear sections: the brief foreground, the flat roof terrace on which the girls sit, and the distant view of blue sea and purple mountains beyond. This was the last of Leighton's paintings modelled by Connie Gilchrist.

PLATE 21

Elijah in the Wilderness
c.1878

Oil on canvas, $92\,^1\!/_2 \times 82\,^7\!/_8$ in / 235.0 × 210.0 cm
Board of the Trustees of the National Museums and Galleries on Merseyside
(Walker Art Gallery, Liverpool)

This was one of eight canvases Leighton exhibited at the Royal Academy in 1879, the first year of his Presidency. First shown in Paris at the 1878 Exposition Universelle, *Elijah in the Wilderness* was one of the last in a series of male nudes. There was much interest in this Old Testament prophet in the Victorian era, perhaps resulting from Mendelssohn's oratorio about him, performed in England for the first time in 1846. In 1863 Leighton painted *Jezebel and Ahab...Met by Elijah*. The subject was taken from *Kings I* in which Elijah escaped from the vengeful Jezebel into the desert of Judah after successfully revealing the power of God on Mount Carmel. Elijah was exhausted by fasting and working. The figure has an anguished corporeal dynamic: according to Leighton's biographer, Emily Barrington, he had put much more energy into this than any other painting, as he felt that biblical themes required a dramatic and forthright approach. Elijah's abandoned pose is directly quoted from the *Barberini Faun*, which Leighton would have seen in Munich as a youth. He has a Baroque robustness and a musculature which recall Caravaggio, and are in contrast to the upright stance of the spiritual, serene angel. The composition is drowned in hues of rose and gold that capture the heat and drought of the sun-baked landscape. The overtly religious theatricality in Leighton's work of this period was not suited to the sensibilities of English taste of the time, as the *Athenaeum* expounded:

> We suppose they may be taken as cosmopolitan; they are the work of a consummate master; they compel our admiration, but they do not sway our hearts, as they would if the artist designed to look down on this poor, workaday England of ours.

BIONDINA
c.1879

Oil on canvas, 20$\frac{1}{2}$ × 16$\frac{1}{4}$ in / 52.1 × 41.3 cm
Hamburg Kunsthalle

Biondina was exhibited at the Royal Academy in 1879 and was bought by Gustave Christian Schwabe who donated it to the Hamburg Kunsthalle in 1886. It was one of a series of half- and three-quarter length paintings, usually executed on a small scale, of young female models dressed in peasant costume. Though naturalistic and painted from life, these paintings have a certain idealized soft-lens effect, particularly in the rendering of the heads. *Biondina*, whose treatment recalls the icons of Venetian masters such as Titian and can be likened to some of Rossetti's contemporary paintings, is innocent without being petulant or coy. Somewhat lacking in charisma, the women in these works are always charming, graceful and ethereal, qualities enhanced by their poetic names.

LIGHT OF THE HAREM
——— c.1880 ———

Oil on canvas, 60 × 33 in / 152.4 × 83.8 cm
Private collection

Harking back to the Oriental subjects that Leighton painted after his visit to Damascus in which the child model Connie Gilchrist appeared, *Light of the Harem* is one of his first works featuring Dorothy Dene, the favourite model he was to 'discover' in the last years of his life. She was to pose for him in some of his most memorable works, often in genre subjects of avowed sentimentality, in Oriental and classical costumes and later nude. These works, and Leighton's obvious affection for the young would-be actress, resulted in rumours that their relationship was more than that of artist and model. Dorothy Dene, whose real name was Ada Alice Pullan, also posed for other artists, including Leighton's friend G. F. Watts. He was especially attracted by her complexion which was described as '…a clouded pallor, with a hint somewhere of a lovely shell-like pink'.

IDYLL
———————— c.1880–81 ————————
Oil on canvas, 41 × 83 ½ in / 104.1 × 212.1 cm
Mr and Mrs Henry Keswick

Leighton has depicted a shepherd, seen from the back, playing pipes
to an audience of two resting dryads (forest nymphs). The entwined
pose of the two female figures recalls the reclining figures on the
Parthenon frieze; one supports herself on her elbow while her
companion rests upon her breast. They lie beneath a wide-spreading
oak on a sloping bank of grass scattered with autumn leaves. The
pastoral setting and the subtle evocation of mood are reminiscent of
George Mason's *Pastoral Symphony*. The title of the painting refers
generally to the *Idylls* of Theocritus. The dryads have been bewitched
by the shepherd's music. He plays to his animals, unaware of his
languid audience who will disappear when night falls and the music
ends. The tanned, robust, corporeal shepherd, outlined by the sea,
contrasts strongly with the rather ethereal nymphs. This, as well as
the colour scheme, closely links this painting to *Cymon and Iphigenia*.
The nymph on the right was reputedly modelled by Lily Langtry, the
mistress of the Prince of Wales.

PLATE 25

WEDDED
———— c.1881–82 ————
Oil on canvas, 57¼ × 32 in / 145.4 × 81.3 cm
Art Gallery of New South Wales, Sydney

One of Leighton's most popular paintings, *Wedded* was one of the first of his paintings to be reproduced as a print, as a result of which it became widely known. In 1882 the original was purchased for £1,500 and sent to Australia. It was acclaimed by Browning, who remarked: 'I find a poetry in that man's work that I can find in no other.' The composition and the subtlety of line and composition was inspired by a variety of sources, including a sketch of a Greek girl who had fascinated Leighton during his visit to Damascus, and a landscape painted on an earlier journey to the Alps. The subject however, is Italian. The dignity of the figures is accentuated by their brilliant drapery. The girl, in a contrapposto pose, is supported by the male figure who is interchangeable with Leighton's *Cymon* – both are strong men before female beauty.

PLATE 26

MEMORIES

———— c.1883 ————

Oil on canvas, 30 × 25 in / 76.0 × 64.5 cm
Private collection

Like *Biondina*, *Memories* belongs to Leighton's series of paintings of professional models to which he appended avowedly sentimental titles such as *Sister's Kiss*, *The Maid with the Yellow Hair* and *Wide, Wondering Eyes*, or girls' first names such as *Serafina*, *Amarilla* and *Catarina*. Like them, this painting has a soft-focus quality that sets it apart from Leighton's more characteristic classical work and appears to be by a quite different hand. The sitter for *Memories* was Edith Ellen Pullan, one of the four sisters of his beloved Dorothy Dene. Leighton often visited the Pullan family, and employed Dorothy's sisters as models.

PLATE 27

CYMON AND IPHIGENIA
———————— c.1884 ————————
Oil on canvas, 64 x 129 in / 162.5 x 327.6 cm
Art Gallery of New South Wales, Sydney

Iphigenia was the daughter of Agamemnon who offered her to
Artemis as a sacrifice to appease the goddess's wrath. Artemis felt
compassion for the innocent victim and snatched her away at the
moment of sacrifice, taking her to Tauris where she became a priestess of Artemis's cult. Victorian spectators may have found the title of
this painting confusing, as it associates Iphigenia from Greek mythol-
ogy with the relatively unknown Cymon, the son of Miltiades. The
title is also that of a poem by Dryden:

> And on the margin of the fount was laid,
> Attended by her slaves, a sleeping maid.
> The fool of nature stood with stupid eyes,
> And gaping mouth that testified surprise,
> Fixed on her face, nor could remove his sight,
> New as he was to love, and novice in delight.

Leighton's haunting depiction of Iphigenia is taken from Boccaccio's
The Decameron in which Cymon, a shepherd, discovers the sleeping
figures of Iphigenia and her attendants, here placed in a visionary
seascape. Momentarily captivated by admiration and beauty, he
reflects upon his own simple existence. Boccaccio wrote: 'From a
labourer, Cymon became a judge of beauty.' Boccaccio's version is
set in spring, Leighton's in late summer, an ideal setting for languor
and the treatment of the themes of immortal beauty and repose. The
transient, surreal lighting of dusk, described by Leighton as '...the
most mysteriously beautiful in the whole twenty-four hours,'
comprising both sunlight and moonlight, surrounds the scene in an
eerie half-light with only Iphigenia's draped form, in an abandoned
pose, cocooned by the remaining luminous glow. Leighton described
the moment: '...the merest tip of the moon has risen from behind the
sea horizon, and the air is haunted still with the flush of the after-
glow from the sun already hidden in the west.' The rectangular,
vertical composition of this painting, which was bought by Sir W. E.
Cuthbert Quilter, emphasizes the diagonal line of the recumbent
figures.

PLATE 28

CAPTIVE ANDROMACHE
c.1888
Oil on canvas, 77½ x 160 in / 197.0 x 406.5 cm
Manchester City Art Galleries

Having planned this painting for several years and executed many preparatory studies, Leighton illustrated a subject which was suggested but not actually described in Homer's *Iliad*: Hector's prophecy about his wife as a lonely captive after the fall of Troy. *Captive Andromache* is a culmination of Leighton's series of processional paintings. It depicts the imprisoned Andromache, one of the most noble characters in the *Iliad*, amongst the women of Epirus. The scene is set in a farmyard of Pyrrhus in Thessaly. The slight narrative may not really justify the huge scale of the painting, but Leighton used the theme as a pretext for representing alienation, the mood indicated by the main figure's sombre drapery and solitary form. Exhibited at the Royal Academy in 1888, the picture was accompanied by lines from Elizabeth Barrett Browning's translation of the *Iliad*:

> Some standing by,
> Marking thy tears fall, shall say 'This is she,
> The wife of that same Hector that fought best
> Of all the Trojans when all fought for Troy.'

Andromache was modelled by Dorothy Dene. Her configuration could be interchanged with that in Leighton's *Day Dreams* and his *Helen of Troy*. Lena Dene, Dorothy's younger sister, posed for the young woman on the left accompanied by children. The pose of the sleeping figure can be seen later in *Flaming June*. Writing in the *Athenaeum*, F. G. Stephens likened the painting to Greek bas-relief. Typically, Leighton designed his own frame, echoing the architectonic elements in the painting. Here it is an integral part of the aesthetic effect of the large-scale piece. *Captive Andromache* was generally well received, the *Magazine of Art* celebrating it as the masterpiece of Leighton's career:

> It has been thoroughly well thought out, and is not only an admirable example of the excellences and faults of its painter...but is in itself a complete exposition of the art of painting...subject, composition, line, character, colour – are all here.

The advent of provincial galleries provided an invaluable new source of patronage for Leighton and his contemporaries. *Captive Andromache* was bought by Manchester City Art Gallery for £6,000 – the record price paid for one of Leighton's paintings during his lifetime – which was raised by subscription. However, the gallery was reluctant to loan the painting when Leighton requested it, at very short notice, as a British contribution to the 1889 Paris Exhibition with which the artist was closely involved.

PLATE 29

GREEK GIRLS PLAYING AT BALL
—————————— c.1889 ——————————
Oil on canvas, 47 × 78 in / 119.4 × 198.1 cm
Dick Institute, Kilmarnock

This was one of Leighton's last paintings in which he attempted to represent the dynamics of movement. He did this by means of the draperies mirroring the actions of the figures and so forming momentary shapes. Leighton may have been influenced by the theories Ruskin expounded in *The Seven Lamps of Architecture*, in which he stated that drapery was only noble and necessary if it expressed motion or gravity. Pictorially this painting recalls Titian's *Rape of Europe*, in which patterns are formed by draperies before a panorama. Leighton had made notes on the subject himself: 'Combination of expressed motion and rest source of fascination in drapery — wayward flow & ripple like a living water together with absolute repose.' In preliminary studies the composition appeared more compressed, with the figures much closer together. As the picture progressed, the girls, reminiscent of works by Michelangelo, drifted apart and one of Leighton's best Mediterranean seascapes was inserted.

PLATE 30

THE BATH OF PSYCHE

———— c.1890 ————

Oil on canvas, 74½ × 24½ in / 189.2 × 62.2 cm
Tate Gallery, London

Psyche, meaning soul in Greek, was a beautiful mythological princess who suffered many traumatic ordeals. Ordered by an oracle to sacrifice her, Psyche's father left her on the summit of a mountain to be devoured by a monster. She was rescued by Zephyrus and taken to a magnificent palace where the man who was destined to be her husband, Eros, would appear to her in the darkness of night. Eros instructed Psyche not to attempt to look at his face, but when she was encouraged to look at him by her envious sisters, she burnt him by accident with lamp oil. On waking, Eros reproached Psyche and vanished, as did the palace. Once again Psyche found herself alone on the rock. Through mysterious divine intervention, she survived a suicide attempt and the jealous Aphrodite's continuing harassment. Finally, Eros implored Zeus to reunite them and make his lover immortal, and they were then married on Mount Olympus.

Leighton depicts the moment where Psyche prepares to bathe for her wedding. Based on his sketches of women undressing for Phryne, this serene depiction of the female form recalls the *Callipygian Venus*, in which a young women exposes her legs and buttocks. Psyche's sensuous corporeality and diaphanous drapery are set against and enhanced by the classical architectural features, her legs reflected in the pool by which she stands. The verticality of the composition, of which she is a formal component, makes her figure appear all the more slender. Here the vulnerable Psyche is exposed for the benefit of the anonymous voyeur, as in the myth where she was offered to an unknown husband. Leighton's contemporaries greatly admired this sensual painting. J. Harlaw, author of *The Charm of Leighton*, describing its eroticism:

> Psyche's contour is perfect and her form is deliciously rounded. The exquisite pearly fairness of the skin must ever make this rendering of the amorous deity the standard of as modelling...Dorothy Dene, Leighton's favourite model, here displays her charms for the admiration of mankind.

Though titillating, the mythological theme and its classical rendering justified the acceptability of the painting, although nudes by contemporary artists such as Alma-Tadema and Poynter were sometimes labelled as salacious. Leighton saw the nude as the pinnacle of classical beauty. The figure bears a close resemblance to that in the ceiling painting of 1888 by Gustav Klimt on the staircase of the Burgtheater, Vienna. A common source, rather than a direct quotation of the Viennese artist, is the most likely explanation for this. Many studies were made for this painting, which was sold to Henry Tate for £1,000 as part of the Chantrey Bequest.

'AND THE SEA GAVE UP THE DEAD WHICH WERE IN IT'

———————————— 1891–92 ————————————

Oil on canvas, 90 in / 228.6 cm diameter
Tate Gallery, London

Commissioned by Henry Tate for his forthcoming gallery of British painting, this is one of Leighton's few biblical subjects on an apocalyptic theme. Depicting a vision of the resurrection of souls on Judgement Day, the subject was taken from the *Book of Revelations*. The first design for the composition was made in the early 1880s as one of eight roundels designed for a scheme of mosaics on the apocalypse for the dome of St Paul's Cathedral. The design was rejected by the Dean of the Cathedral as a result of its supposed unchristian treatment of the subject, and the scheme was abandoned in 1885. Leighton believed this to be his best design to date and worthy of a place in a national collection: '...now this is the work I should wish to be remembered by in our National Gallery', and thus he utilized it to create this painting. Samuel Pepys Cockerell praised the composition and its execution:

> This great group is one which no other painter in this country could have attempted with any chance of success. It shows astonishing mastery, and is worthy to rank with the finest work in the Sixtine [sic] Chapel.

The main group of figures consists of an overwhelmed man supporting his wife and child as they emerge tentatively from the sea and back to life. The colour scheme defines each figure's state of consciousness: the live man is reddening, his unconscious wife has a deathly pallor and their comatose son is merely pale.

PLATE 32

PERSEUS AND ANDROMEDA
———————————— c.1891 ————————————

Oil on canvas, 92 1/2 x 51 in / 235.0 x 129.3 cm
Board of the Trustees of the National Museums and Galleries on Merseyside
(Walker Art Gallery, Liverpool)

Taken from Ovid's *Metamorphoses*, this painting is a narrative sequel to Leighton's *Perseus and Pegasus*, although it is the earlier work. This is a very original treatment of this popular classical theme. Andromeda, daughter of Cepheus, was offered to a sea monster sent by Poseidon to avenge Cepheus's wife Cassiopeia's claim that she was more beautiful than the Nereids. Cepheus consulted the Oracle of Ammon and was told that he must sacrifice his daughter. Perseus arrived to find Andromeda bound to a rock, and fell in love with her. He killed the monster, liberated Andromeda and then married her. Here Andromeda, nude except for drapery around her waist, is bound to the rock. The monster looms above with outstretched scaly wings forming a canopy over his captive. Perseus appears from the clouds on Pegasus, firing arrows. The scene is set in an eerie rocky inlet in a coastline in which vertical cliffs ascend from an inky sea. The landscape is based on sketches made on the Donegal coast of Ireland at Malin Head. Leighton described the setting as '...quite Dantesque in its grim blackness'. The colouring evokes spiritual forces and symbolically distinguishes the nature of the characters, the radiant hero, the life-saving source of light, glowing gold and white, the victim dressed in white, contrasted by the oily green dragon. The dragon was based on studies of prehistoric creatures and Andromeda was modelled by Dorothy Dene. The rather incongruous group of the mounted Perseus on Pegasus was drawn from a model made by Leighton, plagiarizing a print by the Dutch artist Hendrik Goltzius. The action draws the spectator into the distant horizon of the sea. The painting was retouched prior to being exhibited at Oldham in 1894.

PLATE 33

RETURN OF PERSEPHONE
———— c.1891 ————

Oil on canvas, 80 × 60 in / 203.2 × 152.4 cm
Leeds Museums and Galleries

Like *Perseus and Andromeda*, derived from Ovid's *Metamorphoses*, this painting depicts a widely-represented mythological figure. Persephone was the goddess of the Underworld and wife of Hades; her name can be translated as 'she who destroys light'. Before her marriage to Hades, Persephone lived on earth with her mother Demeter, who conceived her by Zeus, and was known as Kore. She was abducted by Hades whilst picking flowers and carried into the Underworld on his chariot. Demeter failed to recover her daughter but accepted the Gods' compromise of Persephone spending part of the year with her on earth. Persephone's iconographic attributes are the bat, the narcissus and the pomegranate. Her cult merged with that of her mother's which had similar rites. This work was shown with *Perseus and Andromeda* at the Summer Exhibition of 1891. In it Leighton depicted Persephone's limp body in shroud-like drapery, being carried towards her mother by Hermes, the messenger of the Gods. Demeter in warm-toned drapery with tanned outstretched arms prepares to embrace her child. The reunion takes place at the mouth of a cave leading to the Underworld, through which we see the bright daylight. The two worlds on either side are symbolized by flora, the sprays of cherry blossom outside contrasting with the darkly menacing non-flowering plants on the inside of the cave. Outside the landscape blooms, Persephone having regained the sunlight. Persephone's upreaching configuration symbolizes the principle of growth, bursting towards the light, while Demeter represents earthly fertility. The mother and child relationship was a recurrent theme in Leighton's work, associated here with summer and winter, light and darkness, and life and death. The painting was purchased by Sir James Kitson for presentation to Leeds City Art Gallery.

The Garden of the Hesperides

———————— c.1892 ————————

Oil on canvas, 66 ½ in / 169.0 cm diameter
Board of the Trustees of the National Museums and Galleries on Merseyside
(Lady Lever Art Gallery, Merseyside)

The Hesperides were the daughters of Hesperus who had the power of everlasting song. They lived at the extreme western limits of the world in a wonderful garden, and protected the golden apples that grew there. Myth suggests that the daughters of Hesperus sang a lullaby to the guardian of the golden apples, the dragon Ladon who was appointed by Juno. Here the dragon, in the form of a serpent recalling the imagery of the Garden of Eden, coils itself around the three young women and the apple tree, with golden fruits hanging from heavy branches above them. The three languid, auburn-haired girls, one of whom was modelled by Dorothy Dene, are draped in richly coloured robes. The central figure is an idealized beauty with a foreshortened body and classical facial features. The somnolent figures are framed by water, the sea behind and by the pool in front, and are surrounded by lush vegetation. This was echoed in Leighton's own picture frame with a circular moulding of foliage and fruit. The tondo composition encloses them in their suspended, cyclical world. The theme of death-in-life relates the painting to Tennyson's poetry, particularly his poem 'The Hesperides'. Other likely sources of inspiration for the theme were Milton's poem 'Comus', Flaubert's erotic and decadent novel *Salammbô* and Ruskin's investigation of the theme in his consideration of Turner's work in *Modern Painters*.

PLATE 35

AT THE FOUNTAIN

c.1892

Oil on canvas, 50 1/4 × 37 1/2 in / 127.6 × 95.3 cm

Layton Art Collection, Milwaukee Art Museum, Gift of Friends of the Layton
Art Gallery

At the Fountain was purchased in 1895 for the Layton Art Gallery. The half-length, single female figure, holding a large water jar under her right arm, is silhouetted against the illuminated marble colonnade behind her. Touches of subtle colour are provided by her fair hair, pale drapery and the lemons hanging from a branch. The painting was purchased in 1895 by the Layton Art Gallery, one of relatively few subjects that were acquired by American collections during Leighton's lifetime. A small colour sketch of the work remains in England, in the Fulham Library.

FATICIDA
———————— c.1894 ————————

Oil on canvas, 60 x 43 in / 152.5 x 109.0 cm
Board of the Trustees of the National Museums and Galleries on Merseyside
(Lady Lever Art Gallery)

Faticida was a prophetess who foretold the future to women. The green-white drapery matches her calm mood, evoked by her relaxed posture and enigmatic facial expression. There is a thick, expressive handling of paint seen in the treatment of the opaque drapery. Faticida leans back with crossed legs, with her head in her left hand, a pose derived from Michelangelo's seated sibyls in the Sistine Chapel. Enclosed in an alcove of purplish stone, Faticida is the most monumental of Leighton's sibyl-type figures. Brighter colour is provided by laurel leaves at her feet, heightened by light reflected in her metal tripod and the gilded ceiling. The painting was exhibited at the Royal Academy in 1894 and acquired by Lord Leverhulme.

THE SPIRIT OF THE SUMMIT
———————— c.1894 ————————

Oil on canvas, 78 × 40 in / 198.1 × 101.6 cm
Auckland City Art Gallery; collection presented by Mr Moss Davis, 1924

This painting was shown at the Royal Academy Summer Exhibition with four other female personifications, ranging from this symbolic work and *Faticida* to a domestic scene in *The Bracelet*. *The Spirit of the Summit* is a representation of the purity of the human spirit. It attests to Leighton's commitment to the truths of art and beauty, and to his aspirations to high ideals. The chaste, fair figure sits regally at the snowy peak of a mountain, gazing towards a starry sky that illuminates her white robes. The background was based on studies made by Leighton in Zermatt in the autumn of 1893. The painting was anticipated by Moritz von Schwind's *Jungfrau*, and follows the German pantheist tradition of interpreting the forces of nature and art. Less monumental than Schwind's personification, this figure conforms to a classical prototype. In the theatrical lighting, she can be likened to a character in a Wagner opera, although the figure was painted from life. The model was the expressive actress Dorothy Dene.

FLAMING JUNE
——————— c.1895 ———————
Oil on canvas, 47½ × 47½ in / 120.6 × 120.6 cm
Museo de Arte de Ponce (The Louis A. Ferré Foundation), Puerto Rico

One of Leighton's best known and most widely reproduced works, *Flaming June* is an exploration in colour and form. Leighton's most abandoned tribute to beauty had been anticipated two decades earlier in the reclining figure in *Summer Moon*, as well as in *Captive Andromache* and is also a possible sequel to his *Summer Slumber* of 1894. Another possible and more contemporary source was *Hope* by G. F. Watts which had been exhibited at the Grosvenor Gallery in 1886. According to Leighton, however, the monumental form, which recalls Michelangelo's *Night* in the Medici Chapel in Florence, was not intentionally arranged but occurred naturally when the fatigued model was resting. The condensed composition was the result of many frenzied preparatory studies. There is no apparent subject matter; this is simply a depiction of a young woman sleeping in brilliant sunlight. Through the unifying curtain of luminous glow, we glimpse the sea with the sun's reflection on it. However all extraneous detail was reduced so that the spectator would concentrate on the confined figure, modelled by Dorothy Dene. Despite the claustrophobic setting, the figure has a certain passivity in the luxuriant ambience. Vibrant orange diaphanous drapery emerges like flames, erupting over the woman's figure and illuminating parts of her face, neck, forearms and foot. Leighton's statements in his Academy notebooks anticipated the execution of *Flaming June*:

A deep slow cumulative execution...is suitable only for subjects of repose...all the qualities of a work of art must be struck in the key and appeal to the order of sensation...suffusion of colour (saturation) gives idea of an overmastering impulse.

L ACHRYMAE
———— c.1895 ————

Oil on canvas, 62 × 24¾ in / 157.5 × 62.9 cm
The Metropolitan Museum of Art, New York, Catharine Lorillard Wolfe
Collection, Wolfe Fund, 1896. (1896.28)

Taken from a watercolour executed in Florence in 1854, *Lachrymae* has no specific mythological or historical reference. Set in the early evening, with a harsh sunset and solemn cypress trees in the background, the mourning figure has been depicted to convey a sense of loss and the theme of grief. The tragic ambience is evoked by Leighton's use of sombre colour and the verticality of the composition. The grieving woman, draped in black, rests on a truncated Doric column upon which stands a funerary urn, her height accentuated by the rising trunk of the yew tree behind. The flickering light emanating from behind the tree suggests a funeral pyre. The verticality of the composition, used in neo-Gothic architecture, in line with Pugin's and Ruskin's theories of design, is symbolic of resurrection and closeness to God. It refers to the ascending spirit of her deceased lover, whom she is unable to follow. The low wall forms a symbolic cross with the column, a compositional device that was frequently used by the Pre-Raphaelites decades earlier and represents the end of continuity and happiness in a phase of life. The configuration of the woman recalls the classical statue of Melpomene in the British Museum, in which a draped figure leans on a plinth.

PERSEUS ON PEGASUS HASTENING TO THE RESCUE OF ANDROMEDA

——————————— c.1895–96 ———————————

Oil on canvas, 72$\frac{1}{2}$ in / 184.2 cm diameter
Leicestershire Museums, Arts and Records Service

Ovid's *Metamorphoses* tells how Polydectes wanted to impress Hippodaemia with various wedding gifts. Much to the relief of jealous Polydectes, the warrior Perseus, his vassal, was anxious for distinction and offered to obtain Medusa's head. The warrior decapitated Medusa with one stroke of his sickle and the winged horse Pegasus sprang from her bloody neck. Perseus then fled on the back of Pegasus carrying Medusa's head. This painting, unfinished when found in the artist's studio on his death, features a theme tackled earlier in his *Perseus and Andromeda* of 1891. Here Leighton used the same bronze model of the figure mounted on horseback, but slightly turned and at closer range. Unlike the first painting which has more dynamism and perspective, the action is classically balanced in the confines of a narrow picture plane.

PRINCIPAL PUBLIC COLLECTIONS CONTAINING
WORKS BY LEIGHTON

AUSTRALIA

Adelaide
Art Gallery of South Australia

Armidale
Teacher's College

Sydney
Art Gallery of New South Wales

CANADA

Ottawa
National Gallery of Canada

GERMANY

Hamburg
Hamburg Kunsthalle

Frankfurt
Städelsches Kunstinstitut

GREAT BRITAIN

Aberdeen
Aberdeen Art Gallery

Bath
Victoria Art Gallery

Birmingham
Birmingham City Art Gallery

Blackburn
Blackburn Museum and Art Gallery

Bournemouth
Russell-Cotes Art Gallery and Museum

Bristol
Bristol Art Gallery

Cambridge
Fitzwilliam Museum

Faringdon
Buscot Park

Grantham
Belton House (National Trust)

Hull
Ferens Art Gallery

Kilmarnock
Dick Institute

Leeds
Leeds Museum

Leicester
Leicester Museum and Art Gallery

Liverpool
Sudley House
Walker Art Gallery

Lode
Anglesey Abbey (National Trust)

London
Fulham Library
Guildhall Art Gallery
Leighton House
William Morris Art Gallery, Walthamstow
National Portrait Gallery
Royal Exchange
South London Art Gallery
Tate Gallery
Victoria and Albert Museum

Lyndhurst
St Michael's Church

Manchester
Manchester City Art Gallery

Oxford
Ashmolean Museum

Port Sunlight
Lady Lever Art Gallery

Scarborough
Scarborough Art Gallery

Stourton
Stourhead (National Trust)

Truro
Royal Institution of Cornwall

INDIA

Baroda
Baroda Museum and Picture Gallery

Hyderabad
Salar Jung Museum

IRELAND

Dublin
Municipal Gallery of Modern Art

ITALY

Florence
Uffizi Gallery

NEW ZEALAND

Auckland
Auckland City Art Gallery

Christchurch
Robert McDougall Art Gallery

PUERTO RICO

Ponce
Museo de Arte de Ponce

UNITED STATES OF AMERICA

Boston, Massachusetts
Museum of Fine Arts

Decatur, Georgia
Agnes Scott College

Hartford, Connecticut
Wadsworth Atheneum

Fort Worth, Texas
Kimbell Art Museum

Milwaukee, Wisconsin
Milwaukee Art Museum

Minneapolis, Minnesota
The Minneapolis Institute of Arts

New Haven, Connecticut
Yale Center for British Art

New York, New York
Metropolitan Museum of Art

Princeton, New Jersey
Princeton Art Musum

SIR JOHN EVERETT
MILLAIS

SIR JOHN EVERETT MILLAIS

1829–96

John Everett Millais was born in Southampton on 8 June 1829, the youngest son of John William and Emily Mary Millais. His father was a prominent inhabitant of Jersey and a long-serving officer in the island's militia. Emily Mary, née Evamy, whose family operated a successful saddlery business in Southampton, was a young widow who had been previously married to Enoch Hodgkinson, by whom she had two sons. Her marriage to John William produced two other children, John's sister Emily, who married John Johnson-Wallack, an American, and emigrated to the United States, and John Everett's elder brother William, who remained his close companion throughout his life.

There had long been Millais residents of Jersey (several landmarks on the island bear the family name), tradition relating that their ancestors had settled there at the time of William the Conqueror. John's early years were spent on the island near St Helier, apart from a spell in Dinan, Brittany, from 1835 to 1837. Following his expulsion from school (after just three days, for biting his teacher's hand), and suffering from poor health, it was decided that he should be educated at home, where he came under the influence of his mother, a powerful personality. At the age of four he began to draw and when he began taking art lessons with a Mr Bessell his prodigious talent became apparent. It was said that by the age of seven, he could stroll on the beach, return home, and draw an astonishingly accurate picture of the scene; he also did portrait drawings of local soldiers. He was encouraged to pursue an artistic career by a number of local dignitaries, who included Sir Hilgrove Turner, former Lieutenant Governor of Jersey (whose signature appears as a tribute on the document held in Millais's later painting, The Order of Release).

To foster their son's burgeoning skill, the Millais family travelled to London in 1838, setting up home in a rented house in Charlotte Street, to the north-west of the British Museum. Carrying a letter of introduction, they took John to Sir Martin Archer Shee, President of the Royal Academy since 1830. He was so disbelieving that someone so young could have produced the drawings he was shown that he asked John to draw a sculpture there and then, and was amazed by the accomplished result.

John became a pupil at Henry Sass's Art Academy in Bloomsbury. His first studies included drawing from casts in the neighbouring British Museum as well as visits to the newly opened National Gallery where he saw works by masters including Rembrandt, Rubens and Titian. Millais won a silver medal awarded by the Society of Arts for his drawing The Battle of Bannockburn when aged only nine. So jealous were his older fellow students of his precocity and

this achievement that they suspended him from a window head down, from where he was rescued in an unconscious state. Millais's family was highly supportive of his métier and they constantly encouraged him, his father even making props and his mother historical costumes for his models.

On 17 July 1840, at the age of eleven, Millais entered the prestigious Royal Academy Schools as its youngest-ever student. He was initially a Probationer, but was enrolled as a full Student six months later. He was known there as 'the Child', a nickname that remained with him into adulthood. He embarked on six years of study, the teaching method placing great emphasis on drawing (he did not attempt to paint in oil until 1841, when he produced his Cupid Crowned with Flowers). In 1843 Millais won a silver medal for drawing from antique sculptures. A year later he met the seventeen-year-old William Holman Hunt at work drawing in British Museum, encouraging him to submit his own work to the Royal Academy, and entering a lifelong friendship with him. Within two years, Millais's first major painting, Pizarro Seizing the Inca of Peru, which had been painted when he was still only sixteen, was shown at the Royal Academy summer exhibition.

On the strength of this early triumph, Millais was commissioned to paint decorations for the Leeds home of John Atkinson. He also entered the competition to design decorations for Westminster Hall with a gigantic canvas depicting The Widow's Mite. He became a member of a drawing group called the Cyclographic Club, along with Hunt and another near-contemporary, Dante Gabriel Rossetti. The following year Millais won a gold medal for his religious painting The Tribe of Benjamin Seizing the Daughters of Shiloh, for which his brother William sat for the male figures.

The year 1848 was marked by revolutions in Europe and by Chartist demonstrations in England, demanding parliamentary reforms and rights for the common people. At this time, Millais was sharing his Gower Street studio with Hunt. There he completed Cymon and Iphigenia, a work based on John Dryden's translation of a poem by Boccaccio, while Hunt worked on his Eve of St Agnes. It was during the course of their work and discussions with like-minded friends that Millais formed the Pre-Raphaelite Brotherhood together with Hunt and Rossetti, along with Rossetti's brother William Michael, Frederic George Stephens, Thomas Woolner and James Collinson. Among their shared aims was a return to the style of fifteenth-century Italian masters and a concern with painting directly from nature, an aspiration derived in part from the theories expounded in John Ruskin's Modern Painters, the first two volumes of which had been published in 1843 and

1846. Millais immediately began to paint in the new style. His first exhibited Pre-Raphaelite work, and the first to bear the then-secret 'PRB' initials, was *Isabella*.

In 1849 Millais began a series of portrait commissions from the Wyatt family (James Wyatt already owned *Cymon and Iphigenia*). His *Isabella* was well received at the Royal Academy, and during the summer he painted the Oxford background to *Ferdinand Lured by Ariel*, the head of Ferdinand modelled by F. G. Stephens. In the same year Millais also executed his curious gothic drawing *The Disentombment of Queen Matilda*, and, while Rossetti painted his *The Girlhood of Mary Virgin*, adopted his own religious theme with *Christ in the House of His Parents*, which was subjected to a vituperative attack by Charles Dickens and from the press of the day. He also embarked on *The Return of the Dove to the Ark* and *Mariana*, based on Tennyson's poem of twenty years earlier. Millais's Wyatt portraits and *Ferdinand Lured by Ariel* were exhibited at the Royal Academy but were scorned by critics. He concentrated on the landscape backgrounds for his *The Woodman's Daughter*, which, with *Mariana* and *The Return of the Dove to the Ark*, was exhibited in 1851 at Royal Academy, but to a poor reception.

Having received repeated critical attacks and being appalled by the vast crowds thronging to London for the Great Exhibition of that year, Millais was now at an emotionally low ebb, and needed all the encouragement he could secure. Ruskin, a hero of the Pre-Raphaelite Brotherhood, provided its members with powerful support through two letters published in *The Times*. Hunt and Millais wrote to thank him, in consequence of which John and his wife visited Millais in his studio, inviting him back the same evening to supper at their Park Street home. Millais had met Mrs Ruskin seven years earlier when, at the age of sixteen, he had attended a dance at Ewell Castle, the Surrey home of Captain William Lemprière, a fellow Jerseyman. She was then Effie Chalmers Gray, a girl of seventeen. Now she was married to John Ruskin, Britain's foremost art critic, who was both wealthy (he was the son of a successful sherry importer) and influential. Effie was a member of a large Scottish family, the daughter of lawyer George Gray and his wife Sophia, one of fifteen children, and a distant cousin of Ruskin. They had known each other since she was twelve and he twenty-one and, despite the opposition of Ruskin's parents, had married on 10 April

1848. The wedding took place at the Grays' home, Bowerswell, near Perth, Scotland.

For reasons, or excuses, of Ruskin's devising, which ranged from not wishing to have children and not wanting his bride's health to be damaged by pregnancy, neither on their wedding night nor on the nights which followed was the marriage consummated. The Ruskins' union was unconventional, even by the puritanical standards of the day. Ruskin was in all probability a manic depressive with a catalogue of psycho-sexual problems, among which he appears to have been horrified to discover that, unlike the classical statues with which he was familiar, his virgin bride had pubic hair. Ruskin's phobias and the abstinence upon which he continued to insist caused severe tensions which, being unable or unwilling to understand, he claimed derived from Effie's mental instability.

On 4 August 1851 the Ruskins returned to Venice, the city in which they had previously spent a year while John Ruskin worked on his monumental book *The Stones of Venice*. There, largely ignored by him, the vivacious and popular Effie had many suitors, but remained entirely faithful to her neglectful husband. After their return to

England, she found her social activities severely restricted and she was compelled to spend time with Ruskin's dour family, who had paid for a house near their own.

Millais spent the summer of 1851 in Kingston painting landscapes with Hunt, and producing *The Bridesmaid*. The next year Millais had Elizabeth Siddal, later Rossetti's wife, sit (or rather, lie) for him as *Ophelia*, which was considered a great critical success, and painted *A Huguenot*, which was even more popular, and was his first painting to be published as an engraving. He worked too on *The Proscribed Royalist*, with fellow Pre-Raphaelite Arthur Hughes posing for the head of the title subject.

In 1853 Millais became friendly with John Leech, the principal cartoonist of the humorous magazine *Punch*. Leech was a keen sportsman whom Millais often accompanied on foxhunting expeditions. In that year, now back in England, Effie Ruskin's constrained life with her husband was relieved when Millais asked her to model for him in *The Order of Release* at his Gower Street studio. The 'release' from the tensions of her relationship with John and his parents may have been accidental, but it was certainly an apt title. This work was exhibited at the Royal Academy together with *The Proscribed Royalist*.

As the friendship between Millais and the Ruskins developed, John Ruskin invited Millais, along with his brother William, to spend a working holiday with them in Scotland. The party stayed first at an inn and then at a schoolmaster's cottage in Glenfinlas, where Millais embarked on a portrait of Ruskin standing on rocks with a waterfall behind, a project that presented many difficulties. Ruskin worked on a speech to be delivered in Edinburgh

Effie with Foxgloves in Her Hair, painted by Millais in 1853.

husband, Effie must have found the young artist amusing and attractive – he was over six feet tall and very slim, an enthusiastic sportsman and, as contemporaries observed, exceptionally strong and agile. Millais gave Effie drawing lessons and during the time they spent alone together she gradually revealed to him details of her marriage, to which Millais responded with a sympathetic ear. As his affection for his mentor's wife grew, Millais wrote to Hunt (who had also been invited on the trip, but had declined), 'Today I have been drawing Mrs Ruskin, who is the sweetest creature that ever lived.' Millais called her 'the Countess', having heard a servant address her thus, and she called him 'Everett', to distinguish him from the other John, her husband John Ruskin. Millais painted numerous sketches, with Effie present in almost all, and executed a sensitive oil study of her with foxgloves in her hair.

Although it was intended for Ruskin, Millais held on to this portrait as a keepsake of their memorable trip and of his love for Effie.

Millais left Glenfinlas on 28 October. Back in London in November, he learned of his election as the youngest-ever Associate of the Royal Academy. The following day Rossetti, ever the most faithful to Pre-Raphaelite principles, wrote in a letter to his sister, the poet Christina Rossetti, '... so now the whole Round Table is dissolved.' Her own response was to write a sonnet outlining the break-up of the group. The

Drawings from Millais's fateful holiday at Glenfinlas: *Two Masters and their Pupils* shows Effie (the 'pupil') with Millais, one of the 'masters' of the title (the portrait of the second master, Ruskin, was cut out after Effie's marriage to him ended). *Awful Protection Against Midges* highlights a hazard of painting that even masks and cigarette smoke did little to alleviate.

and on the massive index for *The Stones of Venice*, publishing the first of three volumes later that year. When not engaged on the troublesome portrait, Millais devoted himself to fishing and producing numerous drawings, while he became increasingly attached to Effie. In contrast to her serious-minded

Pre-Raphaelite Brotherhood had lasted just over five years. Before the year was out, Millais had written to Effie's mother, who was made aware of her daughter's unhappy situation, and expressed his concern for her well-being.

Effie consulted her friend Elizabeth Eastlake, the wife of Charles Eastlake, President of the Royal Academy from 1850, and the daughter of an obstetrician, who seemingly gave her advice about the sexual aspects of marriage previously largely a mystery to her. Effie then wrote to her father explaining her predicament, urging her parents to travel to London and confront Ruskin. On legal advice, the Grays did not meet with him, but arranged for her to leave Ruskin on the pretext that she was visiting them in Scotland. On 25 April 1854, just after the sixth anniversary of her wedding to Ruskin, Effie left their home and travelled to her family's house in Scotland, never to return. Her wedding ring and keys were delivered to Ruskin and legal action was commenced to annul the marriage. At this time, civil courts did not deal with annulment cases, and the matter was duly placed before an ecclesiastical court. When the issue was made public, the scandal eclipsed even news from the Crimea, where war had just broken out. In a well-orchestrated campaign, Elizabeth Eastlake ensured that Ruskin was clearly established as the sole cause of their marital misery. The circumstances of the Ruskin–Millais scandal have been clouded by the partisan accounts of the participants and their respective supporters, and by the censoring and destruction of correspondence relating to the affair, so we shall probably never know for certain that the blame was entirely Ruskin's. However, the later lives of Effie and of Ruskin make it clear that while she had no apparent impediments to settling to normal married life, Ruskin certainly did. Millais's own part in the affair led to many a rumour, including his being banned from the Royal Academy, but the truth was that he was so emotionally disturbed that he could neither bring himself to finish the vexed portrait of Ruskin, nor anything else. Effie was examined by doctors who testified to her virginity, after six years of marriage to Ruskin. By July the case had been heard and her annulment was granted on 15 July 1854, the Decree of Nullity stating the marriage to be void because '... John Ruskin was incapable of consummating the same by reason of incurable impotency.'

Despite these events, Millais doggedly returned to work on Ruskin's portrait, and on learning of the annulment, wrote to Effie remarking, 'This time last year there seemed no more chance of what has happened than that the moon should fall.'

Millais went to Winchelsea in Sussex to paint the background for *The Blind Girl*. Also in 1854, he received a commission to provide illustrations for the so-called 'Moxon Tennyson' (an elegant edition of Tennyson's poems published by London bookseller and publisher Edward Moxon). The Pre-Raphaelite Brotherhood had published four issues of a periodical, *The Germ*, to which Millais and others had contributed engravings. He continued to undertake illustrative work during the 1850s and 1860s, working for six years on *The Parables of Our Lord*, and supplying illustrations for periodicals, including *Once a Week*, as well as realistic scenes of Victorian life for the novels of Anthony Trollope, who became a close friend. Millais's biographer Marion H. Spielmann noted the exceptional quality of his line work: 'His drawing was irreproachable – subtle and suggestive, as well as firm and correct; his line and composition were almost inspired; his black and white has never been excelled.'

He finally finished the hated Ruskin portrait by December 1854 and delivered it. Ruskin told him that he hoped they could remain friends in spite of events – a forlorn hope as Millais made abundantly clear to him.

In January of the following year Millais was inspired by an event he witnessed in the early hours of the morning while returning from a ball in Porchester Terrace. Noticing a glow in the sky, the artist and his brother William asked their cab driver to head in that direction. On arrival at the scene they saw two firemen with a hose standing on a rafter, silhouetted in black against the flames. Suddenly there was an appalling shout as the rafter collapsed into the building below, taking the two men with it. Millais felt compelled to honour these brave and noble men on canvas and decided that the painting would be ready for the 1855 Royal Academy exhibition. After spending almost eighteen months on the Ruskin portrait, Millais executed this, his first contemporary painting, in just three. On hearing that *The Rescue* was complete, Ford Madox Brown noted Millais's remarkable speed of execution, in his diary of 11 April 1855, remarking, '... three weeks ago he had more than half uncovered, they say. How he does it I can't tell.'

Only a Lock of Hair
(1857–58).

Millais was outraged when, after his exhaustive work, the picture was hung above eye level at the Royal Academy, too high to be fully appreciated. He described his anger in a letter to Hunt: 'I almost dropped down in a fit from rage in a row I had with the three hangers, in which I forgot all restraint and shook my fist in their faces, calling them every conceivable name of abuse.' *The Rescue* was lowered by the three inches that Millais demanded, after his threatening to resign from the Royal Academy, the Pre-Raphaelites basking in the rebellion of their colleague. William Michael Rossetti praised *The Rescue* in his 'Art News from London' column in the American periodical *The Crayon*, declaring the painting to be '... beyond compare the great picture of the exhibition ... his most wonderful and consummate work.' The work was also generously praised by Ruskin, who in spite of everything remained objective about Millais's work, later describing him as, among the Pre-Raphaelites, '... always the most powerful of them all'. *The Rescue* was later exhibited in Paris where it was well received.

Effie, who had resisted seeing Millais until February 1855, granted him a brief visit at her Scottish home, and it was agreed that they would marry that summer. Millais spent the evening of 9 June celebrating his coming nuptials at a party organized by Wilkie Collins, the son of a landscape painter and later famed as the author of *The Moonstone* and other popular novels. Afterwards, Millais travelled to Effie's family home and quickly became accepted as a much-loved future son-in-law. On 3 July Millais and Effie were married. As with her marriage to Ruskin, the couple honeymooned in Scotland, before embarking on what was to become a blissful marriage of more than forty years. Ruskin, on the other hand, regressed further and later became infatuated with a ten-year-old girl by the name of Rose La Touche, to whom he proposed marriage. Rose's mother wrote to Effie, who explained how unsuitable a husband Ruskin would make. He became increasingly deranged, dying in 1900.

The newly wed John and Effie Millais divided their time between Annat Lodge, Perth, near Effie's family residence, Bowerswell, and London, where Millais had a studio at Langham Place. On 30 May 1856 their first child Everett was born. Artistically and financially it was a good year: Millais's two masterpieces

Sketch for
The Black Brunswicker
(1859–60).

The Blind Girl and *Autumn Leaves* were completed, and they and *Peace Concluded* were sold for the then substantial total of 2,000 guineas (£2,100). *A Dream of the Past – Sir Isumbras at the Ford* followed in 1857, and was exhibited at Royal Academy, achieving both acclaim and adverse criticism, becoming the victim of a parody by Frederick Sandys. Millais painted *Pot Pourri*, and continued working on *Apple Blossoms*, which he started at Annat Lodge in 1856 and completed in 1859.

Their second child George was born in 1857. Effie and Millais had a large family of four boys and four girls, which was a source of joy to him – and which provided models for many of his paintings. In late autumn they moved to York Terrace, Regent's Park. The next year was marked by the birth of their third child and first daughter, Effie, and, for financial reasons, a move back to Scotland, where *The Vale of Rest* was painted. The late 1850s represent a transitional period in Millais's work, from his Pre-Raphaelite technique to a freer style, with – for him – almost sketchy works such as his small portrait study, *Only a Lock of Hair* (1857–58).

In 1859 *Apple Blossoms*, *The Vale of Rest* and *The Love of James I of Scotland* were exhibited at the Royal Academy.

Red Riding Hood
(1864), a portrait
Millais's daughter
Effie.

Millais's principal painting of 1860 was *The Black Brunswicker*, which featured Kate Dickens, Charles Dickens's daughter, held in the embrace of a dashing officer (Millais's son and biographer John Guille Millais was at pains to explain that at no time did Miss Dickens and the male model actually come into direct physical contact). Its instant success marked Millais's return to popularity, while his growing family and financial pressures led him to paint increasingly sentimental and popular subjects. He left the laborious methods of Pre-Raphaelitism behind as he moved to subjects with a ready market. He felt obliged to defended himself against accusations of 'selling out', writing in a letter to Hunt, 'A painter must work for the taste of his own day. How does he know what people will like two or three hundred years hence? I maintain that a man should hold up the mirror to his own times. I want proof that the people of my day enjoy my work, and how can I get this better than by finding people willing to give me money for my productions?'

In 1862 Millais moved back to London, to a house at 7 Cromwell Place, South Kensington, but from then onwards made an annual visit to Scotland. There he could relax from the pressures of his more 'commercial' subjects and paint landscapes at a leisurely pace, and could take time off for fishing and stag-hunting, two pursuits that he followed with great passion.

Among Millais's notable paintings of the early 1860s were *Trust Me* (1862) and *The Eve of St Agnes* (1863), which were followed in 1863 by *My First Sermon*, an avowedly sentimental subject featuring as model his daughter Effie. In the same year he was elected as a Royal Academician. *My First Sermon* began a long series of similarly sentimental images of attractive children, especially small girls and boys, with works such as his *Girl with a Doll* (a portrait of Lily Noble) of 1864, *Leisure Hours* and *Red Riding Hood* (both 1864), *Cinderella* (1881) and, perhaps most notably,

A Souvenir of Velázquez (1868), Millais's Royal Academy Diploma painting.

Bubbles (1886). He also made a speciality of historical subjects featuring children, with such paintings as *The Boyhood of Raleigh* (1870), *The Princes in the Tower* (1878), *Princess Elizabeth in Prison* (1879), which features his daughter Sophie, and *The Girlhood of St Theresa* (1893). Among other characteristic themes are those of courting couples and contemplative women as in *Yes or No?* (1871).

By the 1870s portraits of women had become an increasingly important part of Millais's repertoire, featuring both named individuals such as *Mrs Bischoffsheim* (1873), *Miss Eveleen Tennant* (1874), *Louise Jopling* (1879), *Miss Beatrice Caird* (1879) and *Dorothy Thorpe* (1882). He also continued to use members of his own family, such as his daughter Alice, who was the model in *The Picture of Health* (1874) and *The Crown of Love* (1875), as well as society ladies, as the casts of genre paintings including his acclaimed *Hearts are Trumps* (1872). To these he added lucrative formal portrait commissions of such eminent personages as Disraeli, Tennyson and Henry Irving.

The success of *My First Sermon* led to *My Second Sermon*, which similarly had the younger Effie as its model. Other works featuring children at sleep and awakening continued with, in 1867, *Just Awake*. One Sunday Millais found a

The Crown of Love (1875), depicting Millais's daughter Alice.

Millais's portrait of Benjamin Disraeli (1881), painted only months before the former Prime Minister's death.

pretty child sitting near him in church and asked her parents for permission to allow her to sit for *A Souvenir of Velázquez*, his 1868 Diploma work for the Royal Academy (the painting presented to the Academy by an artist in commemoration of his election as an Academician).

The Boyhood of Raleigh of 1870 became one of the most famous history paintings and, with later narrative pictures by Millais, familiar to generations ever since from countless reproductions in children's books and prints on school walls. *Chill October*, also dating from 1870, was his first major Scottish landscape and one of his greatest landscape masterpieces. In the same year, Millais drew Dickens as he lay on his deathbed. *The Knight Errant* of 1870 was one of Millais's rare sorties into the type of medieval chivalric subjects popular with Rossetti, Burne-Jones and Pre-Raphaelite followers such as John William Waterhouse. Its associated work, *The Martyr of the Solway*, was first shown in 1871. *Victory, O Lord!*, which Millais completed in 1871, is a rare biblical subject but, lacks the earnestness of Hunt's religious works. According to F. G. Stephens, 'Mr Millais has had this picture in hand during several years past; it does him great honour, and redounds to his credit more than many of his recent works.'

According to Millais's son John Guille Millais, *A Yeoman of the Guard* of 1876 was one of the

artist's favourite paintings and, like his *The North-West Passage* of 1874, appealed to patriotic sensibilities. In 1875 Millais had been commissioned by a dealer to paint a huge canvas depicting Beefeaters undertaking their traditional search of the Houses of Parliament prior to the beginning of a parliamentary session, a work never executed. However, the artist visited the Tower of London to study the guards' uniform and was inspired by their colour and style. Believing that the impact of such a vibrant hue would be diminished by artificial light, Millais opted for a single figure in the open air. He sought a model distinguished enough to suit their costume, and found a retired Yeoman Warder, Major Robert Montagu, who sat for the head and hands. The frail Major, then over eighty, found the sittings very exhausting and had to be sustained by soup every forty-five minutes. Millais painted at great speed, completing his work in just a few days. Marion H. Spielmann wrote warmly of 'The effect of the flesh, neither executed by recipe nor concealed by overpainting', and also noted that the '... management of scarlet, gold and blue – a striking yet not forced harmony – is among the fine things in modern Art.' Despite his limited financial means, the painting was bought by Millais's half-brother Henry Hodgkinson, who also owned *Pizarro Seizing the Inca of Peru* and *The Woodman's Daughter*. He was so delighted and proud to own the painting that he left it to the nation in his will, much to Millais's approval.

In the same year, 1877, Millais painted *Effie Deans*, described by Millais's son as '... one of Millais's most successful pictures in the field of romance'. Inspired by Sir Walter Scott's 1818 novel *The Heart of Midlothian*, the subject depicts the lovers Effie Deans and George Staunton parting in King's Park, Edinburgh. The models were

Arthur Gwynne James, the nephew of Lord James of Hereford (who also posed as the Master of Ravenswood in Millais's other Scott-inspired painting of the same year, *The Bride of Lammermoor*), with Lillie Langtry as the heroine. The next year Millais painted a sensitive portrait of Lillie Langtry under the title *A Jersey Lilly*. Millais's chief work of 1878, *The Princes in the Tower*, was highly praised at the Paris International Art Exhibition, where the artist was awarded the gold Medaille d'Honneur and created Officer of the Légion d'Honneur, a triumph overshadowed by the death of Millais's son George from tuberculosis.

Millais was enormously prolific, painting more than 400 oils in his lifetime. He was hugely energetic and hard-working, yet he managed to find time for educational, charitable and public work, instituting reforms to Royal Academy teaching methods, establishing the Artists' Benevolent Institution with architect Philip Hardwick, and devoting a great deal of energy to promoting the establishment of the National Portrait Gallery in 1889 and encouraging Sir Henry Tate to found the Tate Gallery in 1892. He received numerous accolades in the form of awards and honorary doctorates, and earned increasingly large sums from the sale of his works and of copyright for the production of popular prints. *Cherry Ripe*, an avowedly sentimental subject with which Millais was unhappy, was nonetheless sold to the *Graphic* in 1879. The magazine issued a print of the work as a Christmas supplement, selling a remarkable 600,000 copies. At his peak Millais earned up to £40,000 a year – an enormous amount by nineteenth-century standards, and one that would today put him in the millionaire bracket. His prosperity was made publicly manifest when in 1878 the Millais family moved to 2 Palace Gate, Kensington, a sumptuous neo-classical house designed for him by Philip Hardwick, the son of the architect of Euston Station. Most of the successful painters of the day had grand houses, some, such as those of Leighton and Alma-Tadema, verging on the palatial. Their 'At Homes', at which the distinguished visitors might include the Prince of Wales or Richard Wagner, were part of London social life, with as many as 500 visitors attending an open day (often to the industrious Millais's chagrin). Millais's new establishment was so grand that when visited by Thomas Carlyle (whose portrait Millais painted), he was awestruck, asking, 'Has paint done all this, Mr Millais? It only shows how many fools there are in the world.' In 1881 Millais also took the tenancy of Birnham Hall, Murthly, in Perthshire, thus establishing stately bases in both London and Scotland.

The Liberal leader William Ewart Gladstone sat at Millais's new studio for his portrait in 1879, reportedly revelling in his brief respite from the stresses of political life (he was painted again on subsequent occasions), as did Benjamin Disraeli shortly before his death in 1881 (the last letter he wrote was to Millais). Cardinal Newman sat in the same year and also the Marquis of Salisbury in 1883. In 1885 Gladstone conferred an hereditary baronetcy on Millais, who became the first-ever artist to receive such a high honour. He took the title Baronet of Palace Gate, Kensington, County Middlesex and St Ouen, Jersey, in remembrance of his Channel Islands roots. In that same year, Millais painted *The Ruling Passion (The Ornithologist)*. The ornithological theme featured in this work appears elsewhere in Millais's oeuvre, as in his *Cuckoo* (1880), *Dropped from the Nest* (1883) and *The Nest* (1887).

An exhibition of Millais's collected works was held at the Grosvenor Gallery, London, in 1886, the catalogue containing extracts from Ruskin's varied critiques from the 1850s to 1870s. Edward Burne-Jones wrote to Millais to tell him that visiting the show had '... impressed me, excited me and revived me beyond words.' In that same year Millais produced *Bubbles*, perhaps his most famous though often ridiculed work, and harked back to his earlier historical subjects, most especially *A Huguenot*, with his *Mercy – St Bartholomew's Day, 1572*.

Millais continued to make his annual visits to Scotland, and to paint fine landscapes, such as his *Glen Birnam* (1891), but his formerly robust health was showing signs of failing. In March 1892 he suffered a bout of influenza which hindered his usual output. His illness was exacerbated by a series of exceptionally heavy London fogs, and it was discovered that he had the first symptoms of throat cancer.

He visited the seaside resort of Bournemouth in 1894 in an attempt to recover his strength, and the next year, in the absence of President of the Royal Academy Lord Leighton, who was also ill, addressed the Academy, despite the obvious distress this caused to his throat. A summer spent yachting off Jersey and an autumn visit to Bowerswell did little to alleviate his declining health, and his completion in 1895 of the doom-laden *Speak! Speak!* was hindered by his weakened state. Millais had had the subject in mind for at least twenty-five years. His son John Guille explained the subject, 'A young Roman has been reading through the night the letters of his lost love ... at dawn, behold the curtains of his bed are parted, and there

Portrait caricature of Millais by 'Ape' (1871).

before him stands, in spirit or in truth, the lady herself, decked as on her bridal night ... An open door displays the winding stair down which she has come.'

Leighton died on 25 January 1896, and although Millais was himself terminally ill, he insisted on attending the funeral. Millais succeeded Leighton as President of the Royal Academy on 20 February, whereupon he received a witty letter from his old ally Hunt who remarked, 'You have gone a letter higher – from PRB to PRA.'

At the time of the annulment of her marriage to Ruskin, all Effie's friends had rallied round and supported her, but the strict social etiquette of the day had meant that the merest hint of the scandal attaching to an annulled marriage or divorce caused her to be ostracized at gatherings Queen Victoria might attend, a restriction on their otherwise busy social life which irritated Millais until – almost literally – his dying day. Appeals to the Queen explaining the circumstances of the affair, and Effie's unblemished character, were in vain, and Effie was compelled to remain at home as her husband chaperoned her daughters to debutante balls, a pattern that continued even after Millais had become famous, wealthy, and had been elevated to the baronetcy. As Millais lay dying, however, Queen Victoria sent a message via an equerry asking if there was anything she might do for the artist. He wrote on slate, 'I wish Her Majesty the Queen would see my wife.' After more than forty years of snubbing her, the Queen immediately agreed to receive Effie, who was herself in declining health and now virtually blind, and so she travelled to Windsor Castle to go through the simple but significant ceremony of curtseying to the Queen Empress.

Millais died at home on 13 August 1896 at the age of sixty-seven. Holman Hunt and the actor Sir Henry Irving were among the pall-bearers at his funeral, which took place a week later in the crypt of St Paul's Cathedral. On 7 September the following year Millais's son Everett died of pneumonia, and Effie died on 23 December. She was buried at Kinnoull Church, Perth, the churchyard featured in her husband's 1858 painting, *The Vale of Rest*.

A memorial exhibition of Millais's works was held at the Royal Academy in 1898, and in 1899 his devoted son John Guille Millais published his two-volume *The Life and Letters of Sir John Everett Millais*, which he dedicated 'To the Memory of my Dear Father and Mother'.

Speak! Speak! (1895), a portentous work from Millais's penultimate year.

THE PLATES

1 Pizarro Seizing the Inca of Peru

2 Cymon and Iphigenia

3 Isabella

4 James Wyatt and his Granddaughter

5 Mrs James Wyatt and her Daughter Sarah

6 Ferdinand Lured by Ariel

7 Christ in the House of His Parents (The Carpenter's Shop)

8 Mariana

9 The Woodman's Daughter

10 The Return of the Dove to the Ark

11 The Bridesmaid

12 Ophelia

13 The Huguenot

14 The Proscribed Royalist, 1651

15 The Order of Release, 1746

16 John Ruskin

17 The Blind Girl

18 Autumn Leaves

19 A Dream of the Past – Sir Isumbras at the Ford

20 Apple Blossoms

21 The Vale of Rest

22 The Black Brunswicker

23 Trust Me

24 The Eve of St Agnes

25 My First Sermon / My Second Sermon

26 Leisure Hours

27 The Boyhood of Raleigh

28 Chill October

29 The Knight Errant

30 The Martyr of the Solway

31 Hearts are Trumps

32 The North-West Passage

33 A Jersey Lilly (Lillie Langtry)

34 The Princes in the Tower

35 Louise Jopling

36 Self-portrait

37 Caller Herrin'

38 The Ruling Passion (The Ornithologist)

39 Bubbles

40 Mercy – St Bartholomew's Day, 1572

PLATE 1

PIZARRO SEIZING THE INCA OF PERU
—————————————— 1846 ——————————————

Oil on canvas, 50 1/2 × 67 3/4 in / 128.3 × 172.1 cm
Victoria & Albert Museum, London

This was Millais's debut painting exhibited at the Royal Academy. Derived from a sketch Millais is said to have made on the back of a cheque, the finished work was painted when the artist was only sixteen, but immediately established his reputation, his biographer Marion H. Spielmann noting, '... he was recognized as a marvel and all stood astonished at his work.' The following year Millais was awarded a gold medal for the painting by the Society of Arts. The work depicts the Spanish conquest of Peru at the moment on 16 November 1532 when Francisco Pizarro, the Spanish leader, seizes the Peruvian ruler Atahualpa at Cajamarca. This event led to the slaughter of thousands of Indians by Spanish soldiers. The conquest did indeed occur at sunset, and Millais used this symbolically to represent the twilight of the Inca empire. A Catholic priest, Vincente de Valverde, brandishing a crucifix, almost obscures the disappearing sun. On the right of the composition, a mother with her child quotes the Massacre of the Innocents. History paintings were very popular at the time and Millais may have been influenced by seeing Henry Perronet Briggs's 1826 work, *The First Interview between the Spaniards and the Peruvians*, which was on public display (and is now in the Tate Gallery). The artist would also have seen Sheridan's play *Pizarro* in early 1846 at the Princess Theatre, a venue he often frequented. The actor James William Wallack played the Indian hero Rolla on the stage and was recast by Millais as Pizarro for his painting. Valverde was modelled by the artist's father, John William. Millais may have borrowed costumes and props from the Princess Theatre, although his fellow Pre-Raphaelite painter Holman Hunt said that Millais was lent these by the artist Edward Goodall who had recently returned from a visit to South America.

CYMON AND IPHIGENIA
———— 1848 ————
Oil on canvas, 45 × 58 in /114.3 × 147.3 cm
Private collection

The story of Cymon and Iphigenia came from Boccaccio's *Decameron*.
Cymon was a simple but handsome swain who fell in love with the
beautiful and more refined Iphigenia. They eventually married and he
became a sophisticated gallant. Millais's painting is based on lines
from John Dryden's translation of the story:

> Then Cymon first his rustick Voice essay'd,
> With proffer'd Service to the parting Maid
> To see her safe; his Hand she long deny'd,
> But took at length, asham'd of such a Guide;
> So Cymon led her home.

The subject was very much part of the art-historical canon, having
been painted by such masters as Rubens, Lely and Reynolds, and
later by Leighton. However, artists traditionally depicted the scene in
which the rugged Cymon discovers the sleeping beauty. Stylistically,
the painting was very much influenced by William Etty, the most
revered contemporary figurative painter. Holman Hunt, with whom
Millais worked at this time, executed some of the drapery in return
for Millais's help on his *The Eve of St Agnes*. In early April 1848 this
painting was entered for the Royal Academy summer exhibition, but
was rejected as unfinished. In 1849 the Oxford art dealer and collector James Wyatt, whose portrait Millais later painted, bought the
painting for £60. In 1852 the owner permitted the artist to retouch
the sky, some foliage and drapery, and this is particularly apparent in
the foreground where a greater degree of Pre-Raphaelite detail is
apparent. After Wyatt's death in 1853, the painting was sold at
Christie's and made an important feature in the catalogue. It was
bought for 350 guineas by George Wyatt, James's second son, who
took it home to his home in Newport on the Isle of Wight.

PLATE 3

ISABELLA
──── 1849 ────
Oil on canvas, 40½ × 56½ in /102.9 × 142.9 cm
National Museums & Galleries on Merseyside (Walker Art Gallery)

This was the first major painting to bear the controversial 'PRB' – Pre-Raphaelite Brotherhood – initials. They featured twice, in fact, alongside Millais's signature and in the carving on the side of Isabella's stool, despite which they seem to have gone unnoticed. The work had been started when Millais was nineteen – '... the most wonderful painting that any youth under twenty years of age ever did in the world', according to Holman Hunt. Hung at the Royal Academy next to Hunt's *Rienzi*, *Isabella* (as it was originally titled, although it is sometimes known as *Lorenzo and Isabella*) resulted in a barrage of abuse, though critics were divided. The painting, executed in the early gothic stage of Pre-Raphaelitism, received acclaim for its early Italian, particularly Florentine style. The source of the costumes was Camille Bonnard's *Costumes Historiques*, which had been published in 1829; Isabella's specifically came from an illustration of Beatrice d'Este by Paul Mercuri. The unusual perspective and awkward composition show a conscious affront to academic conventions, which the *Art Journal* felt '... cannot fail to establish the fame of the young painter'. The models for the composition were mostly friends and relatives of Millais, although their identities have been much disputed. The man with the napkin is the artist's father. The art critic Frederic George Stephens sat for the brother holding up the glass, with the American-born artist Walter Howell Deverell to his left in profile. A friend, Jack Harris, is seen on Stephens's right, kicking the dog, and William Hugh Fenn (the subject of a portrait by Millais) peels an apple, while Dante Gabriel Rossetti sits at the back drinking. Lorenzo was modelled by both William Michael Rossetti and Charles Compton and Isabella by Mary Hodgkinson, the wife of Millais's half-brother. The identity of the servant is uncertain, though it may have been either an architect named Wright or a Royal Academy student called A. F. Plass. Alluding to ill-fated love, the painting depicts a passage from Keats's poem 'Isabella or the Pot of Basil', based on a story by Boccaccio:

> Fair Isabel, poor simple Isabel!
> Lorenzo, a young palmer in Love's eye!
> They could not in the self-same mansion dwell
> Without some stir of heart, some malady;
> They could not sit at meals but feel how well
> It soothèd each other to be the other by.

Isabella fell in love with Lorenzo, an employee of her brothers, who were enraged at her choice. Here one of her malevolent brothers raises his glass sarcastically whilst another kicks her dog. This cruel motif, courageous for a British artist to depict, was criticized in the *Athenaeum* as an 'absurd mannerism'. The lovers are shown sharing a symbolic blood orange. Between them lies a majolica plate decorated with a biblical decapitation scene, probably Judith and Holofernes. Later in the story Isabella's brothers murder her lover and bury him in the forest, explaining away his disappearance to their distraught sister. Lorenzo appears to Isabella as a ghost and reveals his tragedy. Isabella then exhumes the body, decapitates the head and plants it in a large pot of basil – in Millais's painting the balcony is prophetically decorated with plant pots. When Isabella's brothers discover what is contained in the pot of basil, they flee with Lorenzo's head, leaving Isabella to die of a broken heart. By 1849 the painting was owned by Benjamin Godfrey Windus, but according to Hunt the picture was bought by three Bond Street tailors for £150 plus a suit. This implies they were William Wethered, who was also an art dealer, with his friends Colls and Wass, the three men who bought William Etty's *Joan of Arc* in 1847.

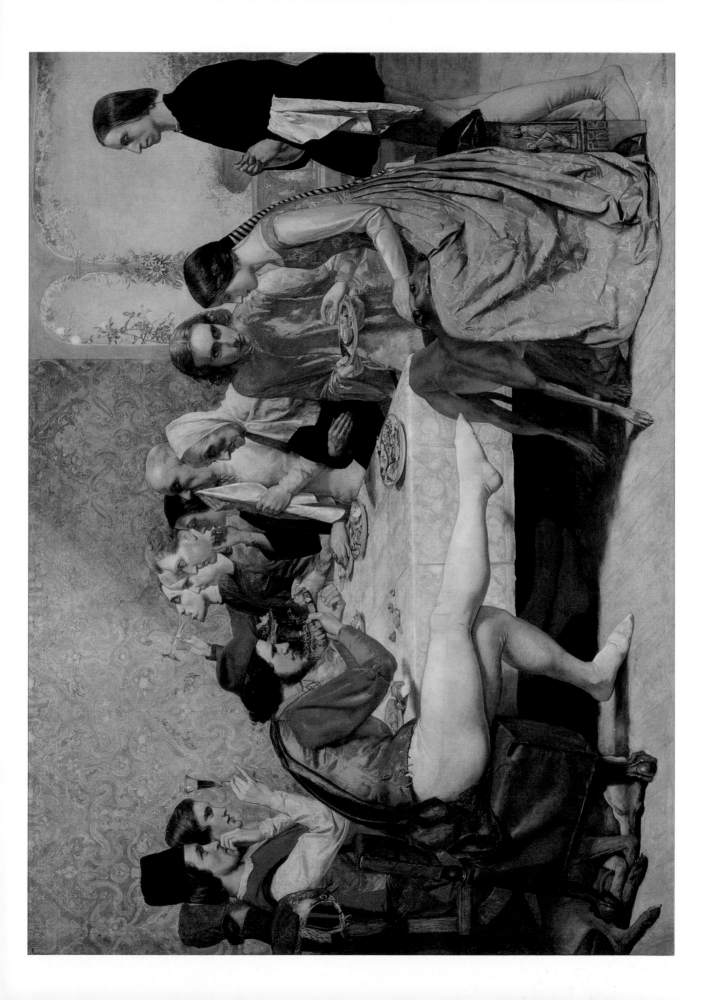

PLATE 4

JAMES WYATT AND HIS GRANDDAUGHTER
——————— 1849 ———————
Oil on panel, 14 × 17 ¾ in / 35.6 × 45.1 cm
Private collection

James Wyatt (1774–1853) had met Millais by 1846 when the artist painted a watercolour of his grandchild Mary and then bought *Cymon and Iphigenia*. Wyatt was a dealer and collector of art as well as being a print publisher, and was Mayor of Oxford in 1842–43. On the strength of his earlier purchase, Wyatt commissioned several small-scale family portraits, which show the transition in technique from Millais's early painting to his evolving Pre-Raphaelite style. A contemporary critic wrote, 'The infinite patience and imitative skill in draughtsmanship, the brilliancy of execution, and the power of reproducing the brightness of sunlight, have manifestly been acquired before the lesson had been learned of harmonious effect and of subordinating the parts to the whole ... This portrait ... is unflinchingly true ... it has all been set down with pitiless and remorseless solicitude. The quaint little Dutch doll-like child has received the painter's most earnest attention.' On the left is a miniature portrait of James's father Frederick Wyatt and in the top right corner a portrait by Sir William Boxall of Eliza Wyatt, James's daughter-in-law, who Millais painted as a companion to this portrait.

MRS JAMES WYATT AND HER DAUGHTER SARAH

———— *c.1850* ————

Oil on panel, 13¾ × 17¾ in / 354.9 × 45.1 cm
Tate Gallery, London

This small-scale double portrait was painted as a companion piece to *James Wyatt and his Granddaughter*. It was probably executed when Millais stayed near the Wyatts in the summer and autumn of 1850, while he was working on *The Woodman's Daughter* and *Mariana*. Eliza Wyatt, née Moorman (1813–95) was James's daughter-in-law. Sarah, later Mrs Thomas, was born on 17 January 1849, so was around twenty months old when this picture was painted. Some family notes give the date of the painting as around 1853; however this is unlikely as the child in the picture is clearly much younger than four years old. On the wall behind the figures are three prints: Leonardo da Vinci's *Last Supper* of 1495, Raphael's *Madonna della Sedia* of 1514 and his *Alba Madonna* of 1511. The latter two are similarly depictions of motherhood, but Raphael's loving mothers are idealized, in contrast to Millais's stiff and cold Mrs Wyatt, who barely touches her child. Her disposition is similar to that of the holy family in Millais's *Christ in the House of His Parents* of the same era and reveals something of his taste for repressed Victorian propriety.

FERDINAND LURED BY ARIEL
—————— 1849–50 ——————

Oil on panel, 25 1/2 × 20 in / 64.8 × 50.8 cm
The Makins Collection

The subject of this painting was taken from Shakespeare's *The Tempest*, in which Prospero's servant, the sprite Ariel, leads Ferdinand to his master. En route, Ariel teases Ferdinand about the death of his father, the King of Naples, in a shipwreck off Prospero's island. In the Royal Academy exhibition catalogue, the painting was accompanied by lines from the play. Here the sprite is carried through the air by surreal green bat-like creatures, holding a shell to prove his story. Ferdinand, modelled by the long-suffering F. G. Stephens, who had to endure a day-long sitting without a rest, stands in an odd pose, almost as if he is dancing. This was apparently derived, along with the design of his costume, from a plate entitled *Jeune Italien* dating from 1400 in Millais's much-used copy of Bonnard's *Costumes Historiques*. The luminosity of colour was obtained by the use of the Pre-Raphaelite 'wet white' technique, which consisted of applying paint to a freshly primed surface that was not allowed to dry. This was Millais's first attempt at *plein-air* painting. The background was executed in the summer of 1849 during a visit to a friend, George Dury, at Shotover Park in Oxfordshire. The landscape was meticulously depicted, Millais claiming, 'I have done every blade of grass and leaf distinct.' During the progress of the painting, the dealer William Wethered made some kind of commitment to purchase the picture, but subsequently withdrew the offer as a result of Millais's treatment of Ariel and the bats. Victorians were fascinated by fairies and no doubt Wethered expected a typically erotic sylph-like depiction of the sprite. Despite this rejection, Millais sold the painting prior to its exhibition for £150 to the collector Richard Ellison. Some time after Millais's death in 1896, but before it entered the Makins Collection, Hunt restored the painting as it had been what he described as 'ignorantly varnished'.

CHRIST IN THE HOUSE OF HIS PARENTS
(THE CARPENTER'S SHOP)
—————————— 1849–50 ——————————

Oil on canvas, 34 × 55 in / 86.4 × 139.7 cm
Tate Gallery, London

When this painting was exhibited in 1850, its contemporary audience found the graphic detail in the treatment of the biblical subject offensive and its warts-and-all treatment blasphemous. The critic in *Blackwood's Magazine* exclaimed, 'We can hardly imagine anything more ugly, graceless and unpleasant ... such a collection of splay feet, puffed joints and misshapen limbs was assuredly never before made ... We have great difficulty in believing the report that this unpleasing and atrociously affected picture has found a purchaser at a high price.' The painting was sold for £150 to dealer Henry Farrer and later to Thomas Plint, a Pre-Raphaelite collector who lived in Leeds. *The Carpenter's Shop* was shown with Hunt's *A Converted British Family*, but bore the brunt of abuse directed at the Pre-Raphaelite Brotherhood. It was so controversial that Queen Victoria had the painting removed from the exhibition for a private viewing. The holy family were meticulously depicted as ordinary people. Charles Dickens, who would later become an ardent admirer of Millais, was possibly the painting's most vociferous critic, finding it '... mean, revolting and repulsive'. It was accompanied by lines from the Old Testament Book of Zechariah, interpreted by theologians as pre-figuring Christ's passion, 'And one shall say unto him, what are these wounds in thine hands? Then he shall answer, Those with which I was wounded in the house of my friends.' The taut, Rossetti-inspired composition is loaded with elaborate and evocative biblical symbolism that is typical of the Pre-Raphaelites. The set-square refers to the Holy Trinity, while the white dove on the ladder is symbolic of the descent of the holy spirit from Heaven at Christ's baptism. The red flower represents Christ's blood and his crucifixion is prophesied by the wood, nails and stigmata imagery. The Virgin was modelled by Mary Hodgkinson, seen previously as Isabella, and described by Dickens as '... a woman so hideous in her ugliness that ... she would stand out from the rest of the company as a Monster in the vilest cabaret in France or in the lowest gin-shop in England.' Christ was based on Nöel Humphreys, the son of a medievalist book illustrator, who Dickens claimed was a '... hideous wry-necked, blubbering, red-haired boy, in a bed gown'. There was some historical precedent for depicting Joseph, here a composite of Millais's father's head and the body of an unknown carpenter, working at carpentry, although he was customarily accompanied by Mary sewing or spinning. Other biblical figures such as St Anne and St John the Baptist, modelled here by Edwin Everett, an adopted cousin of the artist, were rarely included. Millais, however, had undoubtedly seen Herbert's *Our Saviour, Subject to His Parents at Nazareth*, which was exhibited at the Royal Academy in 1847.

PLATE 8

MARIANA
———— 1850–51 ————
Oil on panel, 23½ × 19½ in / 59.7 × 49.5 cm
The Makins Collection

Millais exhibited this painting with *The Woodman's Daughter* and *The Return of the Dove to the Ark*. It was then untitled but accompanied by lines from Tennyson's 1830 poem 'Mariana':

> She only said, 'My life is dreary,
> He cometh not,' she said;
> She said, 'I am aweary, aweary,
> I would that I were dead!'

Tennyson was one of the most popular poets of the Victorian era and had been made Poet Laureate in 1850; in 1857 Millais was to illustrate an edition of his poems. *Mariana* was in turn inspired by Shakespeare's *Measure for Measure*; in which the lonely heroine has spent five years in a moated grange after her marriage dowry was lost in a shipwreck. She was rejected by her lover Angelo with whom she was still in love. Eventually Mariana is reunited with the officious Angelo after he has become Deputy to the Duke of Vienna. Millais's languid Mariana, having been working on an embroidery, stretches with boredom. She looks out of a stained-glass window, based on the windows of Merton College Chapel, Oxford, depicting an Annunciation scene. This vignette of the Virgin's fulfilment provides a distinct contrast to Mariana's plight. The motto above translates as 'In Heaven there is rest', alluding to her suicidal inclinations at this point of the story. The heraldry was invented by Millais for its symbolism, the snowdrop signifying consolation; it is also associated with 20 January, St Agnes's Eve, when legend says women will have visions of their future lovers. The mouse in the bottom right corner is mentioned in Tennyson's poem. The small altar in the background holds a silver caster seen also in *The Bridesmaid* and *The Eve of St Agnes*. The garden, painted from Thomas Combe's Oxfordshire garden, is not faithful to Tennyson's poem which describes a gloomy view broken merely by a poplar tree. *Mariana* was bought for £150 just before its completion by the dealer Henry Farrer, who also bought *The Carpenter's Shop*. Farrer then sold it on to the collector Windus. The painting inspired Burne-Jones who visited Windus's house with William Morris: '... we saw ... a beautiful little picture of a lady in black by Millais ... and we came away strengthened and confirmed.' The dress, made from silks and velvets bought in London in December 1850, was actually deep blue, contrasting with the intensely vivid shades in the Rossetti-inspired stained glass. After being in the collection of Windus, the painting entered the collection of Henry Makins who requested Hunt to do some restoration work on it after Millais's death, as it had become dull.

PLATE 9

THE WOODMAN'S DAUGHTER
——————— 1851 ———————

Oil on canvas, 35 × 25 ½ in / 88.9 × 64.8 cm
Guildhall Art Gallery, Corporation of London

Based on a poem of the same title by Coventry Patmore (1823–96), which appeared in his first volume of poems, published in 1844, *The Woodman's Daughter* refers to a relationship between Maud, the daughter of a woodman called Gerald, and the son of the local squire. Because of the difference in their social rank, they are thwarted in their desire to marry. Maud bears a child, which she drowns in a pond and goes insane. The painting illustrates the burgeoning of their childhood friendship:

> He sometimes, in a sullen tone,
> Would offer fruits, and she,
> Always received his gifts with an air
> So unreserved and free,
> That half-feigned distance soon became Familiarity.

The painting was 'assembled' from elements painted at different locations, from nature and in Millais's studio. Staying first with James Wyatt in Oxford, Millais moved to lodgings with a grocer called King at Botley from where he made excursions to Wytham Wood to paint the background for the painting. He asked Mrs Combe, a friend in Oxford, to buy the boots of Esther, a girl living in a lodge at the entrance to Lord Abingdon's estate, so that he could paint them as the woodman's daughter's footwear, also telling her, 'If you should see a country-child with a bright lilac pinafore on, lay strong hands on the same, and send it with the boots.' The strawberries proffered by the boy were purchased in Covent Garden market in March 1851. The models' identities are unknown. The painting was shown at the Royal Academy in 1851, but remained unsold until being acquired by Millais's half-brother Henry Hodgkinson. In 1886, at his request, Millais repainted parts of it, including the girl's face, which had been criticized by several observers, with results that are clearly visible on the canvas.

THE RETURN OF THE DOVE TO THE ARK
—————————————— 1851 ——————————————

Oil on canvas, 34 1/2 × 21 1/2 in / 87.6 × 54.6 cm
Ashmolean Museum, Oxford

This biblical painting from Genesis is related in subject to Millais's *The Eve of the Deluge* and Charles Landseer's painting of the same title exhibited in 1844, depicting one of Noah's wives holding the returned dove to her breast. Millais had intended a three-figure composition, including Noah, praying in front of a menagerie of birds and animals. Noah and the animals were subsequently rejected some time between February and April 1851. The painting was much admired by Ruskin who apparently wished to purchase it, but Millais had already sold it to his patron Thomas Combe. Millais always had Combe in mind as a buyer for this picture as he wanted it to hang in his prestigious collection with Hunt's *A Converted British Family*. Millais and Pre-Raphaelite associate Charles Allston Collins had stayed at Combe's home in Oxford, both painting portraits of their patron and his wife's uncle William Bennet. Combe had bought Collins's *Convent Thoughts*, which was close in dimensions to this painting, with a complementary theme: hope contrasted by sacrifice. Perhaps Millais intended his painting to be a pendant to his colleague's, and for both of these to form a triptych with Hunt's painting, thus representing three theological virtues, Faith, Hope and Charity. The woman who holds the bird to her breast wears robes of green, the colour of hope. Prior to sending the picture to its owner, Millais advised Combe to hang the painting near a window, tilted slightly forward to show it off advantageously.

THE BRIDESMAID
———— 1851 ————

Oil on panel, 11 × 8 in / 27.9 × 20.3 cm
Fitzwilliam Museum, Cambridge

Millais depicts an old superstition which states that if a bridesmaid passes a small morsel of wedding cake through the wedding ring nine times, she will have a vision of her future lover. In this context, the painting is very much linked to both *The Eve of St Agnes* and *Mariana*, in which the same silver caster features. The girl's chastity is symbolized by the orange blossom at her breast, its colouring accentuated by the fruit and the shade of her hair. The symbolic flowers and fruit, as well as the luxuriant tenor of this painting, are reminiscent of Rossetti's sensual, half-length paintings of women of the same decade. The model, according to the *PRB Journal*, was a Miss McDowall. Millais depicted the same subject again in 1879, but on this occasion in very different style and content in a conventional portrait of his daughter Mary as bridesmaid to his eldest daughter Effie. This painting has often been variously but incorrectly entitled *The Bride* and *All Hallow's E'en*; *The Bridesmaid* was bought by B. G. Windus, who sold it as *The Bride* at Christie's in 1862. It is uncertain whether this Pre-Raphaelite collector was the first owner, though Ford Madox Brown definitely saw it in Windus's home in March 1855. In 1868 it was bought by Ernest Gambart, the foremost picture dealer in Europe.

OPHELIA
———— 1851–52 ————

Oil on canvas, 30 × 44 in / 76.2 × 111.8 cm
Tate Gallery, London

The subject of *Ophelia* was taken from Shakespeare's *Hamlet*, in which Ophelia's death is described by Queen Gertrude:

> There is a willow grows aslant a brook,
> That shows his hoar leaves in the glassy stream;
> There with fantastic garlands did she come ...
> When down her weedy trophies and herself
> Fell in the weeping brook. Her clothes spread wide,
> And, mermaid-like, awhile they bore her up;
> Which time she chanted snatches of old tunes.

It was innovative of Millais to depict this stage of the story where Ophelia, driven mad by her lover Hamlet killing her father, falls into a stream and decides to let herself drown. Much copied, *Ophelia* inspired Arthur Hughes's eerie painting of the same title exhibited in the same year. Fully clothed in what Millais described as 'a really splendid lady's ancient dress' for which he had paid £4, Dante Gabriel Rossetti's future wife Elizabeth Siddal modelled for Ophelia by laying in a bath of water heated by lamps below. She caught an extremely bad cold as a result of the lamps going out and her father threatened to sue Millais until he promised to pay her doctor's bills. Millais went to great lengths to achieve accuracy in the painting, taking four months to complete the figure alone. According to William Michael Rossetti, *Ophelia* was the best likeness of Lizzie Siddal. Ruskin wrote to the artist on seeing the painting during his first visit to the Royal Academy in 1852, 'I came home last night with only *Ophelia* in my mind and wrote to my son nearly as follows. Nothing can be truer to Shakespear [sic] than Mr Millais's *Ophelia* and there is a refinement in the whole figure – in the floating and sustaining dress – such as I never saw before expressed on canvas. In her most lovely countenance there is an Innocence disturbed by Insanity and a sort of Enjoyment strangely blended with lineament of woe.' The background was painted in a field belonging to Effie's friend Mr Gadesden on the River Hogsmill at Ewell in Surrey. There is a great deal of botanical accuracy, but the multitude of symbolic flora, which allude to Ophelia's situation, would not all have bloomed at the same time. Millais had originally used daffodils for touches of yellow until Tennyson advised that if combined with wild roses, it might be taken as meaning false hope. The willow alludes to forsaken love, as do the pansies which refer to an earlier scene of the play. The violets around Ophelia's neck, symbolic of faithfulness, are also referred to earlier in *Hamlet*. The nettle and daisy are symbolic of pain and innocence respectively. The death-symbol, the poppy, was not mentioned by Shakespeare, but was an addition by Millais. The robin is that from one of the songs she sings, 'For bonny sweet Robin is all my joy'. The purple loosestrife in the upper-right corner alludes to the 'long purples' in the play, although Shakespeare actually meant the purple orchid. On the left of the loosestrife, the meadowsweet represents the futility of her death. Ophelia's sorrow is symbolized by the pheasant's eye and the fritillary floating on the surface of the water. There was originally a water-rat in the composition, but Millais painted it out as it was deemed inappropriate for the melancholic mood of the scene. Beside the self-explanatory forget-me-nots, the chiaroscuro forms the outline of a skull, referring both to Ophelia's death and Hamlet's famous graveyard scene which follows.

THE HUGUENOT
—————— 1851–52 ——————
Oil on canvas, 36½ × 24½ in / 92.7 × 62.2 cm
The Makins Collection

The Huguenot depicts an incident from the Massacre of St Bartholomew's Day. In August 1572 in Paris, French Catholics led by the Duke of Guise slaughtered thousands of Protestants, known as Huguenots. In another subject of ill-fated love, a Catholic girl attempts to prevent her Huguenot lover's death by persuading him to wear the white armband used to identify Catholics, but he is unwilling to compromise his principles even in the face of death. Millais was inspired by seeing the actress Pauline Viardot as Valentine in Giacomo Meyerbeer's opera *Les Huguenots* (1836), which was performed annually at Covent Garden after 1848. In it, after the Huguenot Raoul de Nangis refuses to deny his faith, his loyal lover Valentine converts to Protestantism and they marry, but both fall victim to the massacre. Huge crowds flocked to see this painting, probably due to its anti-Catholic implications, as there was much religious paranoia throughout Europe at this time. Millais embarked on the picture during his stay with Holman Hunt at Worcester Park Farm, originally intending to illustrate a line from Tennyson's poem 'Circumstance'. Hunt persuaded him that this was trite and Millais recalled the incident with the white cloth, applying it to his whispering lovers in a garden. Again he used symbolic flora: the ivy is symbolic of constancy or friendship in adversity, the Canterbury bells represent faith, and the nasturtiums, symbolic of patriotism, refer to Raoul's loyalty to his faith. Arthur Lemprière, the teenage son of Millais's friend William Charles Lemprière, modelled for the head of the Huguenot. The body was based on a professional model known as Child. Valentine was sat for by the beautiful model Anne Ryan, whose dark hair was changed to blonde. After being exhibited at the Royal Academy, *The Huguenot* was sent to Liverpool Academy where it was awarded a £50 prize. In March 1852 the picture and its copyright were purchased by the dealer D. T. White, who gave Millais £250 initially and then another £50 after the engraving was published. By April 1852 the painting had been acquired by his patron B. G. Windus. Millais was concerned about the deadening of colour tone in his paintings soon after their completion, and in January 1854 the artist Thomas Linnell advised him, 'I think the grounds you paint on must be too absorbent for I remember your saying that your picture of the Huguenot deadened in the same way and I have found that when a picture is painted on such ground it requires varnishing a good many times before it will bear out. I think you will find that all your pictures require is re-varnishing.' This good advice is attested by the lasting quality of Millais's paintings.

PLATE 14

THE PROSCRIBED ROYALIST, 1651
————— 1852–53 —————

Oil on canvas, 40$\frac{1}{2}$ × 28$\frac{1}{2}$ in / 102.9 × 72.4 cm
Private collection

Lewis Pocock, the Honorary Secretary of the Art Union of London, commissioned this painting in May 1852 for his own private collection. Desiring a subject of ill-fated love as in *The Huguenot*, the artist and patron had discussed a scene from *Romeo and Juliet*, particularly since Pocock had bought Shakespearean oil sketches by Hunt, although a Civil War context was eventually agreed upon. The couple here are from Vincenzo Bellini's 1835 opera *I Puritani*, which Millais saw at Covent Garden. She is Elvira, a Roundhead and he, Arturo, a Cavalier. The compositional device of hiding the young man in an oak tree, an emblem of valour, may have been inspired by the myth that Royalists avoided confrontation with their enemy by these means. The scene was painted from one of the most ancient trees on West Wickham Common, later known as the 'Millais Oak'. The artist stayed at The George Inn in Hayes near Bromley (for which he painted a new signboard), taking a week off to return to Gower Street to nurse a bad cold caught outdoors. Effie Ruskin was originally supposed to model for Elvira but was replaced by Anne Ryan from *The Huguenot*. Her period costume was painted from a dressed lay figure; the lace cuff, found for Millais by the ever-helpful Mrs Combe, was previously seen in *The Huguenot*. The artist's mother sewed the costume of Arturo, whose head was painted from Millais's friend Arthur Hughes.

THE ORDER OF RELEASE, 1746
──────────── 1852–53 ────────────

Oil on canvas, 40 ½ × 29 in / 102.9 × 73.7 cm
Tate Gallery, London

Originally entitled *The Ransom*, *The Order of Release* is set in a prison waiting-room.
The work was probably entirely studio-painted as there is little reference to a
setting, apart from the door. Millais had looked at the Tower of London for a suitable door or gateway, as well as researching churches, but was disappointed.
Although the subject was invented by Millais, it was probably inspired by the
novels of Sir Walter Scott. The rebel Scottish clansman, imprisoned after the defeat
of Bonnie Prince Charlie at Culloden on 16 April 1746, is led by the jailer to his
wife and child, dressed in the Drummond Tartan of the mother. His pet Collie
jumps up at his master, its feet on his Gordon Tartan kilt. The Highlander was
modelled by Westall, a deserter from a dragoon regiment who went on to become
a famous model. He was later arrested in an artist's studio and imprisoned. When
he had served his sentence, Westall was bought out of the army with funds raised
by artists. Effie Ruskin modelled for the wife in the spring of 1853. Ironically, it
was a prophetic picture for the artist and his female model, who was delighted to
be released from her elderly in-laws, the Ruskins. Millais worked his model to an
exhausting schedule from just after breakfast to nightfall with just one break for
lunch. Effie wrote on the 20 March 1853, 'He found my head like everyone else
who has tried it immensely difficult and he was greatly delighted last night when he
said he had quite got it! He paints so slowly and finely that no man working as he
does can paint faster.' John, the son of the artist and model, described it as a
perfect likeness of his mother with the exception of her hair colour, since Effie's
auburn locks were changed to black to contrast with those of the child. The prim-
roses symbolize the child's youth and set the scene in spring. The woman's
ambiguous expression implies that she prostituted herself to secure her husband's
liberty, but despite her loss of virtue is self-possessed and has an inner strength.
This was typical of the mid-nineteenth-century obsession with women's virtue. It
was felt that virtuous wives and mothers were the very backbone of society and the
key to British success. Effie was criticized for modelling by some of her then
husband's friends who felt that this behaviour was inappropriate for a virtuous
woman, but she believed it was justified as it was 'a painting of expression and of
human sympathy and incident'. Millais found the child and dog to be very difficult
models, 'All the morning I have been drawing a dog, which in unquietness is only
surpassed by a child, both of these animals I am trying to paint daily, and certainly
nothing can exceed the trial of patience they incur.' This controversial work
required a police guard to control crowds at the Royal Academy. Andrew Lang
wrote, 'As a piece of realistic painting it may challenge comparison with anything
else in the world … The work is saved by expression and colour from the realism
of a photograph.' *The Order of Release* was bought by Joseph Arden, a lawyer friend
of the novelist William Makepeace Thackeray, for £400; Arden also later bought
The Rescue. In 1878 it was sold to James Renton for £2,853 and on Renton's death
acquired by Henry Tate for £5,000.

JOHN RUSKIN

───────── 1853–54 ─────────

Oil on canvas, 31 × 26¾ in / 78.7 × 68.0 cm
Private collection

Commissioned by the subject, this portrait by the river at Glenfinlas was begun in the summer of 1853. According to Ruskin, Millais had '... fixed on his place, a lovely piece of worn rock, with foaming water and weeds and moss, and a noble overhanging bank of dark crag ... I am sure the foam of the torrent will be something quite new in art.' The setting reflects the sitter's interests in geology and botany. Ruskin was trying to convert Millais to his style, providing preparatory studies of rock for the painting. The artist usually worked very fast but found this painting virtually impossible to execute, in March 1854 writing to Effie's mother, 'If only I had myself to consult, I should write immediately and refuse to go on further with the portrait, which is the most hateful task I ever had to perform.' Ruskin was seemingly unaware of Millais's distress, and in October wrote to his father, 'Millais has done some glorious bits of rock ... with all their lichens gleaming like frosted silver – most heavenly. He is delighted with it himself.' This discrepancy indicates that by this stage Millais was not wholly committed to the principles of Pre-Raphaelitism. After a break, and rather bizarrely, Millais suggested completing the waterfall in Wales rather than at the original site, but Ruskin insisted that the rocks were quite different and so Millais reluctantly returned to Scotland. The background was eventually finished in June 1854 and both artist and subject had to endure two further sittings. Millais was extremely relieved on the completion of portrait and received £350 in payment from the sitter's father. Ruskin was fairly pleased with the finished portrait, with the exception of a couple of small elements: he did not like the yellow flower and nor did he appreciate the sparkle in his right eye, 'making me slightly squint'. It was during this working holiday that Millais and Effie's relationship developed. The unconsummated marriage of Ruskin and Effie was annulled in 1854, and she married Millais the following year.

THE BLIND GIRL
——— 1854–56 ———
Oil on canvas, 32 1/2 × 24 1/2 in / 82.6 × 62.2 cm
Birmingham City Museums and Art Gallery

Perhaps Millais's most highly acclaimed painting, *The Blind Girl* was retrospectively considered by many critics as a key picture in British art, and a graphic justification of Pre-Raphaelite principles. Another simple composition without much symbolic meaning, it is a sensitive evocation of affliction and the contemporary social issue of young and disabled vagrants. It depicts a blind girl of about eighteen years old and a young female companion resting at the roadside as they wait for a shower of rain to pass. The models were Matilda Proudfoot (as the blind girl) and Isabella Nicol, two young girls from Perth seen also in *Autumn Leaves*. The background is believed to be a view of Winchelsea in Sussex from the East (though according to the artist's son, John Guille Millais, portions were painted at Barnhill near Perth). The melancholy mood is accentuated by the evocative land-scape and leaden sky with the double rainbow and the thunder clouds. Rossetti described it as '… one of the most touching and perfect things I know'. The brilliance is for the benefit for the viewer's unimpaired eyes, making one's sympathy for the girl all the more poignant. Denied the beauty of such light, she is surrounded by objects that accentuate her other senses such as wet grass and forget-me-nots, and in her lap is a concertina, described by Ruskin as her '… poor instrument of musical beggary'. The concertina was lent by a Mr Pringle, whose daughter had died six months earlier, on the understanding that no one would play it. The girl's petticoat was originally red, but as it clashed with the other colours, it was replaced by a striped yellow and brown one that was still not ideal. Millais decided that he needed one in a shade of amber, and when Effie (to whom he was now married) saw a woman at her local butcher wearing one of the right colour she asked her poultry woman Jean Campbell to request its loan. Millais kept it for two days and his wife then returned the petticoat to the bemused woman along with a shilling. Ruskin celebrated the luminosity of Millais's palette: 'The freshly wet grass is all radiant through and through with the new sunshine; the weeds at the girl's side as bright as a Byzantine enamel, and inlaid with blue Veronica.' Not all contemporary critics were so favourable in their analysis: *The Times* condemned the painting as '… another study of red hair … pretty obvious … not very original', a pedantic writer in the *Art Journal* attacked the order of the colours in the rainbow and several influential Royal Academicians commented adversely. Millais was convinced of a conspiracy against him that resulted from innate jealousy, 'I have the whole Royal Academy (with one or two exceptions) against me.' The painting was sold to Ernest Gambart for 400 guineas with an additional 200 guineas for copyright as the painting was to be engraved.

PLATE 18

AUTUMN LEAVES
———— 1855–56 ————
Oil on canvas, 41 × 29 in / 104.1 × 73.7 cm
Manchester City Art Galleries

Four years prior to the execution of this painting, Millais asked, 'Is there any sensation more delicious than that awakened by the odour of burning leaves? To me nothing brings back sweeter memories of the days that are gone; it is the incense offered by departing summer to the sky, and it brings on a happy conviction that Time puts a peaceful seal on all that has gone.' The subject of this highly acclaimed picture was simple and unpretentious. It depicts four girls, modelled by Effie's sisters Alice (holding the basket) and Sophie, with Matilda and Isabella from *The Blind Girl*, piling leaves to be burned in a field. The redhead Matilda Proudfoot leans on either a broom or a rake, while young Isabella, dressed in purple, holds the apple. According to Millais, Rossetti was '... aghast with admiration, saying he would rather have the Autumn Leaves than any picture he ever saw.' *The Times* compared the painting with *The Return of the Dove to the Ark* and noticed a development in the force of the handling. The art world celebrated Millais's technical ability and treatment of colour, led by Ruskin who felt Millais had surpassed Giorgione: 'By much the most poetical work the painter has yet conceived ... the first instance existing of a perfectly painted twilight. It is as easy ... to give obscurity to twilight, but to give the glow within its darkness is another matter.' This twilight tonality can be seen later in *Sir Isumbras*. Millais, having intended to imbue the work with a philosophical meaning, was rather disappointed when the apparent religious symbolism went unnoticed: 'I have always felt insulted when people have regarded the picture as a simple little rustic episode chosen for effect and colour, as I intended the picture to arouse by its solemnity the deepest religious reflection.' The melancholic atmosphere, created by the subtle themes of transience and death, is a precursor to Symbolism, using motifs of dead leaves, smoke and the sunset. The girls' youth and innocence will soon be gone. T. S. R. Boase in the *Athenaeum* felt that *Autumn Leaves* and *The Blind Girl*, exhibited at the same time, '... have a unique place in British art.' Millais may have been inspired by helping sweep up and burn dead leaves at Tennyson's home, Farringford, on a visit in November 1854. Painted in Millais's garden at Annat Lodge, Perth, the horizon in the background, behind which the sun is setting, is a view of the hills looking towards the peak of Ben Vorlich. The spire of St John's Kirk can also be seen. A collector of genre paintings, James Eden, had agreed to buy the painting before its completion but tried to get out of his promise. Millais held him to his word and received £700 for it.

A Dream of the Past – Sir Isumbras
at the Ford
——————————— 1857 ———————————

Oil on canvas, 49 × 67 in /124.5 × 170.2 cm
National Museums & Galleries on Merseyside (Lady Lever Art Gallery)

This transitional work, possibly influenced by Albrecht Dürer, was Millais's largest painting to date. Executed near Annat Lodge at the Bridge of Earn, it depicts an aged knight crossing a stream on horseback accompanied by two woodsman's children carrying sticks. The models included Millais's son Everett and a Colonel Campbell for the knight. The evocative, brooding natural setting contains an almost Impressionist treatment of water. The exhibition catalogue entry included lines reputedly from *The Metrical Romance of Sir Ysumbras*. Indeed there was a metrical romance of this name, but it did not feature these lines. They were written specifically for the painting by Tom Taylor, a friend of Millais and later the editor of the humorous weekly *Punch*. Naïvely, Millais anticipated a positive review from *The Times*, which dedicated nearly an entire column to the artist, but the response was not as he expected: 'Much of the picture is carelessly painted, while the composition invites criticism, so daringly does it depart from all received notions of agreeableness and grace.' The tenor of this passage was similar to the criticism vented by most journals. Ruskin, who appreciated the noble subject-matter while suggesting that at its very deepest level the painting could personify the 'Christian Angel of Death', found nothing else to praise in the picture: 'The change in manner, from the years of *Ophelia* and *Mariana* to 1857 is not merely Fall – it is a Catastrophe; not merely a loss of power, but a reversal of principle.' Having been executed directly from nature, close to Pre-Raphaelite principles and much admired by Hunt, he predicted the painting would not be well received. The proud artist blamed disparaging reviews on art world jealousy and animosity, but was reassured by his public popularity. Critically, the painting fared better retrospectively, the landscape being particularly praised. The infamous painting inspired several jokes and caricatures, the most famous by a then unknown illustrator from Norwich, Frederick Sandys, who later became a friend of Rossetti. Prior to the opening of the exhibition, Millais had hastily refused an offer of £800 from Gambart and consequently suffered the humiliation of having to transport the unsold painting from Burlington House. It was eventually bought by the novelist Charles Reade for less than half the amount offered by Gambart.

PLATE 20

APPLE BLOSSOMS
——— 1856–59 ———

Oil on canvas, 43¹/₂ × 68 in / 110.5 × 172.7 cm
National Museums & Galleries on Merseyside (Lady Lever Art Gallery)

In late April 1856 Millais wrote to Effie saying he wanted to paint apple blossoms. This very large canvas was begun at Annat Lodge, Perth, in the autumn of 1856 and took nearly four years to complete. Originally planned as a woman sitting under a tree watched by a knight in the background, it was to have been entitled *Faint Heart Never Won Fair Ladye*. The project was abandoned in the spring of 1857 as a new tenant prohibited the artist from painting in the grounds as it would disturb her friends' walks. He then painted trees from neighbouring orchards near Annat Lodge and Bowerswell. The frieze-like picnic scene that replaced the earlier medieval subject was taken from an earlier sketch. *Apple Blossoms*, or *Spring*, as it was originally titled, has no symbolic content and Hunt thought it a fine example of its genre. But the eight girls picnicking in an orchard of apple trees in full blossom were considered ugly and vulgar by the critics. The reviewer of the new periodical *Bentley's Quarterly* described them as '... clothed skeletons, every one of them ugly and ungraceful, with hard features, strained skins, and in broad day with cheeks and lips painted as if for the footlights.' The models included a celebrated beauty named Georgiana Moncrieff, later Lady Dudley, for the kneeling central figure. On her left is Sophie Gray. Alice Gray is shown twice, resting on her elbow and lying on her back on the right. This pose was later used for an etching entitled *A Day in the Country*. The second figure from the right is Helen Moncrieff, later Lady Forbes. The girl in the red cloak is probably Agnes Stewart, described by the artist as 'that little humbug', and the girl second from left was apparently Henrietta Riley. The artist wrote to Hunt accusing Arthur Hughes of stealing his idea of painting an orchard in bloom in his *The King's Orchard*. Effie enthused, 'When the picture of *Spring Flowers* was on the easel out of doors, and in broad sunlight, the bees used often to settle on the bunches of blossom, thinking them real flowers from which they might make their honey.' *Apple Blossoms* was criticized by reviewers for a decline in the quality of Millais's work, particularly the landscape which shows a marked move away from Pre-Raphaelite attention to detail. Millais had trouble selling the painting. It remained unsold at the end of the Royal Academy exhibition and then at the Liverpool Academy in 1859. Gambart bought it in early May 1860 and had to auction it at Christie's a year later. The first collector to purchase the painting was Jacob Burnett of Newcastle in 1861.

PLATE 21

THE VALE OF REST
——— 1858 ———

Oil on canvas, 40½ × 68 in / 102.9 × 172.7 cm
Tate Gallery, London

The title was from a Felix Mendelssohn song which contains the line 'the vale of rest where the weary find repose', which Millais had heard his brother singing and felt was appropriate for his painting. It is a milestone piece in the development of his career, with Pre-Raphaelite attention to detail given what his son described as a 'greater breadth of treatment'. The painting is another with a death theme, set at twilight in a convent graveyard. One nun digs a grave while another sits looking at the sky in contemplation, having noticed a coffin-shaped cloud – a warning of death according to an old Scottish superstition – and with a skull hanging from her rosary. Effie described the origins of the painting: 'It had long been Millais's intention to paint a picture with nuns in it ... we imagined to ourselves the beauty of the picturesque features of the Roman Catholic religion, and transported ourselves back to the times before the Reformation had torn down, with bigoted zeal, all that was beautiful from antiquity, or sacred from the piety and remorse of the founders of old ecclesiastical buildings in this country.' Much of the painting was executed in the open air outside their home at Bowerswell during intense cold as winter set in. The graveyard section was painted later at Kinnoull Church in Perth. Retrospectively described by Millais as his favourite painting, *The Vale of Rest* received mixed reviews. Some felt that the narrative was unremittingly morbid and inappropriate. Ruskin, however, argued that had the nuns been beautified, the picture would have lapsed into sentimentality and lost its realistic power. In spring 1859, Millais offered the painting to Thomas Combe for 1,000 guineas, but Combe decided to buy Hunt's *Finding of Christ*, then unfinished, and could not afford both. Millais felt that his painting was far superior but did not speak publicly on the matter, not wanting to be accused of envy. This had been called Millais's last truly Pre-Raphaelite painting. It was sold to a Mr White, a dealer on behalf of Windus for £700. This sale helped the artist's two other paintings of this year to sell and boosted his confidence. Indeed, he received about £1,200 worth of commissions for new work on the strength of the picture. The face of the nun on the right was retouched after the exhibition making it slightly more appealing, using a Mrs Paton as the model, and then again in 1862 from the head of a Miss Lake.

PLATE 22

THE BLACK BRUNSWICKER
1859–60

Oil on canvas, 39 × 26 in / 99.1 × 66.0 cm
National Museums & Galleries on Merseyside (Lady Lever Art Gallery)

The Black Brunswicker depicts a young officer parting from his English fiancée, modelled separately, she by Charles Dickens's daughter Kate (Millais was on good terms with the Dickens family, despite Dickens's savage attack on *Christ in the House of His Parents*), and he by a private in the First Life Guards who died of consumption a year later, on the eve of Waterloo. Millais needed money and his dealer suggested executing a piece similar to *The Huguenot*. The painting is set in the Napoleonic era in Brussels on the night of the Duchess of Richmond's ball. The officer was from the Prussian cavalry regiment that wore black uniforms with skulls and cross-bones. His lover tries to prevent him leaving by holding the door shut, given moral support by her dog. Behind the couple is an equestrian portrait of Napoleon by David. It is more melodramatic and sentimental than *The Huguenot*, but was popular and emotive for its contemporary audience who would have been aware that nearly the whole regiment was killed in the battle after displaying great valour. Millais was helped by William Russell, a contemporary pioneering war journalist, who gave advice on military matters. This painting was intended as a pendant to the 1852 painting, although it is not of such a high standard. There is some precise detail, for example the creased wallpaper raising from the wall, the sheen and drapery of her satin dress and the hero's uniform copied from a real Prussian one. The treatment of the dog was favourably compared to the work of the great animal painter Edwin Landseer. The artist had trouble with the depiction of Miss Dickens's face. It was restarted when the model noted some exaggeration, after her chaperone refused to make a judgement. This was Millais's only Royal Academy entry in 1860 and he was optimistic about its reception: 'I have it all in my mind's eye, and feel confident that it will be a prodigious success.' The painting was still unsold in early June, though Millais had anticipated selling it for 2,000 guineas. However shortly after this Gambart paid a more realistic price of 1,000 guineas and sold it on to Thomas Plint. An engraving of the picture was made in 1864 by T. L. Atkinson.

PLATE 23

TRUST ME

──── 1862 ────

Oil on canvas, 44 × 30½ in / 111.8 × 77.5 cm
The Forbes Magazine Collection, New York

Genre paintings containing hints of clandestine love affairs were extremely popular among the Victorian public, and may be seen as the visual equivalents of the novels of the period. *Trust Me*, in particular, bears close affinities to the illustrations to the novels of Anthony Trollope that Millais had begun in 1860 with six drawings for *Framley Parsonage*. In 1862 he was at work on illustrations for *The Small House at Allington*. The action of the novels is set in the fictitious county of Barset, and here Millais has indicated that the location is rural, rather than urban, by showing the man dressed for the hunt. The *Art Journal* was convinced that the painting was designed to inform us that '... a young lady has received a letter, which her father desires to see.' It was impressed too by Millais's ability to convey the story with clarity, noting, 'Nothing can surpass the clearness of the narrative; this, indeed, is what Mr Millais always strives for, and wherein he most frequently succeeds.' However, the subject of the painting remains enigmatic: is the man the woman's father or husband? is her stance demure or defiant? is the letter she clutches from a lover? and, finally, who is declaring (or asking) the 'trust me' of the title?

PLATE 24

THE EVE OF ST AGNES
————— 1862–63 —————

Oil on canvas, 46½ × 61 in / 118.1 × 154.9 cm
Her Majesty Queen Elizabeth The Queen Mother

Here Madeline disrobes in the moonlight as her voyeuristic lover Porphyro watches secretly from a closet. This scene was inspired by the Keats poem of the same name which had inspired Hunt's final Pre-Raphaelite painting, specifically the stanza that contains the lines:

> Anon his heart revives: her vespers done,
> Of all its wreathèd pearls her hair she frees;
> Unclasps her warmèd jewels one by one;
> Loosens her fragrant bodice; by degrees
> Her rich attire creeps rustling to her knees.

However, Millais's version is far removed from Pre-Raphaelite principles as it is so historically inaccurate as to be anachronistic. The girl, who looks contemporary, stands in a Jacobean rather than a fourteenth-century room. F. G. Stephens wrote in the *Athenaeum*, 'There is a charm of execution … which carries thought away from its absurdity. The anachronism is so thorough … We cannot fail to see that the idea is as much the artist's own as that of Keats.' Millais's setting was the King's Bedroom in England's largest private house, Knole in Kent, featuring the bed of King James I with its opulent bed linen and original silver fittings. He painted late in the evening in full moonlight to obtain realistic atmospheric effects, enduring freezing conditions that numbed his fingers. The picture was executed at great speed in just five-and-a-half days – three and a half at Knole and two at home, using a bull's-eye lantern to create a similar lighting effect. Despite the adverse conditions under which it was executed, *The Eve of St Agnes* was considered to be one of Millais's greatest paintings, and one which shows a complete reversal of previous principles. At Knole, Effie sat for Madeline, whose figure was finished from the professional model Miss Ford. Unfortunately, when the picture was exhibited, the audience found the Madeline unattractive and rigid, Tom Taylor unkindly describing her as 'scraggy' and Sir Frances Grant complaining, 'I cannot bear that woman with the gridiron' (a reference to the pattern on the floor). The painting was bought for £800 by Gambart who sold it on to Charles Lucas by 1865. It was then acquired by the artist Val Prinsep who was very enthusiastic about his purchase, describing it as '… essentially a painter's picture'.

MY FIRST SERMON
───── 1863 ─────
Oil on canvas, 36 ¹/₂ × 28 ¹/₂ in / 92.7 × 72.4 cm
Guildhall Art Gallery, Corporation of London

My First Sermon was Millais's first sentimental depiction of a child,
and marks the beginning of a long and profitable series of similarly
attractive works featuring young girls. It was modelled by his
five-year-old daughter Effie, the first time she had sat for a painting.
She later became Mrs James, the mother of the young boy subject of
his celebrated *Bubbles*. When the picture was exhibited at the Royal
Academy, in a speech at the Academy banquet the Archbishop of
Canterbury used the picture to exemplify the 'piety of childhood'.
The high-backed pew (no longer extant) was painted in a church at
Kingston-on-Thames where the artist's parents lived. The popularity
of the picture led to a sequel being painted in the following year.
Millais had already painted a highly finished oil copy in August 1863,
completing it in just two days and selling it for £180, commenting, 'I
never did anything in my life so well or so quickly.' A watercolour
of the subject was bought by Charles Langton. The original work was
in the collection of Charles Gassiot by 1886, and was bequeathed to
the Guildhall in 1902, along with its sequel.

MY SECOND SERMON
───── 1864 ─────
Oil on canvas, 36 × 28 in / 91.4 × 71.1 cm
Guildhall Art Gallery, Corporation of London

Begun in January 1864, this was painted to capitalize on the success
of *My First Sermon*. It was rejected by the Royal Academy Committee,
however, on the grounds of its plagiarism of the earlier painting. This
painting was similarly mentioned in a speech by the Archbishop of
Canterbury, 'I see a little lady here … who, though unconscious
whom she has been addressing … has in truth, by the eloquence of
her silent slumber, given us a warning of the evil of lengthy sermons
and drowsy discourses. Sorry indeed should I be to disturb that sweet
and peaceful slumber, but I beg that when she does awake she may
be informed who they are who have pointed the moral of her story.'
As with its companion, Charles Langton owned a watercolour
version. The original was owned by Charles Gassiot who bequeathed
it to the Guildhall with *My First Sermon*.

LEISURE HOURS
—— 1864 ——

Oil on canvas, 33 × 46 in / 83.8 × 116.8 cm
Detroit Institute of Arts (Founders Society Purchase, Robert H. Tannahill
Foundation Fund)

This is a double portrait of Anne (on the right) and Marion (on the left), the daughters of Sir John Pender of Middleton Hall, Linlithgow, and his second wife Emma, *née* Denison. Pender was the Liberal Member of Parliament for Totnes in Devon, as well as a businessman involved in both textiles and telegraphy. Anne (1852–1902) never married; Marion (1856–1955) married Sir George William Des Voeux in 1875. The rich red and green, also seen in his anecdotal sermon paintings, were typical of Millais's work at this time. The screen recalls hangings in *Mariana* but has a very different ambience, this being wholly populist and aimed at the print market. The tense, eerie mood is reminiscent of *Autumn Leaves*. The goldfish bowl is symbolic of the artifice in the lives of upper-middle-class girls like the Pender sisters. Sir John Pender collected modern British art, having recently bought Millais's *The Proscribed Royalist* and *The Parable of the Tares*. Until recently the painting was still owned by the Pender family by descent.

PLATE 27

THE BOYHOOD OF RALEIGH
—————— 1870 ——————
Oil on canvas, 47½ × 56 in / 120.7 × 142.2 cm
Tate Gallery, London

The subject was suggested to the artist on reading the historian James Anthony Froude's 'England's Forgotten Worthies' in the *Westminster Review* of 1852. The young Raleigh and his brother listen keenly to the tales of an old Genoese sailor's adventures on the Spanish main. The artist's sons Everett and George sat for the two boys and a professional model took the part of the elderly sailor. The seascape was painted on the Devon coast close to Exeter, Raleigh's home town, on the land of Lady Rolles. F. G. Stephens wrote, 'This work glows in the warm light of a Devonshire Sun ... The young Walter sits up on the pavement ... and with fixed, dreaming eyes, seems to see El Dorado, the islands of the east and west, the palms and temples of the south ... ships, gold, the hated Spaniards, and ... the "fountain of youth" were before his fancy.' The toy boat in the bottom left corner is prophetic of the young Walter's maritime adventures as an adult.

PLATE 28

CHILL OCTOBER
———— 1870 ————
Oil on canvas, 55 1/2 × 73 1/2 in / 141.0 × 186.7 cm
Collection of Sir Andrew Lloyd Webber

This was Millais's first autumnal Scottish landscape. The wild and
isolated terrain is a backwater of the River Tay known locally as
'Seggy Den', five miles from Perth, just below Kinfauns. Millais
wrote, 'The scene, simple as it is, had impressed me for years before
I painted it. I made no sketch for it, but painted every touch from
Nature, on the canvas itself, under irritating trials of wind and rain.'
The amateur critic, Lord Justice James, recognized Millais's evocation
of autumn: 'Every true painter is a poet. A good landscape is especially a descriptive poem, and in this landscape the artist has shown
us how well he has seen, how thoroughly he has felt, and how truly
he has followed nature.' Probably his best landscape, *Chill October* was
one of Millais's most popular paintings, though not unique: during
the 1870s the artist produced a pure landscape almost annually.
There are no sophisticated allusions to atmosphere, but there is a
great degree of botanical accuracy in the treatment of the reeds,
rushes, willows, the stream, the sky and the background hills, Millais
altering nothing from the scene in front of him. Marion H.
Spielmann remarked, 'Millais could paint the time of day; he could
moreover draw a tree, as few of his contemporaries could do; and
sky and grass and dew-drenched heather, luminous screen of cloud
and tangled undergrowth – he painted them all, not only with love,
but with an enthusiasm which he had the happy faculty of imparting
to the spectator.' A bemused local railway porter helped the artist
carry his canvas and easel. On reading that the painting had been sold
to Samuel Mendel for £1,000 in 1871, he remarked that he would
not have given half-a-crown for it. In 1875 it was bought at
Christie's by Agnew for £3,253, and in 1883 was made the subject of
an engraving by Brunet Debaires.

PLATE 29

THE KNIGHT ERRANT
— 1870 —
Oil on canvas, 72 1/2 × 53 1/4 in / 184.2 × 136.3 cm
Tate Gallery, London

The 1886 Grosvenor Gallery exhibition of Millais's works describes the action depicted in this unusual subject: 'Attacked by robbers! Such has been the fate of the damsel in the picture. Not content with stealing all her valuables, the thieves have tied her naked to a tree, leaving her clothes in a heap on the ground. A knight wandering about, ever ready to avenge misfortune, sees her plight, and is on the point of releasing her. The pale crescent of the new moon light the picture, and we see the retreating figures of her assailants.' *The Knight Errant* was one of Millais's very rare nude scenes. According to his son John Guilles Millais, 'Mrs Grundy was shocked, or pretended to be so, and in consequence it remained long on the artist's hands, no one daring to buy it. At last (in 1874) a dealer purchased it, and (with this "hall mark") it at once gained the favour of the public.' Painted from professional models, with the background painted at Wortley Chase, Millais originally depicted the woman facing toward the spectator, but was dissatisfied with the effect and even threatened to destroy it. Having removed that portion of the canvas, which he reworked as *The Martyr of the Solway*, however, he then repainted the head, turning it away as if in shame, with a result he found acceptable.

PLATE 30

THE MARTYR OF THE SOLWAY
— 1871 —

Oil on canvas, 27 ¾ × 22 ¼ in / 60.3 × 56.5 cm
National Museums & Galleries on Merseyside (Walker Art Gallery)

This painting depicts Margaret Wilson of Wigtownshire (1667–85) who was a Covenanter. Refusing to acknowledge the Episcopacy, she was sentenced to execution by drowning in the Solway. Millais's illustration of this subject, showing Margaret Wilson in a full-length pose, was published in the journal *Once A Week* in July 1862. The head and bust of the figure in this painting originally belonged to the woman in Millais's *The Knight Errant* of 1870, which he cut out and replaced with a new piece of canvas, painting the woman facing away. The original piece of canvas was then pasted on to a new canvas and her nude figure clothed to create this work.

HEARTS ARE TRUMPS
———— 1872 ————

Oil on canvas, 65¼ × 86½ in / 165.7 × 219.7 cm
Tate Gallery, London

This scene of contemporary life depicts three beautiful and glam-orously attired young women sitting around a card table. The spectator participates in the game of Dummy Whist, being shown the good hand of the player on the right. This compositional device was common in nineteenth-century domestic realism. The models were the daughters of the inventor and industrialist Sir William Armstrong, Elizabeth, Diana and Mary, later Mrs Tennant-Dunlop, Mrs Secker and Mrs Blennerhasset. Inspired by Millais's *Sisters*, Armstrong, co-founder of the armaments company Vickers Armstrong, requested a portrait of his daughters, price being no object. On 5 August 1871 Millais wrote to Effie, 'They know the price and are prepared to give anything I ask.' In 1875 it was bought by Armstrong for 200 guineas. Millais himself designed the opulent dresses and executed them with a triumph of technique in a masterpiece of fashion portraiture, its delicate handling of textures on a par with Leighton. The arrange-ment of the sitters is reminiscent of Sir Joshua Reynold's *Three Ladies Waldegrave*, also a triple portrait, which hung at Strawberry Hill, then the home of the Countess of Waldegrave. The background shows the influence of oriental arts, *Japonisme* being a fashionable style in 1870s Britain. *Hearts Are Trumps* received enthusiastic and positive reviews when exhibited at the Royal Academy. The Athenaeum critic wrote, 'Mr Millais will hold a position second to none this year, principally through his superb portraits, conspicuous among which is the picture styled *Hearts Are Trumps* ... the painting is as brilliant, lucid and formidable as a Velasquez, and as broad as a Reynolds. It contains what, on the whole, are the best portraits Mr Millais has produced.' In 1878 the painting was shown at the Exposition Universal in Paris. It inspired John Singer Sargent's portrait of the three daughters of Colonel Thomas Vickers.

PLATE 32

THE NORTH-WEST PASSAGE
— 1874 —
Oil on canvas, 69 1/2 × 87 1/2 in / 176.5 × 222.3 cm
Tate Gallery, London

This unusually serious painting for Millais was imbued with sincere middle-class patriotism. Extremely popular, it was always surrounded by a crowd at the Royal Academy. Millais received a letter from Sir George Narks, who commanded the expedition to the North Pole in 1879, praising the painting's effect on national morale. The work was subtitled 'It might be done and England should do it'. In this period it was hoped that a safe shipping passage from the Far East via the north of Canada would be established. An aged mariner sits in a room of nautical paraphernalia, with an open map and a glass of brandy. His daughter, modelled by the woman who also appeared in *Stitch! Stitch! Stitch!* of 1876, reads to him from an account of one of his expeditions. He remembers his own past experiences at sea, his weather-beaten face clearly moved with nostalgia. The old man was modelled by Captain Edward John Trelawny, an eccentric friend of Byron and Shelley, about both of whom he reminisced in his autobiography *Adventures of a Younger Son*. Among his many adventures he had been captured by Greek pirates who took him ashore; after marrying the daughter of the chief, he spent his honeymoon in a cave. At first this authentic ancient mariner refused to sit for Millais because he despised contemporary culture. Even after Trelawny introduced himself to Millais at the funeral of a mutual friend, John Leech, the artist was afraid to ask him again. Effie decided to confront this awkward old man and they eventually agreed upon a bargain. Trelawny would sit for six sessions as long as Effie agreed to take six Turkish baths, accompanied by his niece, the elderly sailor having an interest in a company promoting Turkish baths in London. Surprisingly, the old sea dog did not drink alcohol and complained about the proposed tumbler of brandy in the composition. The artist waited for the completion of the six sittings before he painted in the controversial glass. Trelawny was angered when he saw the completed canvas in the Academy, fearing recognition. At one stage of the painting's execution, two children, modelled by the artist's own offspring, were introduced in the right corner looking at a globe. Millais decided that the children ruined the simplicity of the story and the composition. The canvas was then cut and a new section stripped in on which the children were replaced by an old English flag.

PLATE 33

A JERSEY LILLY (LILLIE LANGTRY)

——— 1878 ———

Oil on canvas, 43½ x 33½ in / 110.5 x 85.1 cm
Jersey Museum Service

This is a portrait of the famous actress Lillie Langtry (1853–1929) at her most beautiful. Not only was she a close friend of Millais's family, but she also had a shared ancestry with the artist, descending, like Millais, from an old Jersey family. Born Emilie Charlotte Le Breton, she was the daughter of William Le Breton, the Dean of Jersey. In 1874 she married Edward Langtry, the son of a wealthy shipowner, and moved to London where she acquired the nickname 'Jersey Lily'. There she became celebrated as a society beauty and as the mistress of the Prince of Wales, later Edward VII. She entered this role in 1877, when she first posed for Millais in the title role of *Effie Deans*, a painting based on Sir Walter Scott's novel *The Heart of Midlothian* (1818). The following year Millais painted this formal portrait, which was exhibited at the Royal Academy along with his equally famous *The Princes in the Tower*. She became well-known as an actress in Britain and the USA, and died in France, but was buried in the churchyard of St Saviour's in her native Jersey.

PLATE 34

THE PRINCES IN THE TOWER
—————— 1878 ——————

Oil on Canvas, 58 × 36 in / 147.3 × 91.4 cm
Royal Holloway and Bedford New College, University of London

This historical painting depicts the sons of King Edward IV who were imprisoned in the Tower of London by Richard Duke of Gloucester, who claimed the throne for himself. One is Edward V, the rightful heir to the throne, then aged thirteen, and his younger brother Richard, the Duke of York, aged ten in 1493, the year of their father's death. In this tense composition, the boys are caught at a moment just prior to their murder. The painting was extremely popular, the mezzotint being widely distributed, but Millais was criticized for the morbid nature of the subject. It was popularly believed that the boys were suffocated in their sleep with pillows, and in 1674 the skeletons of two children were found under the staircase in the White Tower, hence Millais's setting, perhaps also inspired by an 1831 Paul Delaroche painting of the same subject. Millais's son John had sketched in the Bloody Tower, but on finding the staircase too small and the wrong way round, Millais went to sketch there himself. He had already painted a background for this painting at St Mary's Tower at Birnam, but rejected it, although this incomplete canvas provided the background for *The Grey Lady* of 1883. Prince Edward wears the Order of the Garter on the advice of James Robinson Planché, an eminent costume historian and heraldic expert. A year later Millais executed a companion painting, *Princess Elizabeth in Prison at St James's*. It depicts the second daughter of Charles I and Henrietta Maria who spent most of her short life imprisoned in St James's Palace. She is shown writing a letter to Parliament requesting to be reunited with her servants. Princess Elizabeth was moved to Carisbrook Castle on the Isle of Wight, where she died in 1650, aged fifteen. These two paintings are more exceptional than Millais's usual child themes, not only because they depict historical figures (although he had already painted Sir Walter Raleigh as a boy), but because all three children died in captivity. The princes had provided a common subject in British art since the eighteenth century, but were shown at a less tense moment by artists such as Opie and Northcote. *The Times* reviewer wrote, 'The painter has admirably expressed in these young faces the trouble of continued fear bent with the agitation of sudden alarm, and it is greatly to his praise that ... his work should awaken no thought of plagiarism. The execution is consummate, and thoroughly carried through the picture.'

LOUISE JOPLING
———— 1879 ————
Oil on canvas, 48 1/2 × 29 1/2 in / 123.2 × 74.9 cm
Private collection

Millais painted numerous portraits of the eminent men and women of the day, among them writers and poets including Carlyle and Tennyson, Prime Ministers Gladstone, Disraeli and the Marquis of Salisbury, and actors and actresses such as Sir Henry Irving and Lillie Langtry. This simple and elegant portrait was, according to his son John Guille Millais, 'One of the finest that ever came from his brush'. Louise Goode (1843–1933) was first married to Frank Romer, the private secretary of Baron Rothschild. While living in Paris, the Baroness encouraged her to take painting lessons. Following the death of Romer, she married Joseph Middleton Jopling, a painter and a close friend of Millais (like Millais, 'Joe' Jopling was a shooting enthusiast, representing England in competitions), and as Louise Jopling achieved celebrity as a portrait painter.

S E L F - P O R T R A I T
———— 1880 ————
Oil on canvas, 33 ¾ × 25 ½ in / 86.0 × 65.0 cm
Uffizi Gallery, Florence

Along with contemporaries such as Alma-Tadema and Leighton, Millais was invited to paint himself for the Uffizi's collection of artists' self-portraits. Millais executed the painting in just a few days with ease, using the huge mirror from his Palace Gate studio beside his canvas. He explained, 'You see, it is done very quickly, for as I know exactly when to keep still, I'm a pretty good sitter.' Millais depicted himself full of health and vitality. The self-portrait was generally regarded as the best representation of the artist, one contemporary critic describing it as 'Holding its own with singular power among the auto-portraits of the great masters of the world, from the mighty painters of Italy down to the present day.' Unlike more bohemian artists, the conservative Millais dressed in the style of a successful businessman. He had once visited a phrenologist named Donovan, who from Millais's manner deemed him to be uncreative, logical and a shrewd businessman, much to the artist's indignation. The Garrick Club holds a copy of this work. Millais also painted a self-portrait three years later for the collection of artists' self-portraits founded by Alexander McDonald of Aberdeen.

CALLER HERRIN'
—————— 1881 ——————
Oil on canvas, 43 1/2 × 31 in / 110.5 × 78.7 cm
Private collection

The 1886 exhibition of Millais's paintings at the Grosvenor Gallery provided a description of this work: 'A beautiful young fisher girl is resting for a moment as she carries home her load of fish. She is gazing over the sea, thinking perhaps of her absent lover. Every detail is carefully rendered; the scales of the herrings on the basket glitter in the bright sunlight.' In his *Art of England* John Ruskin drew special attention to the work: '... a picture which, as a piece of art, I should, myself, put highest of all yet produced by the Pre-Raphaelite school – in that most noble picture, I say, the herrings were painted just as well as the girl, and the master was not the least afraid that, for all he could do to them, you would look at the herrings first.'

PLATE 38

THE RULING PASSION
(THE ORNITHOLOGIST)
―――――― 1885 ――――――

Oil on canvas, 63¼ × 85 in / 160.7 × 215.9 cm
Glasgow Art Gallery and Museum

Millais was inspired to paint this work, which he painted in the year that he became a baronet, after paying a visit to the home of John Gould (1804–81), a distinguished ornithologist, who was noted as a curmudgeonly invalid. He did not begin it until after Gould's death, finishing it in time for the 1885 Royal Academy show. T. Oldham Barlow, an engraver and fellow Royal Academician, sat for the figure of the aged ornithologist, while Millais's own grandchildren, William (the subject of *Bubbles*) and George James, modelled the small children. Ivor Byng, the son of the Reverend Francis Byng, the former chaplain to the House of Commons, sat for the boy in a sailor suit, and a professional model (who appeared later in *The Nest*), as the girl on the left. Millais was delighted with the picture, which was warmly praised by Ruskin, who wrote, 'I have not seen any work of modern Art with more delight than this.' It remained unsold, however, causing Millais to speculate on whether he should '… trouble the critics and public any more with what is called "an important picture".'

PLATE 39

BUBBLES

———— 1886 ————

Oil on canvas, 43 × 31 in / 109.2 × 78.7 cm
Elida Gibbs Collection

Originally entitled *A Child's World*, this is a portrait of the artist's grandson William, born in 1881. The son of Effie junior and Major William James, he went on to become Admiral Sir William James. Millais saw his grandson playing with a pipe and soap bubbles and was inspired to paint him, 'bubbles and all', for his own pleasure. The child was happy to sit, anticipating being told fairy stories by his grandfather. The bubbles, described by his son as 'too evanescent for portraiture', proved too challenging and were painted from glass spheres manufactured for the purpose. Beatrix Potter noted in her journal of 15 November 1885 that Millais had visited her home to ask her father to photograph Willie, so that he could compare the photograph to life. The painting was purchased, with copyright, by Sir William Ingram for the *Illustrated London News* for its Christmas 1887 issue presentation plate, as they had done with *Cherry Ripe* in 1879. However, before publication the copyright was sold to Messrs A. and F. Pears, who used it as an advertisement for their transparent soap, adding the soap to the coloured reproduction. Millais, accused of commercialism, was furious and protested – though in vain as he knew they had every right to do as they wished. He was criticized in 1895 by the novelist Marie Corelli who has a character in her novel *The Sorrows of Satan* remark, 'I am one of those who think the fame of Millais as an artist was marred when he degraded himself to the level of painting the little green boy blowing bubbles of Pears' soap.' She later apologized to the artist by letter when he corresponded about the facts of the sale, observing, 'I have seen and loved the original picture – the most exquisite and dainty child ever dreamed of, with the air of a baby poet as well as of a small angel – and I look upon all Pears posters as gross libels, both of your work and you ... I hope you will forgive me my excessive zeal; for now that I know you had nothing to do in the "soap business", I will transfer my wrath to the dealer, and pray you to accept my frank apologies.' The novelist agreed to alter the dialogue in the next edition of her novel.

MERCY – ST BARTHOLOMEW'S DAY, 1572

—————— 1886 ——————

Oil on canvas, 72 1/2 × 51 1/2 in / 181.6 × 130.8 cm
Tate Gallery, London

Millais had a decade of productive work ahead of him when he executed this painting. He occupied his remaining years with landscapes, portraits of wealthy clients such as Vanderbilts and Rothschilds, and the occasional genre picture, but with few exceptions it is clear that the days of his great masterpieces were drawing to a close. *Mercy – St Bartholomew's Day, 1572* was in effect a reprise of *The Huguenot* of thirty-five years earlier in a depiction of an imaginary incident during the St Bartholomew's Day Massacre. The models were the Marchioness Granby as the nun, Geoffroy Millais as the cavalier and the Reverend Richard Lear as the priest. It was reportedly one of the most troublesome pictures Millais had attempted. He wrote dejectedly to the painter Briton Riviere on 11 July 1886, 'I have done the picture. That is, I have only, I hope, small things to complete it. I am sometimes happy over it, but oftener wretched ... People pass it, and go to a little child-picture, and cry "How sweet!" Always the way with any attempt at something serious. Bring Calderon [the painter Philip Hermogenes Calderon] with you if he cares to see an old hand's last performance. I feel a very poor old thing.'

PRINCIPAL PUBLIC COLLECTIONS
CONTAINING WORKS BY MILLAIS

AUSTRALIA

Adelaide
National Gallery of South Australia

Melbourne
National Gallery of Victoria

Perth
Perth City Art Gallery
Western Australian Art Gallery

CANADA

Ottawa
National Gallery of Canada

GERMANY

Hamburg
Hamburger Kunsthalle

GREAT BRITAIN

Aberdeen
Aberdeen Art Gallery

Birmingham
Birmingham City Art Gallery

Bristol
City of Bristol Museum and Art Gallery

Cambridge
Fitzwilliam Museum

Edinburgh
National Galleries of Scotland

Egham
Royal Holloway and Bedford New College

Glasgow
Glasgow Art Gallery

Jersey
Jersey Art Gallery

Leeds
Leeds City Art Gallery

Liverpool
Walker Art Gallery

London
British Museum
Guildhall Art Gallery
National Portrait Gallery
Royal Academy
Tate Gallery
Victoria & Albert Museum
William Morris Gallery

Manchester
Manchester City Art Gallery

Oldham
Oldham Art Gallery

Oxford
Ashmolean Museum

Plymouth
Plymouth City Art Gallery

Port Sunlight
Lady Lever Art Gallery

Sheffield
Sheffield City Art Galleries

Wolverhampton
Wightwick Manor (National Trust)

ITALY

Florence
Uffizi Gallery

SOUTH AFRICA

Johannesburg
Johannesburg Art Gallery

UNITED STATES OF AMERICA

Detroit, Michigan
Detroit Institute of Arts

Minneapolis, Minnesota
Minneapolis Institute of Arts

New Haven, Connecticut
Yale Center for British Art

New York, New York
The Pierpoint Morgan Library

DANTE GABRIEL ROSSETTI

Portrait of Elizabeth Siddall, 1850–65

DANTE GABRIEL ROSSETTI

1828–82

Dante Gabriel Rossetti's romantic self-portrait, drawn at the age of 18, in March 1847

Gabriel Charles Dante Rossetti was born in London on 12 May 1828 in the family house at 38 Charlotte Street, a run-down area to the north-west of the British Museum. His mother was Frances Polidori, the sister of Byron's physician John William Polidori, who came from an Anglo-Italian literary family. His father was Gabriele Rossetti, from Neapolitan peasant stock but with strong poetic leanings and a lifelong obsession with the poet Dante – hence the exotic name conferred on his first-born son.

Gabriele had attended the University of Naples and had subsequently held various positions – including that of a librettist to Rossini at the Naples Opera House and a museum curator – but after becoming a political exile he had travelled to Malta and then on to London, where he settled in 1824. There he worked as a teacher, and in 1831 he was appointed Professor of Italian at King's College. By then all four of his children had been born: Gabriel (or Dante Gabriel, as he reversed his name to give precedence to his poetic namesake); his elder sister Maria, who became an Anglican nun (the religion followed by the women of the household); his younger brother William Michael, who worked in a government department but developed a second career as a critic and historian of the Pre-Raphaelite movement; and their younger sister Christina, a poet celebrated for her authorship of religious and other poems, including *Goblin Market* and the Christmas carol *In the Bleak Mid-winter*.

After home tuition and attendance at a local school, with his brother William, Dante Gabriel Rossetti went to King's College School in 1837. The rigorous education provided there taught him Latin and Greek but he was a restless and academically unsuccessful pupil, and left at the age of 13. What he lacked in formal learning, however, he more than made up for through his reading and the cultural stimulation he received in the bilingual and intellectual Rossetti household. His parents were also unusually liberal for the

time, so that when he announced that he intended to become a painter he was positively encouraged: in fact, torn between his twin passions for poetry and painting, he decided to pursue both. He was ultimately to combine his two aspirations by appending self-penned sonnets to the frames of his paintings.

Rossetti began his study of art at a private school known as 'Sass's', a sort of preparatory school for those intending to enter the Royal Academy. His four years there were no more successful than his schooldays, however, as he found the school's emphasis on formal technique incompatible with his temperament. His next move, to the Antique School of the Royal Academy, was similarly unsuccessful, although Rossetti's charismatic personality began to be revealed to the circle of admirers that gathered round him. His sense of humour was a notable feature, coupled with his skill in caricature and writing impromptu and witty limericks about his friends and enemies. His dashing Italianate looks are presented without exaggeration in a self-portrait drawing dating from 1847, while a contemporary's recollection quoted by his biographer Henry C. Marillier could have described many an art student of today:

'Thick, beautiful, and closely-curled masses of rich, brown and neglected hair fell about an ample brow, and almost to the wearer's shoulders; strong eyebrows marked with their dark shadows a pair of rather sunken ·eyes, in which a sort of fire, instinct with what may be called proud cynicism, burned with a furtive sort of energy. His rather high cheekbones were the more observable because his cheeks were roseless and hollow enough to indicate the waste of life and midnight oil to which the youth was addicted. Close shaving left bare his very full, not to say sensuous lips and square-cut masculine chin. Rather below the middle height [he was 5' 7" tall] and with a slightly rolling

Rossetti's sister Christina and their mother Frances, 1877

gait, Rossetti came forward among his fellows with a jerking step, tossed the falling hair back from his face, and, having both hands in his pockets, faced the student world with an insouciant air which savoured of thorough self-reliance. A bare throat, a falling ill-kept collar, boots not over familiar with brushes, black and well-worn habiliments including not the ordinary jacket of the period but a loose dress-coat which had once been new – these were the outward and visible signs of a mood which cared even less for appearances than the art student of those days was accustomed to care, which undoubtedly was little enough!'

Rossetti's appearance was in keeping with the prevalent mood of the age, with its romantic revival, but he was ahead of the public at large in his appreciation of, for example, the poems of John Keats, who was then unfashionable, and William Blake. In 1847, while still a student, he acquired one of Blake's notebooks from George Palmer, a British Museum attendant, for 10 shillings, and contributed an essay on Blake's art to a biography.

He left the Royal Academy before his twentieth birthday and before moving on, as was customary, to the Academy's Life School. This abandonment of his training has been seen by some, unfairly, as explanation for his supposed inability to paint nude figures that are anatomically correct: in fact he did continue his studies, attending classes at which he painted from life models, elsewhere.

At this stage he had a vague idea of relinquishing painting in favour of poetry (the métier that his sister Christina was now pursuing), writing his poem *The Blessed Damozel* and translating the works of Italian poets. At this crossroads in his professional life he sought the advice of several eminent men: the poet and painter William Bell Scott; Leigh Hunt (who dissuaded him from attempting to earn a living as a poet); and the then little-known painter Ford Madox Brown.

Brown was one of a number of hopeful young artists who four years earlier had entered a competition to paint the murals in the new Houses of Parliament. Rossetti had seen his entries and other works by him, and he wrote such an effusive letter to him that Brown assumed he was the victim of a hoax, and allegedly visited his unknown admirer armed with a stick. Such was Rossetti's charm, however, that the two men became immediate friends, Brown accepting Rossetti as his pupil without charge.

Rossetti began working in Brown's studio, but quickly tired of painting the still lifes that Brown set him as lessons, so that although Brown remained an ally and mentor, he very soon changed teachers. He had seen his fellow Academy pupil Holman Hunt's *The Eve of Saint Agnes* (Guildhall Art Gallery, London), based on the poem by his beloved Keats, when it was exhibited at the Royal Academy in 1848. Rossetti warmly praised it, ingratiated himself with Hunt and moved to his studio, where he started his first major oil painting, *The Girlhood of Mary Virgin*.

Brown had been influenced by the Nazarenes,

The Meeting of Dante and Beatrice in Paradise, c.1852, a watercolour from Rossetti's medieval period.

Study for a portrait of Rossetti by his friend Holman Hunt, 1853

a group of contemporary German painters who followed a style that emulated early Italian masters. Their artistic intentions became a component of discussions between Brown, Hunt, Rossetti and other like-minded men, as a result of which the Pre-Raphaelite Brotherhood was founded in September 1848, holding its inaugural meeting at the home of the parents of John Everett Millais, in his studio (a converted greenhouse at the back of the house). 'Pre-Raphaelite' described their aspiration to return to the style before Raphael, while the notion of its being a 'Brotherhood' was probably suggested by Rossetti. More than 25 years before the Impressionists did so by exhibiting in public, the Pre-Raphaelite Brotherhood was the first group avowedly to set itself up against the artistic establishment. Rossetti's father had inculcated in him a belief in Freemasonic conspiracies and told him tales of secret societies, such as the Italian Carbonari; and he was probably the one who urged on the group the need to keep their innocuous revolution to themselves. Thus it was decided that the only outward sign of their membership of the Brotherhood would be the three initials, P.R.B., added to their paintings. Their ideals were simply set out in a short manifesto:

1. To have genuine ideas to express;
2. To study Nature attentively, so as to know how to express them;
3. To sympathize with what is direct and serious and heartfelt in previous art, to the exclusion of what is conventional and self-parading and learned by rote;
4. And most indispensable of all, to produce thoroughly good pictures and statues.

One of Rossetti's numerous haunting portraits of Elizabeth Siddal, 1854.

Its founder membership consisted of seven men, not all of them painters: Dante Gabriel Rossetti and his brother William Michael, James Collinson (for a while Christina Rossetti's fiancé), William Holman Hunt, John Everett Millais, Thomas Woolner, a sculptor, and Frederic George Stephens. Ford Madox Brown excluded himself.

The P.R.B. members' choice of subjects was broad, encompassing religious, medieval, literary and contemporary themes, with an underlying ideal rooted in moral values or commentary on current social problems such as emigration, drunkenness, gambling and sexual vice. Paradoxically, however, in many of their works – especially Rossetti's – they adopted an idealized and escapist view of an imaginary 'golden age' rooted in the medieval world, with its traditions of courtly love and chivalric duty. While this reflected one of the passions of the Victorian age – an omnivorous hunger for the past that manifested itself in literature, with the popularity of Walter Scott and other romantic authors, and in the Gothic revival in architecture and decoration – it was essentially detached and morally neutral, as its critics noted.

As a focus for the artistic aspirations of a number of individuals, the Pre-Raphaelites and their influence lasted far longer than the Brotherhood itself, which had all but ceased to exist within five years, as each member pursued his own interests. Millais, for example, became immensely successful, exhibiting at the Royal Academy and achieving great wealth and fame; Collinson resigned when he decided to become a Roman Catholic priest; F. G. Stephens turned his attention to writing and art criticism; while Woolner emigrated to Australia to seek his fortune as a gold prospector (he failed to do so and soon returned to England, where he became a moderately successful establishment sculptor, and ultimately a Royal Academician).

Rossetti's *The Girlhood of Mary Virgin* was the first painting ever exhibited with the mysterious P.R.B. initials. It was shown at the Free Exhibition that opened in London on 24 March 1849, pre-empting the opening of the annual Royal Academy exhibition, which opened the following month. It was generally well received and was acquired by the Marchioness of Bath (a friend of his mother's family) for £80. With the proceeds from this, his first sale, Rossetti travelled to France and Belgium with Hunt, and was profoundly affected by the medieval religious paintings he saw.

Back in London, with several new recruits to his group, in January 1850 Rossetti founded *The Germ*, a journal devoted to the Pre-Raphaelites' interests in art, literature and poetry. It contained poems by Christina Rossetti (writing under the pseudonym Ellen Alleyne) and Rossetti's poem *The Blessed Damozel*, but it was a financial failure and only four issues were published. In the same year several artists exhibited works with the P.R.B. acronym at the Royal Academy. Rossetti rashly explained its meaning to an outsider, the secret came out, and they were criticized for their audacity in a number of publications. The next year, however, the art critic John Ruskin leapt to the group's defence both in letters to *The Times* and in subsequent lectures, so that just as the Pre-Raphaelite Brotherhood began to break apart its component artists started to achieve public recognition.

To Rossetti and his friends, any strikingly attractive woman was a 'stunner' (an expression that first appeared in print in 1848, the year the Pre-Raphaelite Brotherhood was formed). Elizabeth Siddal was the first of the stunners who were to dominate his paintings. Rossetti had met Elizabeth, or Lizzie, Siddal (or Siddall, as her father spelled his name) late in 1849. She was born in London on 25 July 1829, the daughter of a Sheffield cutler whose family claimed noble ancestry but lived in a modest home in London. Lizzie worked as an assistant in a milliner's shop. It is hard to comprehend today, but in the nineteenth century women working in this trade – partly because they were poorly paid – had a reputation for being sexually promiscuous, as is implied in paintings of milliners by artists such as Degas and Tissot. Although Miss Siddal was decidedly not such a woman, she was 'discovered' there by somebody who was probably seeking one who was, the Irish poet William Allingham. He described her to the American-born painter Walter Howell Deverell (an associate of the group, he had just missed being elected to the Brotherhood on the departure of Collinson, and was to die in 1854 at the age of 26). Deverell, who was searching for just such a woman to model for a painting, observed the proprieties of the day by having his mother visit Lizzie's shop, and once Mrs Deverell had established that she was a respectable girl – and she that Walter had no ulterior motives – Lizzie was asked to visit his studio in Kew to pose as Viola for his *Twelfth Night* (Forbes Magazine Collection). She was soon in demand among other members of the group, for her appearance, according to William Michael Rossetti, was that of 'a most beautiful creature with an air between dignity and sweetness with something that exceeded modest self-respect and partook of disdainful reserve; tall, finely formed with a lofty neck and regular yet somewhat uncommon features, greenish-blue unsparkling eyes, large perfect eyelids, brilliant complexion and a lavish heavy wealth of coppery-golden hair.'

Lizzie appeared in Holman Hunt's *A Converted British Family Sheltering a Christian Priest from the Persecution of the Druids* (1850, Ashmolean Museum, Oxford) and as Sylvia in

Rossetti's drawing, believed lost, of Elizabeth Siddal in his Blackfriars studio, 1855.

his *Valentine Rescuing Sylvia from Proteus* (1851, Birmingham City Museum and Art Gallery); in paintings by Ford Madox Brown; and most famously as Ophelia in Millais's painting of that title (1852, Tate Gallery). She posed for Millais lying fully clothed in a bath of water kept warm by lamps beneath it (despite which she caught a severe cold – perhaps pneumonia – and her father threatened to sue the artist until he agreed to pay her doctor's bills). Her state of health was always delicate, but never properly diagnosed, and has been much speculated on: consumption (tuberculosis) is the commonest suggestion, but both her exceptionally slender appearance and the clinical progress of her illness, which departed from that experienced with TB, suggest that she was suffering from anorexia.

Nude study for *Ecce Ancilla Domini!*, c.1849.

Rossetti first met Lizzie while Deverell was painting her, and, as he later told Brown: 'when he first saw her he felt his destiny was defined.' He encouraged her to leave her employment and agree to model exclusively for him, and he taught her to draw and paint, which she did with great competence – although his influence is evident. Rossetti produced hundreds of drawings of her (so significant a body of work that they have become the subject of a recent book), and she haunted his canvases for the next decade. Christina Rossetti's sonnet *In An Artist's Studio*, written on Christmas Eve 1856, sums up his obsession:

One face looks out from all his canvases,
One selfsame figure sits or walks or leans;
We found her hidden just behind those screens,
That mirror gave back all her loveliness.
A queen in opal or in ruby dress,
A nameless girl in freshest summer-greens,
A saint, an angel – every canvas means
The same one meaning, neither more nor less.

He feeds upon her face by day and night,
And she with true kind eyes looks back on him,
Fair as the moon and joyful as the light:
Not wan with waiting, not with sorrow dim;
Not as she is, but when hope shone bright;
Not as she is, but as she fills his dream.

Rossetti moved from his parents' house to Chatham Place, near Blackfriars Bridge, with Lizzie in constant attendance. Visitors were discouraged as the two became an increasingly self-absorbed couple. In 1853 Rossetti sold his second painting, *Ecce Ancilla Domini! (The Annunciation)*, to Francis MacCracken, a patron whom – like most of his successors – Rossetti resented and spoke of derogatorily.

After his first two major religious works Rossetti's art became secular in tone, as did that of the majority of his colleagues, and the early 1850s found him producing, and occasionally selling, watercolours with increasingly rich colouring representing medieval themes, especially those featuring his hero Dante. These included pictures such as *The First Anniversary of the Death of Beatrice*, which Ruskin considered 'a thoroughly glorious work'. Ruskin assisted Rossetti and Lizzie financially, and, perhaps reacting to his benefactor's criticism that his paintings failed to convey any moral 'messages', Rossetti began to paint *Found*. His only truly 'moral' picture, it mirrored his inability to come to terms with his personal life in that it remained unfinished throughout his career.

Meanwhile, Rossetti's relationship with Lizzie was troubling him emotionally. He clearly revered her, but respected her chastity and aloofness – a protective barrier she maintained deliberately to save herself from becoming one of the numberless women whose virtue had been ruined by sinking (the popular, and generally accurate, term) into the morally reprehensible profession of 'artist's model'. It is clear that he thought of their affair – platonic at this stage – as paralleling that of Dante and Beatrice, with Lizzie as the desirable yet unobtainable woman, her ethereal spirit symbolized by one of his nicknames for her, 'Dove'. (He also called her 'The Sid', while their pet name for each other was 'Guggum'.) But at the same time his desires were undeniable, and he sought release elsewhere. By the curious standards of Victorian morality this was by no means unusual, though his choice of partners was not always well advised. As well as visiting prostitutes (the subject of *Found*), while his friend Holman Hunt travelled to Egypt and Palestine in 1854–55 (where he was to paint his notable work, *The Scapegoat*), Rossetti took the opportunity to conduct a liaison with Hunt's fiancée Annie Miller – as a result of which, his previously warm friendship with Hunt not surprisingly cooled.

This was not the only sexual scandal to affect the Pre-Raphaelite Brotherhood at this time: in 1854 Ruskin's young wife Effie left him, the marriage was later annulled on the ground of non-consummation, and Effie married Millais. It was in 1854 (the year in which Rossetti's father Gabriele died) that Rossetti and Ruskin met and became friends. Ruskin introduced Rossetti to several influential patrons, such as Charles Eliot Norton of Harvard University, and Ellen Heaton, for whom he produced a number of commissioned works. Ruskin also advanced money to Lizzie, but his attempt to control her output of pictures taxed her nervous disposition, and the arrangement soon ended. Ruskin persuaded Rossetti to teach at a Working Men's College, and he continued in this voluntary labour for at least six years, during which he was to meet Edward Burne-Jones, whom he encouraged to paint, and William Morris, whom he guided into poetry. Though only a few years younger than him, both men revered Rossetti and the two, with others whom Rossetti similarly influenced, were to carry the mantle of Pre-Raphaelitism into the next generation.

Fanny Cornforth in an unfinished oil version of *Found*.

In 1855 Rossetti began creating designs for woodcuts, including those for *The Maids of Elfen-Mere* (the work that had led Burne-Jones to visit Rossetti), and in 1856 he started work on illustrations to Tennyson's poems for a book published the following year. Although he was characteristically dissatisfied with both productions, and the so-called 'Moxon Tennyson' (named after the publisher Edward Moxon) was not commercially successful, the latter undoubtedly made him better known to the public. For these subjects he sought inspiration from medieval manuscripts, which in turn led him to produce the watercolours of Arthurian scenes that were to preoccupy him in the next phase of his work: medieval chivalric subjects and doomed romantic themes, with Dante and Beatrice as the dominant characters. His poetry was not neglected though, and examples were published in the Morris-funded *Oxford and Cambridge Magazine*.

In the summer of 1857, during a temporary break in his on-off relationship with Lizzie, Rossetti, along with Burne-Jones, Morris and others, worked on a series of murals in the Oxford Union. Rossetti's favoured Arthurian themes, based on Sir Thomas Malory's *Morte d'Arthur*, were scoured for subjects but it proved an ill-fated project that was never completed, and it suffered from the fact that none of them knew enough about the techniques of fresco painting. It was while work was progressing, though, that two further influential individuals entered Rossetti's life: he met the poet Algernon Swinburne (who modelled for his *Sir Galahad*, and later lived in Rossetti's house) and Jane Burden, whom the group had spotted at a theatre in Oxford. She entered the circle as a model, appearing in Rossetti's *The Wedding of Saint George and Princess Sabra*, and marrying William Morris two years later.

At about this time Rossetti met Fanny Cornforth. A striking, large woman (Rossetti nicknamed her 'Elephant', and depicted her as one in caricatures) with floor-length blonde hair, her married name was

Money to the House, one of Rossetti's elephant caricatures from his illustrated letters to Fanny Cornforth.

Sarah Cox. She worked on the fringes of prostitution and as an artist's model, and soon numbered Rossetti among her many lovers. His first painting of her, *Bocca Baciata* (1859, Museum of Fine Arts, Boston), which translates as 'lips that have been kissed', marks his return to the oil-painting medium that he had largely neglected since *Ecce Ancilla Domini!* Having mastered the medium of watercolour in these intervening years, however, the transition was easy and the results remarkable. His triptych for Llandaff Cathedral, on which he continued to work in the early 1860s, marks, in Holman Hunt's words, 'the turning point from his first severity of style to a sensuous manner'.

It had taken five years, until 1855, for Rossetti to introduce Lizzie to his family, and although they were nominally engaged, marriage terrified him: almost ten years after they had met it seemed as distant a prospect as ever. But in 1860, when Lizzie was ill and attempting to recover her strength at the Sussex resort of Hastings, Rossetti – perhaps sensing that she had not long to live – finally made the commitment she had sought since they met, and on 23 May, with no guests on either side, they were married. Lizzie recovered sufficiently to embark on a honeymoon in Paris (the intention to travel with Burne-Jones and his new bride Georgiana was thwarted when Burne-Jones, ever susceptible to stress-inducing occasions, fell ill). It was in Paris that Rossetti drew his haunting *How They Met Themselves*, an image that conveys a mood of impending death. In September Lizzie announced that she was pregnant, and for the first time in years her health seemed to improve.

In 1861 Rossetti became a shareholder in Morris's newly founded firm, and began contributing stained-glass designs. Then on 2 May Lizzie gave birth to a stillborn daughter. After their bereavement she became increasingly melancholy and subject to unpredictable behaviour, and was

The young Algernon Swinburne in an 1861 watercolour portrait by Rossetti.

How They Met Themselves, ominously drawn on the Rossettis' honeymoon.

Fair Rosamund (1861), the mistress of Henry II, ironically modelled by Rossetti's own mistress, Fanny Cornforth.

by the notion that he should have devoted more time to his wife's welfare than to his work, placed with her a notebook containing the sole complete collection of his poems (in emulation of a story by Christina, written 12 years earlier). Lizzie was buried at Highgate cemetery in the Rossetti family tomb; Christina Rossetti would be buried alongside her in 1894.

Rossetti spent the last 20 years of his life tormented with guilt and plagued by insomnia. With the poets Algernon Swinburne and George Meredith he moved to Tudor House, 16 Cheyne Walk, facing the Thames at Chelsea, where many notable artists lived, including Turner and Whistler. His was an eccentric household, his home filled with *objets d'art* and exotic animals, from his favourite wombats to kangaroos, as well as peacocks which proved so noisy that later leases prohibited tenants from keeping them. Although he gradually recovered some of his former *joie de vivre*, and was able to produce self-mocking caricatures such as one bewailing the death of one of his wombats, he became increasingly reclusive, only occasionally showing his work publicly, preferring to sell direct to a handful of dedicated collectors, and was extremely sensitive about criticism. Fanny Cornforth moved in with the euphemistic title of 'housekeeper', consolidating her role as mistress – which she had been, on and off, since they first met.

Rossetti's memorial to Lizzie, and effectively his last painting of her, was his *Beata Beatrix*. Thereafter his oil paintings became ever more sensuous and erotic, featuring loosely draped or naked women, typically with exaggerated masses of hair – a classic ingredient of the imagery

Rossetti's self-parodying *Death of a Wombat*, 1869.

Society photographer W. Downey's portrait of Rossetti in 1862, the year of Elizabeth Siddal's death.

taking increasing doses of laudanum, a powerful opiate. Rossetti was occupied with a number of projects: his translation *The Early Italian Poets from Ciullo d'Alcamo to Dante Alighieri…together with Dante's 'Vita Nuova'*, done when he was 20 and lately revised, was published; and he began work on illustrations for Christina's *Goblin Market*, which proved to be a success. (His curious caricature of the characteristically placid Christina in a tantrum, smashing orna-

Christina Rossetti jokingly depicted by her brother, 1862.

ments and furniture, was produced as a punning reference to a review in *The Times* that used the phrase 'could not easily be mended'.)

On the night of 10 February 1862 Rossetti dined in a restaurant with Lizzie and Swinburne. After leaving early and returning home with Lizzie, Rossetti went out again – perhaps to visit Fanny Cornforth. When he returned at 11.30, he found Lizzie unconscious, having apparently taken approximately ten times the fatal dose of laudanum. A doctor was called but was unable to save her, and at 7.20 on the morning of 11 February, Lizzie died. There seems little doubt that her overdose was deliberate, but an inquest returned a verdict of 'accidental death' (a common practice, to avoid the stigma of suicide).

While Lizzie's coffin lay open, Rossetti, obsessed

Jane Burdon drawn by Rossetti in 1858, the year before her marriage to William Morris.

associated with the *femme fatale* – wearing sumptuous costumes and surrounded in almost claustrophobic proximity by decorative details that were a world apart from the simplicity of the medieval subjects that had preceded them. As Holman Hunt observed: 'He executed heads of women of voluptuous nature with such richness of ornamental trapping and decoration that they were a surprise, coming from the hand which had hitherto indulged itself in austerities.' These highly decorative later works have often been criticized, but Rossetti himself regarded them as his finest. In a letter of 21 October 1877 he wrote to Frederic Shields:

'I am quite certain that I have, as an artist should, made solid progress in the merit of my work, such as it is, and this chiefly within the last five years, during which I have supplied by application some serious qualities which had always been deficient in my practice, and produced, I will venture to say, at least a dozen works (among those covering the time) which are unquestionably the best I ever did.'

This transition was not without its rewards: by 1867 Rossetti was earning £3,000 a year, a substantial amount by the standards of the day. Yet he managed permanently to live beyond his means, and was eternally troubled. In 1868, while staying with William Bell Scott at the castle in Penkill, Ayrshire, that was the home of Scott's companion Alice Boyd, he seems to have considered suicide.

What kept him alive was his next great love – for Jane Morris. She began sitting regularly for him from the mid-1860s, and her distinctive visage can be seen in the paintings of his final years. As his photographs of her reveal, his canvases did not overstate Jane's beauty. The writer Henry James recalled:

'*Je n'en reviens pas* – she haunts me still. A figure cut out of a missal – out of one of Rossetti's or Hunt's pictures – to say this gives but a faint idea of her, because when such an image puts on flesh and blood, it is an apparition of fearful and wonderful intensity. It's hard to say whether she's a grand synthesis of all the Pre-Raphaelite pictures ever made – or they are a "keen analysis" of her – whether she's an original or a copy. In either case she is a wonder. Imagine a tall lean woman in a dress of some dead purple stuff, guiltless of hoops (or of anything else I should say), with a mass of crisp black hair, heaped into great wavy projections on each of her temples, a thin pale face, great thick black oblique brows, joined in the middle and tucking themselves away under her hair, a mouth like the "Oriana" in our illustrated Tennyson, a long neck, without any collar, and in lieu thereof some dozen strings of outlandish beads. In fine complete.'

Rossetti's relationship with her developed, apparently without complaint from William Morris. Meanwhile, his poetry experienced a resurgence when, inspired by Jane, he wrote a series of poems called *The House of Life*. In 1869 he decided to issue a collection of his unpublished poems, but although he had given copies of many to friends, he was unable to track most of them down, and it was with horror that he realized that the only complete collection was enclosed within Lizzie's coffin in Highgate cemetery. The only way to recover them was to have her body exhumed. After much procrastination he arranged for her disinterment – while he himself was away from

Pandora, a chalk study (1869) based on an 1865 photograph of Jane Morris.

London. The grisly task was managed by his friend and agent, the somewhat disreputable Charles Howell, and carried out on 5 October, by night and by the light of bonfires. According to Howell's imaginative description, Lizzie's body was 'perfectly preserved'; he even claimed that her luxuriant hair had grown so considerably after death that her tresses had to be cut to disentangle the book. He doused it in disinfectant, carefully separated the pages, and dried the volume. *Poems*, which included the sonnet 'Nuptial Sleep', was published to great acclaim in 1870, but its author experienced yet another wave of guilt for defiling Lizzie's grave. Suffering worse insomnia than ever, he began taking the newly invented hypnotic drug chloral hydrate, to which he rapidly became addicted.

His brother William Michael Rossetti and F. G. Stephens, two of the founding fathers of Pre-Raphaelitism, had both by then become respected critics, and both had naturally praised Rossetti's paintings and his poetry, a line that was generally followed by other reviewers. It therefore came as a shock when the success of his poems in 1870 was followed in 1871 by a vicious attack on the sensual elements of his work (with 'Nuptial Sleep' as a focus of the onslaught), published in an article entitled 'The Fleshly School of Poetry', by Robert Buchanan, writing pseudonymously as Thomas Maitland. In his weakened state Rossetti reacted with a sense of outrage and became convinced that he was the victim of a campaign of personal vilification and persecution. He retaliated with an article, 'The Stealthy School of Criticism' (*The Athenaeum*, 16 December 1871), and attempted to commit suicide by precisely the same method as Lizzie, but without success.

During the period from 1871–74 Rossetti shared the tenancy of Kelmscott Manor in Oxfordshire with William

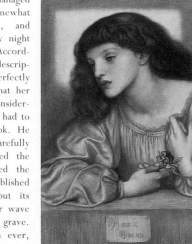

Morris, while his relationship with Jane Morris continued (with the tacit consent of her husband). Jane Morris dominates Rossetti's late works, in which she appears in various guises, but generally as a powerful woman or a goddess. However, alarmed at his addiction and concerned for her children (one of whom had been discovered to be epileptic), she eventually terminated her relationship with Rossetti and returned contritely to her husband. She outlived William Morris (who died in 1896), dying in 1914.

Rossetti occupied himself during the remainder of the 1870s largely alienated from his friends, except Ford Madox Brown and Fanny Cornforth, his perception clouded by his intake of chloral, which he kept as secret as possible for fear that his reputation might be marred. In a letter to his friend Frederic Shields, he observed: 'As to the eternal drug, my dear Shields, if I suffer at times from morbidity, it is also possible for others to take a morbid view of the question... To reduce the drug as far as possibility admits is most desirable...but if an opinion were to get abroad that my works were subject to a derogatory influence which reduced their beauty and value, it would be most injuring to me.'

In 1882 he visited Birchington-on-Sea, a resort near Margate in Kent, with a new friend, Thomas Hall Caine, and there he died on Easter Day, 9 April. He was buried in the village in All Saints' churchyard with a Celtic cross monument designed by Brown, while memorial windows by Frederic Shields, based on one of Rossetti's own watercolours, *The Passover of the Holy Family: Gathering the Bitter Herbs* (Tate Gallery), were installed in the church.

Writing in the year of Rossetti's death, the critic William Tirebuck considered that many of his subjects were so obscure that 'his pictures not only require titles but footnotes'. His richly coloured medieval subjects, however, provided Pre-Raphaelitism with its distinctive identity, and the remarkable portraits of his later years stand alone as a highly charged and personal art. He has also been criticized for abandoning any attempt to deal with the social issues that were one of the stated tenets of the Pre-Raphaelite Brotherhood in favour of the aesthetic principle of 'art for art's sake'. In doing so he has been seen as a precursor of the Aesthetic Movement, and in works such as *Astarte Syriaca* as a pioneer Symbolist, thereby extending his influence into the twentieth century. In recent times his work has become increasingly appreciated, both aesthetically and commercially: the most expensive Pre-Raphaelite painting of all time is Rossetti's *Proserpine*, which sold in 1987 for £1,300,000, while a replica of *La Ghirlandata* was sold in 1993 for £420,000.

THE PLATES

1. The Girlhood of Mary Virgin

2. Ecce Ancilla Domini! (The Annunciation)

3. The First Anniversary of the Death of Beatrice

4. Found

5. Paolo and Francesca da Rimini

6. The Blue Closet

7. The Tune of Seven Towers

8. The Wedding of Saint George and the Princess Sabra

9. The Seed of David

10. Before the Battle

11. The Salutation of Beatrice

12. Dantis Amor

13. Saint George and the Princess Sabra

14. Fazio's Mistress

15. Morning Music.

16. How Sir Galahad, Sir Bors and Sir Percival
were fed with the Sanc Grael; but
Sir Percival's Sister Died by the Way

17. Venus Verticordia

18. Il Ramoscello

19. The Beloved

20. Regina Cordium

21. Monna Vanna

22. Sibylla Palmifera

23. Lady Lilith

24. La Pia de' Tolomei

25. Mariana

26. La Donna della Fiamma

27. Dante's Dream at the Time of
The Death of Beatrice

28. Veronica Veronese

29. The Bower Meadow

30. Beata Beatrix

31. La Ghirlandata

32. Proserpine

33. Sancta Lilias

34. La Bella Mano

35. Astarte Syriaca

36. The Blessed Damozel

37. A Sea Spell

38. A Vision of Fiammetta

39. La Donna della Finestra

40. The Day Dream

PLATE 1

THE GIRLHOOD OF MARY VIRGIN
1848–49
Oil, 32 ¾ x 25 ¾ in / 83.2 x 65.4 cm
Tate Gallery, London

Executed when he was 20 years old, and shown at the Free Exhibition that opened on 24 March 1849, this was Rossetti's debut painting and the first to bear the P.R.B. initials in public. It was well received by critics and was sold for £80 to the Dowager Marchioness of Bath as a result of the intervention of Rossetti's aunt Charlotte Polidori, who had been her governess and was later her companion. The style is less naturalistic than the work of Rossetti's contemporary Pre-Raphaelite artists, being likened to 'Early Christian Art' by Ford Madox Brown. Brown supervised the painting with Holman Hunt, who shared Rossetti's Cleveland Street studio.

The Girlhood of Mary Virgin is steeped in religious symbolism. The seven-leaved palm branch on the ground is tied to a seven-thorned briar by a scroll, the inscription on which predicts the forthcoming Passion of Christ. There is a cross in the lattice work; a dove, symbolic of the Holy Spirit; and a red cloak representing the Robe of Christ. The vine signifies the sacrifice of Christ's life. The titles of the six large books stacked on the ground represent the three cardinal virtues and three of the theological virtues – although Justice was omitted. Rossetti explained the subject in an 1848 letter to his godfather Charles Lyell:

'The subject is the education of the Blessed Virgin, one which has been treated at various times by...other painters...they have invariably represented her as reading from a book under the superintendence of her mother, St. Anne... In order, therefore, to attempt something more probable and at the same time less commonplace, I have represented the future Mother of our Lord as occupied in embroidering a lily – always under the direction of St Anne; the flower she is copying being held by two little angels.'

The original intention to include two angels was rejected because of the problematic child model, and, as it was, the angel's head was repainted in July 1849. Christina, Rossetti's sister, sat for Mary; his mother for Saint Anne; and Old Williams, a family handyman, stood patiently in an uncomfortable pose with upraised arms as Saint Joachim. The identities of the figures are inscribed in gilt haloes above their heads. As portraits of the sitters, these were considered very accurate. Two sonnets, printed on gold paper, were attached to the frame of the picture and are now on the back. Amendments were made in 1864 when Rossetti borrowed the painting from its then owner, Lady Louisa Fielding, who was given it by her mother, the Marchioness of Bath.

PLATE 2

ECCE ANCILLA DOMINI!
(THE ANNUNCIATION)
──────── 1849–50 ────────

Oil, 28⅝ x 16½ in / 72.7 x 41.9 cm
Tate Gallery, London

Rossetti's simplistic sequel to *The Girlhood of Mary Virgin* is stripped of its traditional grandiose iconography and its unaffected naïveté was admired by the other Pre-Raphaelites. The potentially risqué position of the Virgin on the bed without covers was justified in the context of the hot climate in which the composition is set. This painting contains the completed embroidery that Mary was working on in the previous work on the Mariological theme and was pre-empted by the lines of one of the sonnets on the frame of its predecessor:

> She woke in her white bed, and had no fear
> At all – yet wept till sunshine, and felt awed;
> Because the fulness of the time was come.

Christina Rossetti sat again for the Virgin in preparatory studies, but Rossetti later sought a red-haired woman to model, finding a Miss Love to sit for the hair. The archangel is a composite of various models employed by Rossetti, as well as his brother William.

The painting, which remained unsold during the next three years and was repeatedly amended, had been exhibited at the Portland Gallery in 1850 and received bitter public criticism. Rossetti's resulting outrage initiated a lifetime avoidance of public exhibitions, except on rare occasions, and a subsequent rejection of religious themes. In 1851 Lady Bath suggested, through Charlotte Polidori as an intermediary, that Rossetti should exhibit the painting in Liverpool, but he refused. The other members of the Pre-Raphaelite Brotherhood resented Rossetti for not exhibiting at the Royal Academy and for his consequent evasion of the storm of abuse that was directed at them. The title was later changed to *The Annunciation*, in fear of anti-Catholic recrimination, and it was eventually sold for £50 to an Irish Protestant shipping agent, Francis MacCracken (ungraciously described by Rossetti as 'an Irish maniac!'). It was sold at auction in 1874 for £388 10s, then in 1886 it was acquired by the Tate Gallery for £840.

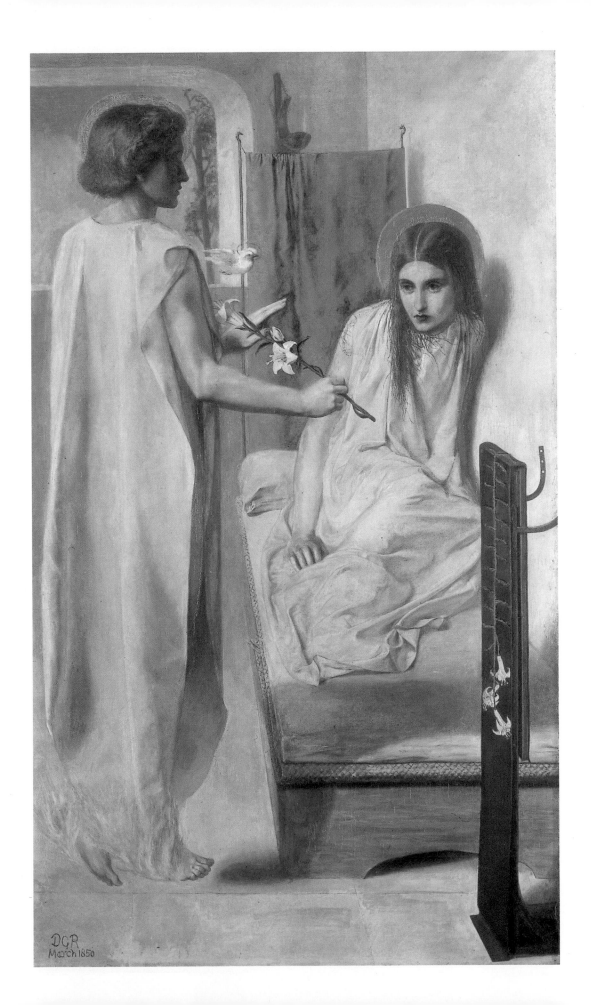

THE FIRST ANNIVERSARY OF THE DEATH OF BEATRICE

——————— 1853–54 ———————

Watercolour, 16 ½ x 24 in / 41.9 x 61 cm
Ashmolean Museum, Oxford

This illustration to Dante's *Vita Nuova*, which Rossetti had completed translating in 1848, is his largest watercolour. It depicts Dante drawing an angel in memory of Beatrice, interrupted by sympathetic visitors. The subject-matter was explained in the inscription below:

'On that day on which a whole year has completed since my lady had been born into the life eternal, remembering me of her as I sat alone, I betook myself to draw the resemblance of an Angel upon certain tablets. And while I did this, chancing to turn my head, I perceived that some were standing beside me to whom I should have given courteous welcome and that they were observing what I did; also I learned afterwards that they had been there a while before I perceived them. Perceiving whom, I arose for salutation and said: "Another was with me."'

Lizzie Siddal posed for the young woman in her first subject modelled for Rossetti, and Old Williams for the elderly gentleman. Dante's features resemble those of William Rossetti. Rossetti's use of relatively dramatic chiaroscuro contrasts the sunlight with Dante's sombre gown and rich glowing drapery, and the influences of both Dürer and Memling can be seen. This painting was one of the works that became a catalyst for a second phase of Pre-Raphaelitism in the mid-1850s, inspiring Burne-Jones and William Morris. It was described by Ruskin, who first encountered Rossetti at this time, as 'a thoroughly glorious work – the most perfect piece of Italy, in the accessory parts, I have ever seen in my life'.

The angularity of the figures was characteristic of contemporary Pre-Raphaelite Brotherhood work, particularly that of Millais, the first owner of the picture. A greater attention to detail than in his earlier works is also clear. Rossetti had executed an earlier drawing of the same subject, finished in May 1849, that was compositionally very different; in the earlier version there was no female visitor. The woman in this version is probably intended to represent Gemma Donati, Dante's later wife, who appears again in Rossetti's *La Donna della Finestra*. Amongst the wealth of literary symbolism in the work, a crossbow, hanging on an easel next to a quill and ink bowl, represents Dante's active life, while the lute, skull and ivy symbolize *vanitas*.

FOUND

—————— 1854– (unfinished) ——————

Oil, 36 x 31 ¾ in / 91.4 x 80 cm

Delaware Art Museum: Samuel and Mary R. Bancroft Memorial

Rossetti, determined to paint a contemporary social subject, was preoccupied by *Found*, which remained unfinished, all his life. It was originally commissioned by MacCracken in 1854, then cancelled, and commissioned again in 1859 by James Leathart, a lead merchant in Newcastle. By 1867 the exasperated Rossetti was prepared to reimburse Leathart the money that he had advanced and relinquish the commission because so little progress had been made. Yet he took up the struggle again in both 1869 and 1879, hoping to prove that despite his being a poetic painter he was also able to paint naturalistic subjects. On Rossetti's death the incomplete painting entered the possession of William Graham, a Glasgow MP, who in 1869 had agreed to purchase *Found* for £800.

Rossetti's tackling the theme of the 'fallen woman' – a subject often treated in both literature and art by his contemporaries – indicated his untypically relaxed attitude toward sexuality in a climate of fervent morality. Prior to and during the execution of the painting, he wrote two poems on the subject. His *Jenny* of 1848 described an encounter with a prostitute – 'Lazy laughing languid Jenny / Fond of a kiss and fond of a guinea' – while his sonnet of 1881, written when he was completing the figures, speaks of the moment of truth captured by the painting, with the woman exclaiming, 'Leave me – I do not know you – go away!'

The choice of such an overtly moralistic theme reveals a dutiful attempt to follow the Pre-Raphaelite Brotherhood line on realism. F. G. Stephens analysed the imagery thus: 'the girl crouches against a wall of a church-yard – "where the wicked cease from troubling, and the weary are at rest"; the brightening dawn symbolizes, as it may be, peace (with forgiveness) on earth, or in Heaven, after sorrow.' The prostitute is discovered by a farmer, her former lover. Having executed the wall in situ in Chiswick, Rossetti spent much of the winter of 1854 with the Madox Browns in Finchley, where he laboured to paint the calf and cart. He wrote:

'As for the calf, he kicks and fights all the time he remains tied up, which is five or six hours daily, and the view of life induced appears to be so melancholy that he punctually attempts suicide at 3½ daily P.M.'

According to her own (and possibly fanciful) account – as told later to the painting's eventual owner, the American textile tycoon and collector Samuel Bancroft Jr – Rossetti, seeking a model for this painting, met Fanny Cornforth while out walking with friends. One of his party knocked her golden hair and sent it cascading down her back, and she was asked to sit for *Found* the next day. As she recalled it: 'he put my head against the wall and drew it for the head in the calf picture.'

PAOLO AND FRANCESCA DA RIMINI
—————— 1855 ——————
Watercolour, 9¾ x 17½ in / 24.8 x 44.5 cm
Tate Gallery, London

This painting, illustrating a story from the fifth Canto of Dante's *Inferno*, depicts Francesca, who with her lover and brother-in-law Paolo Malatesta, was murdered by the Tyrant of Rimini. The depiction of the lovers reading was possibly inspired by the poem *The Story of Rimini* by Leigh Hunt. The composition is a three-part narrative beginning with the lovers' fatal kiss. In the centre, against a flat background, Dante and Virgil observe sympathetically as the entwined couple, on the right, float eternally through the flames of Hell. Based on preparatory studies made at least six years earlier, the work has a simplistic linearity, typical of early Pre-Raphaelite work.

Rossetti associated the tragic story with his own ill-fated relationship with Lizzie Siddal, who sat for Francesca. He painted three other versions of this subject in watercolour. This, the earliest version, has a particularly convoluted provenance. Later owned successively by William Morris and George Rae, a banker, it was originally bought by Ruskin for £35 after being hurriedly painted in just one week when Rossetti urgently needed money to relieve Lizzie, who was stranded penniless in Paris. Ruskin sent the watercolour with Rossetti's *Rachel and Leah* of 1855 to Ellen Heaton with the request that she choose either one. Miss Heaton selected *Rachel and Leah* (now in the Tate Gallery), probably under the moral guidance of Ruskin, who observed in November of that year that *Paolo and Francesca da Rimini* was 'a most gloomy drawing – very grand but dreadful – of Dante seeing the soul of Francesca and her lover!... Prudish people might perhaps think it not quite a young lady's drawing. I don't know. All the figures are draped – but I don't quite know how people would feel about the subject.'

PLATE 6

THE BLUE CLOSET
———— 1856–57 ————
Watercolour, 13 1/2 x 9 3/4 in / 34.3 x 24.8 cm
Tate Gallery, London

Painted in the style of medieval illuminations, a number of Rossetti's watercolours of this period were inspired by medieval romances – predominantly those of Malory – and represent themes of ill-fated love. One such work, *The Blue Closet*, probably completed in late 1856 and exhibited at the Pre-Raphaelite show in Fitzroy Square in 1857, was one of five watercolours purchased by William Morris who commented 'These chivalric Froissartian themes are quite a passion of mine.' Rossetti, like many of his contemporaries, had a profoundly idealized view of the Middle Ages. This painting inspired Morris to write a poem of the same title, published the following year, in a collection entitled *The Defence of Guenevere*, which links the red lily in the foreground with death. At this time Rossetti's art and Morris's poetry were interdependent on each other for inspiration, Rossetti explaining that 'the poems were the result of the pictures, but don't at all tally to any purpose with them though beautiful in themselves.'

This watercolour depended predominantly upon colour and form for its meaning, as well as in its anticipation of musical subjects, and in this can be seen as a precursor to the Aesthetic Movement of the 1890s. Set in a brilliant blue-tiled chamber, it depicts two queens playing a clavichord with two attendants singing from sheet music. The symmetrical composition harks back to medieval scenes of musical angels, such as Orcagna's panel in Christ Church, Oxford. The sun and moon on the instrument, motifs common in Rossetti's work, refer to the passage of time. The holly on top of the clavichord indicates the time of year at which the picture was executed.

THE TUNE OF SEVEN TOWERS

— 1857 —

Watercolour, 12 ³⁄₈ x 14 ³⁄₈ in / 31.4 x 36.5 cm
Tate Gallery, London

Rossetti added strips to either side of this picture, initially a square composition, to make it rectangular. Still in its original frame, *The Tune of Seven Towers* is another of Morris's purchases that inspired a poem of the same name in his collection *The Defence of Guenevere*. The woman, modelled by Lizzie Siddal, sits in a tall oak chair playing an instrument that lies across her knees. The composition, divided diagonally by a banner, was derived from an 1853 drawing entitled *Michael Scott's Wooing*, but here the medieval setting is more complex and enigmatic. On the left an orange branch, symbolic of marriage, is placed on a bed by a maid. The meaning here is partly autobiographical. Rossetti, who was finally considering marriage, was anxious about Lizzie's potentially fatal illness, as indicated by the inclusion of the dove on the right, Rossetti's sign and pet name for her. The heroine wears a scallop shell around her neck, symbolizing pilgrimage and perhaps referring to Lizzie's travels in search of a cure. The pennant that hangs on the left is decorated by a border of a seven-towered castle, a motif echoed in gold on the top of the man's seat. The unusual medieval 'built-in' furniture was undoubtedly influenced by William Morris's aesthetic interests and the furniture made for his London showrooms in 1856. The subject may have been inspired by the contemporary relevance of the issues of medieval songs and tales such as Morris's favourite, the thirteenth-century courtly love story *Aucassin and Nicolette*.

THE WEDDING OF SAINT GEORGE
AND THE PRINCESS SABRA
—————— 1857 ——————
Watercolour, 13½ x 13½ in / 34.3 x 34.3 cm
Tate Gallery, London

This picture was executed at a time of close contact with William
Morris and Burne-Jones in Oxford, when marriage was particularly
pertinent to all three men; Burne-Jones produced a stained-glass
decoration on the same theme. Painted for William Morris, *The
Wedding of Saint George and the Princess Sabra* is typical of Rossetti's
work in this period in terms of its title, small scale, heraldic patterns
and colouring, and the romantic theme taken from medieval literature. It was eventually bought by Thomas E. Plint, a Leeds
stockbroker who was a patron of Ford Madox Brown.

As well as medieval manuscripts that Rossetti saw in the British
Museum, and the collection owned by Ruskin, a source of inspiration
could have been a ballad entitled *Sir George and the Dragon* in Thomas
Percy's *Reliques of Ancient English Poetry* (1765):

> Therein with his dear love he liv'd
> And fortune did his nuptials grace:
> They many years of joy did see
> And led their lives at Coventry.

James Smetham, an artist on the periphery of the Pre-Raphaelite
Brotherhood, described the painting as 'one of the grandest things,
like a golden dim dream'. The claustrophobic composition is crammed
with medieval motifs. Princess Sabra, enveloped in Saint George's
arms, cuts a lock from her hair as he kisses her. Saint George, in
profile, is enclosed in a series of right angles. Two angels, behind a
hedge, play bells to the couple, perhaps luring them to the bed in the
background.

THE SEED OF DAVID (TRIPTYCH)
———————————— 1858–64 ————————————

Oil, 90 × 60 in / 228.6 × 152.4 cm (centre);
73 × 24½ in / 185.4 × 62.2 cm (wings)
Llandaff Cathedral, Wales

In early 1856 Rossetti was commissioned by John P. Seddon, a friend of John Ruskin and the architect responsible for the restoration of Llandaff Cathedral, Wales, to paint an altarpiece for £400. Rossetti described the work, which heralded his move back to painting in oils, as 'a big thing which I shall go into with a howl of delight'. In painting the only Pre-Raphaelite work that related directly to their Italian predecessors – specifically Veronese's *Adoration of the Magi* of 1573, which had been acquired by the National Gallery in 1855 – Rossetti used the traditional triptych composition with a central nativity scene. Tintoretto's *Nativity* of 1581 was possibly a source of inspiration, as well as his *Annunciation* of 1583–87, although Rossetti explained that: 'The centrepiece is not a literal reading of the event of the Nativity, but rather a condensed symbol of it.'

The work was first executed in watercolour in 1856, and there is a vast difference in size, technique, style and composition in the final oil version completed eight years later. The figures in the watercolour were in Rossetti's medieval style in contrast to the figures in the oil painting, all of whom are more monumental and with a more developed musculature. The semi-nude David in the left panel is almost classical in his contrapposto pose, his body having been modelled by Timothy Hughes, Fanny Cornforth's husband, and the head by William Morris. Swinburne sat for the king and Burne-Jones for the shepherd, while Arthur Hughes's daughter Agnes modelled for the child. The Virgin's body was based upon Fanny Cornforth; her head was originally copied from Ruth Herbert but was changed to depict Jane Morris in 1861.

BEFORE THE BATTLE
———— 1858 ————

Watercolour, 16 ⅝ x 11 in / 42.5 x 28 cm
Special Picture Fund, Courtesy Museum of Fine Arts, Boston

Before the Battle was commissioned in 1858 and purchased for £50 by Charles Eliot Norton of Harvard University. The original drawing for the piece was probably completed when Rossetti was staying with Lizzie at Matlock in 1857. Two years earlier Lizzie herself had painted a watercolour of a woman attaching a pennant to a knight's lance (*Lady Affixing a Pennant to a Knight's Spear*, 1856, Tate Gallery). Rossetti sent his completed picture four years later, having retouched it under the guidance of Ruskin, who was concerned about the artist's reputation in the United States. Ruskin wrote to Norton in 1862:

'Rossetti was always promising to retouch your drawing and I, growling and muttering, suffered him still to keep it by him in the hope his humour would one day change. At last it has changed; he has modified and in every respect so much advanced and bettered it... It is exceedingly full and interesting in fancy, and brilliant in colour.'

In his diary Ford Madox Brown made the following observation about Rossetti's paintings of this period:

'They form an admirable picture of the world of our fathers with its chief characteristics – religion, art, chivalry and love. His forte, and he seems to have found it out, is to be a lyrical painter and poet, and certainly a glorious one.'

THE SALUTATION OF BEATRICE
—— 1859 ——

Oil on two panels, both 29 1/2 x 31 1/2 in / 74.9 x 80 cm
National Gallery of Canada, Ottawa

This work consists of two panels that originally decorated a settle in Morris's Red House, painted between 16 and 25 June 1859, and which were brought together in a frame designed by Rossetti when the house was abandoned in 1865. The first panel portrays the first meeting of Dante and Beatrice in Florence, as described in Dante's *Vita Nuova*, and was modelled by Jane Morris, Fanny Cornforth and Mary, Morris's housekeeper at Red Lion Square in London. Underneath, Rossetti added a quotation from a sonnet in the *Vita Nuova*: 'My lady carries love within her eyes.' A gold figure on the frame between the panels, symbolizing love, holds a sundial whose shadow is cast at nine o'clock, the time of Beatrice's death. Love extinguishes the flame of his torch to symbolize her death, the date of which, 9 June 1290, is inscribed above. The second panel depicts Dante's meeting with Beatrice in Eden, as described in the *Divine Comedy*, accompanied by the inscription 'Guardami ben: ben son, ben son Beatrice', meaning 'Look on me well: I indeed, I indeed am Beatrice.' Rossetti wrote: 'The subjects are treated from the real and not the allegorical side of Dante's love story.'

Commissioned by Richard Leyland, the Liverpool shipowner who also owned Whistler's celebrated Peacock Room, Rossetti began a later version in 1880 that remained unfinished at his death and was acquired by Leyland. In a letter of February 1881 Rossetti told Jane Morris: 'It seems to enchant everyone who sees it.'

DANTIS AMOR
———— 1859–60 ————
Oil, 29 1/2 x 32 in / 74.9 x 81.3 cm
Tate Gallery, London

Dantis Amor was originally a third central panel to decorate the settle
at Red House, placed between *Dante Meeting Beatrice in Florence* and
Dante Meeting Beatrice in Paradise. The panels were separated a few
years after execution, the other two possibly being sold to raise capital for Morris's new firm. Another theme from Dante, it portrays a
red-haired angel, here symbolizing love, holding a sundial and bow
and arrow. Christ's head on the left is the sun in contrast to Beatrice
encircled by the moon. This central panel symbolizes Beatrice's
death, the transition between earth and heaven. Rossetti's message
here is that love is the generating force of the universe. The combination of the inscriptions around the sun and moon form the concluding words of the *Vita Nuova*, translated as: 'That blessed Beatrice
who now gazeth continually on His countenance, who is through all
ages blessed.' The inscription that separates night and day was taken
from the *Divine Comedy*: 'Love who moves the sun and the other
stars.' Rossetti connected this with Dante's vision of Love in the *Vita
Nuova*. Some authorities have suggested that only the heads in this
unfinished composition were executed by Rossetti himself.

PLATE 13

SAINT GEORGE AND THE PRINCESS SABRA
─────────── 1862 ───────────
Watercolour, 20⅝ x 12⅛ in / 52.4 x 30.8 cm
Tate Gallery, London

In late December 1861 Rossetti had begun a watercolour for Ellen
Heaton that had been delayed as a result of Lizzie's poor health.
Lizzie had continued to sit for him until early February of the following year while he made several studies, but shortly afterwards she
died tragically of a laudanum overdose. Here Saint George washes his
hands, having slain the dragon. A crowd (seen through the window)
gathers outside, triumphantly carrying the dragon's head. Rossetti,
anxious about this vignette in the composition, wrote to Miss
Heaton:

'I trust you will not be disappointed with the out-of-window bit,
which however is not very bright in effect. Being altogether in one
corner, & no bright colour occurring anywhere else in the picture, it
would hardly have been practicable without endangering the balance
of the light & shade, to have adopted an effect...where the outdoor
light is central.'

FAZIO'S MISTRESS
——— 1863 ———
Oil, 17 x 15 in / 43.2 x 38.1 cm
Tate Gallery, London

Begun in 1863, this oil was primarily a study in colour and shows Fanny Cornforth plaiting her hair. Ten years later it was substantially retouched, glazed and given the additional title *Aurelia*. Rossetti wrote to Fanny at that time:

'I have got an old picture of you here which I painted many years ago. It is the one where you are seated doing your hair before a glass. Rae [the banker George Rae], to whom it belongs, has sent it me as it wants some glazing, but I am not working at all on the head, which is exactly like the funny old elephant [Rossetti's nickname for her], as like it as any I ever did.'

Fazio's Mistress is one of a group of Venetian-inspired bust-length paintings from this period, the culmination of which was his *Lady Lilith* of 1864–68. The title was taken from a poem by Fazio degli Uberti that described the seductive beauty of his lover. This allure, seen in all Rossetti's paintings of this group, is manifested in her sensual mouth, white neck and voluptuous arms. Titian's *Alphonse Ferrara et Laura de Dianti* in the Louvre was particularly influential, but as well as this precedent, links can be seen in the drapery of Whistler's contemporary work. Rossetti began this oil as 'chiefly a piece of colour'.

MORNING MUSIC
—————— 1864 ——————
Watercolour, 11⅝ × 10½ in / 29.5 × 26.7 cm
Fitzwilliam Museum, Cambridge

The subject of this watercolour, a beautiful woman having her hair
dressed to musical accompaniment, harks back to Rossetti's earlier
works such as *A Christmas Carol* of 1857–58. Like *Fazio's Mistress*,
however, this picture is infinitely more sensual, and here again the
use of colour is predominantly white with brilliant touches of gold,
blue and red, in line with the Venetian model. William Etty's painting *The Duet*, shown at the International Exhibition of 1862, may also
have been an influence. Like his friend Swinburne, Rossetti believed
that art should be sensually gratifying, and in his group of 'toilette'
paintings his commitment to 'art for art's sake' is highly apparent
and in contrast to the founding ideals of the Pre-Raphaelite
Brotherhood. Rossetti gained decadent literary inspiration from
Fitzgerald, Baudelaire, de Sade, and Gautier, the last of whom wrote
in his preface to *Mademoiselle de Maupin*: 'enjoyment seems to me to
be the end of life, and the only useful thing in the world. God has
willed it so. He who created women, perfumes and light, lovely
flowers, good wives, lively horses.'

How Sir Galahad, Sir Bors and Sir Percival were fed with the Sanc Grael; but Sir Percival's Sister Died by the Way

——————————— 1864 ———————————

Watercolour, 11½ x 16½ in / 29.2 x 41.9 cm
Tate Gallery, London

The design of one of Rossetti's most brilliant medieval watercolours was based on the mural *The Attainment of the Sanc Grael*, painted for the Oxford Union in 1857. It was commissioned by Ellen Heaton, to whom Rossetti wrote in late June 1864:

'Its price is, as we agreed, 100 guineas; and I would be much obliged if you could kindly let me have £55 (the remainder going to discharge my too long outstanding debt) on the day of your visit, as I am obliged to go out of town...for a day or two, to avoid a summons on the Grand Jury(!) which would otherwise absorb my time & annihilate my olfactory nerves for a month to come.'

He succeeded in realizing in watercolour the colours he had striven for unsuccessfully in the Oxford murals, and the composition is similar to that of *Sir Galahad, Sir Bors and Sir Percival Receiving the Sanc Grael*, incorporating a row of red-haired, crimson-winged angels, with Sir Galahad modelled by Swinburne, whom Rossetti met during the murals enterprise.

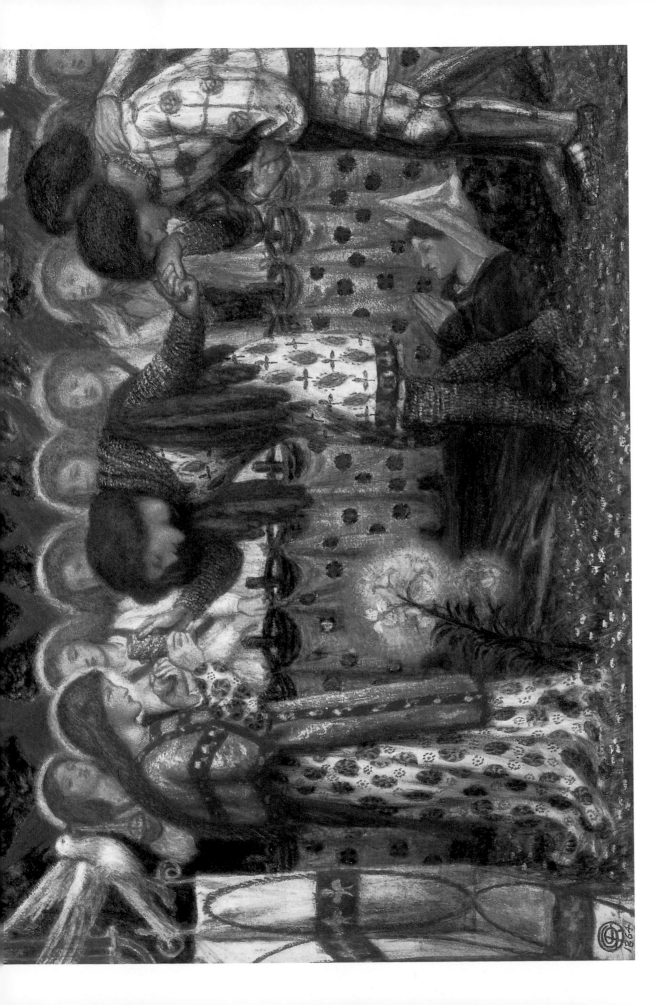

VENUS VERTICORDIA
———— 1864–68 ————

Oil, 38⅝ x 27½ in / 98.1 x 69.9 cm
Russell-Cotes Art Gallery and Museum, Bournemouth

Commissioned by John Mitchell of Bradford, this is one of very few nudes painted by Rossetti. He did several versions of the subject, including a watercolour for William Graham in 1868. That version was based on his 1863 chalk study modelled by a statuesque cook whom he had noticed in the street, whereas this final version in oil, repainted in March 1867, was modelled by Alexa Wilding, a dressmaker whom Rossetti 'discovered'.

Venus is surrounded by honeysuckle and roses, her auburn hair topped by a halo. Rossetti struggled with the flowers, having difficulty in finding exactly what he wanted at a fair price. Ruskin, appalled by the sensuality of the painting, but too prudish to voice the precise subject of his complaint, condemned the coarseness of the flowers. One of Rossetti's patrons, Graham Robertson, wrote later to a friend:

'I suppose he is reflecting upon their morals, but I never heard a word breathed against the perfect respectability of a honeysuckle. Of course roses have got themselves talked about from time to time, but really if one were to listen to scandal about flowers, gardening would become impossible.'

Rossetti wrote a sonnet on the same subject:

> She hath the apple in her hand for thee,
>   Yet almost in her heart would hold it back;
>   She muses, with her eyes upon the track
> Of that which in thy spirit they can see.
> Haply, 'Behold, he is at peace,' saith she;
>   'Alas! the apple for his lips,—the dart
>   That follows its brief sweetness to his heart,—
> The wandering of his feet perpetually.'
>
> A little space her glance is still and coy;
>   But if she give the fruit that works her spell,
> Those eyes shall flame as for her Phrygian boy.
>   Then shall her bird's strained throat the woe foretell,
>   And her far seas moan as a single shell,
> And her grove glow with love-lit fires of Troy.

PLATE 18

IL RAMOSCELLO
— 1865 —
Oil, 18¾ x 15½ in / 47.6 x 39.4 cm
Harvard University Art Museums, Fogg Art Museum,
Bequest of Grenville L. Winthrop

F. G. Stephens was one of the founding members of the Pre-Raphaelite Brotherhood and later became the art critic of *The Athenaeum*. Rossetti, in an attempt to control the criticism of his work, gave Stephens exclusive rights to describe his major paintings and Stephens's writing provided Rossetti with a vehicle for his own interpretations of his work to become known. On 21 October 1865 Stephens reviewed Rossetti's contemporary work including *Il Ramoscello*:

'Of late, the artist in question has, to some extent, resumed that practice of oil painting; the results we have now to describe, in the hope that the public may, ere long, be able to judge for itself of the order of their invention, originality and technical merit. The scale of the pictures is almost that of life.'

According to William Rossetti, *Il Ramoscello* was a portrait of William Graham's daughter Amy, later Lady Muir MacKenzie. It was originally known by the title of *Belle e Buona* but was renamed in 1873 when Rossetti borrowed and repainted much of it, adding the new title to the background. Graham had most of the amendments removed but left the new title.

THE BELOVED
——————— 1865–66 ———————
Oil, 32^1/$_2$ x 30 in / 82.6 x 76.2 cm
Tate Gallery, London

Commissioned by George Rae in 1863 for £300 and also known as *The Bride*, this painting is an elaborated version of *The Blue Bower* and was initially intended to be a Beatrice for Ellen Heaton. However, the colouring of the model, Marie Ford, resulted in a change of concept to the Bride of the Canticles (in the biblical 'Song of Solomon'). In July 1863 Rossetti wrote to Miss Heaton:

'The model does not turn out to be a perfect Beatrice, and at the same time I do not like to risk spoiling the colour by altering it from another model. I have got my model's bright complexion, which was irresistible, & Beatrice was pale... I propose to find another subject to suit the figure – the Bride from Solomon's Song is specially in my head... The present Beatrice must, I now find, be turned without remedy into Solomon's Bride, which however is a subject I myself delight in and have always had an eye to.'

Here a bride, about to meet her groom, is surrounded by five attendants in a composition that consciously recalls the setting of a jewel. The woman on the right was Keomi, the gypsy mistress of the painter Frederick Sandys. In March 1865 a mulatto girl on the left was replaced by a black boy, Rossetti explaining: 'I mean the colour of my picture to be like jewels and the jet would be invaluable.' This change could have been influenced by Manet's *Olympia*, which Rossetti may have seen on a visit to Manet's Paris studio in 1864. The painting was substantially retouched in 1873. The less glossy surface may indicate the beginning of Rossetti's descent into drug and alcohol abuse. The elaborate frame, probably also dating from 1873, is inscribed with an erotic quotation from the 'Song of Solomon' that accentuates the sensual intensity of the painting:

> My Beloved is mine and I am his.
> Let him kiss me with the kisses of his mouth:
> for thy love is better than wine.
> She shall be brought unto the King
> in raiment of needlework: the virgins
> that be her fellows shall bear her
> company, and shall be brought unto thee.

F. G. Stephens praised the then incomplete painting in *The Athenaeum*:

'The subtle rendering of expression, upon which the picture relies for much of its effect, is admirable, and thoroughly original in its tenderness. The beautiful drawing...would be remarkable in a production of any school, and is still more so in that of England, where thoroughness and respect is rare indeed.'

REGINA CORDIUM

—— 1866 ——

Oil, 23¹/₂ x 19¹/₂ in / 59.7 x 49.5 cm
Glasgow Museums: Art Gallery and Museum, Kelvingrove

On their honeymoon in Paris in 1860 Lizzie had sat for studies for
an oil portrait on a panel with the same title, on which Rossetti later
based this version of *Regina Cordium*, for which Alexa Wilding sat.
This is one of the last in the artist's group of luxuriant bust-length
pictures of women in confined spaces. The title, which is inscribed
on the painting, allowed Rossetti to depict a beautiful young woman
with emblems of love, contrasting nature and artifice. Naturalistic
roses in the foreground are juxtaposed with stylized flat plants on
the parapet. On the gold background there is a heart-shaped medal-
lion of a cupid in a blindfold. This subject may have been influenced
by Bellini's *Doge Loredan* or Van Eyck's *Leal Souvenir*, both of which
were bought by the National Gallery in the mid-nineteenth century.
In an 1858 letter to William Bell Scott, Rossetti wrote:

'Even among the old good painters, their portraits and simpler pictures are almost always their masterpieces for colour and execution,
and I fancy if one kept this in view one must have a better chance of
learning to paint at last.'

The 1860 version of *Regina Cordium* (which is translated as *The Queen
of Hearts*) is a study in pinks and reds that has the quality of a
playing-card with a decorative scheme of hearts and kisses. Its first
owner was probably Ruskin. The *Regina Cordium* of 1866 was painted
for J. Hamilton Trist, a Brighton wine merchant, and sold for £170.
Ironically the painting – which is currently still in its original frame
– was at one stage owned by Fanny Cornforth who, at the time of
the honeymoon, was ill in London, distraught as a result of
Rossetti's marriage to Lizzie.

REGINA CORDIVM

1866

PLATE 21

MONNA VANNA
—— 1866 ——
Oil, 35 × 34 in / 88.9 × 86.4 cm
Tate Gallery, London

Originally entitled *Venus Veneta*, this picture was renamed after its completion to add Italian connotations, Monna Vanna being a character from both Boccaccio and Dante's *Vita Nuova*. Rossetti here portrays the Venetian ideal of feminine beauty, modelled by Alexa Wilding. The opulent sleeve, which may have been inspired by Raphael's *Portrait of Giovanni of Aragon* in the Louvre, was made from the same fabric as that seen in *Monna Rosa* and other paintings Rossetti did during this period. The spiral pearl clasp and red necklace, which echo the circular composition of the picture, were decorative motifs frequently used by Rossetti at this time, the necklace for example also appearing in *Regina Cordium*. The artist initially offered the painting to John Mitchell, who owned *Venus Verticordia*, because he thought 'It would be a splendid match to your more classical Venus'. However, the first owner of *Monna Vanna* was W. Blackmore from Cheshire, who owned *Fazio's Mistress*. It was subsequently purchased by the owner of *The Beloved*, George Rae. In 1873 the painting was retouched at Kelmscott and retitled *Belcolore*, a name that Rossetti felt was more appropriate to the relatively modern look of the picture.

SIBYLLA PALMIFERA
———————— 1866–70 ————————

Oil, 37 x 32½ in / 94 x 82.6 cm
Board of Trustees of the National Museums and Galleries on Merseyside
(Lady Lever Art Gallery, Port Sunlight)

Commissioned in 1866 by George Rae, this painting was originally called simply *Palmifera*; adding *Sibylla* was an afterthought. In a letter to his brother William, Rossetti explained that: 'The title Palmifera was adopted to mark the leading place which I intend her to hold among my beauties.' In 1869 Rossetti wrote to the artist James Smetham, asking him to help with the perspective of the background, but the degree of assistance given, if any, is unknown. Leyland requested a replica (a common practice, and one that Rossetti often undertook), but no duplicate of this painting is known. The model here, Alexa Wilding, represents 'the Palm-giver, i.e. the Principle of Beauty', as he described her – but the beauty of the soul in contrast to the beauty of the body in *Lady Lilith*. Rossetti composed this accompanying sonnet:

> Under the arch of Life, where love and death,
>   Terror and mystery, guard her shrine, I saw
>   Beauty enthroned; and though her gaze struck awe,
> I drew it in as simply as my breath.
> Hers are the eyes which, over and beneath,
>   The sky and sea bend on thee,—which can draw,
>   By sea or sky or woman, to one law,
> The allotted bondman of her palm and wreath.
>
> This is that Lady Beauty, in whose praise
>   Thy voice and hand shake still,—long known to thee
>   By flying hair and fluttering hem,—the beat
>   Following her daily of thy heart and feet,
>   How passionately and irretrievably,
> In what fond flight, how many ways and days!

LADY LILITH
——— 1868 ———

Oil, 37 1/2 x 32 in / 95.3 x 81.3 cm
Delaware Art Museum: Samuel and Mary R. Bancroft Memorial

According to Talmudic legend, Lilith was the beautiful and elegant, yet evil, wife of Adam before Eve. Viraginous women were a popular subject in art and literature of the period, and here Rossetti captures his subject's aloofness. The picture has a cold ambience reminiscent of *Monna Vanna*, her luscious hair used effectively as a symbol of sexual power (a motif that was later taken up by Symbolist and Art Nouveau artists). Rossetti's poem *Lilith* explains the subject:

> Of Adam's first wife, Lilith, it is told
>   (The witch he loved before the gift of Eve,)
>   That, ere the snake's, her sweet tongue could deceive,
> And her enchanted hair was the first gold.
> And still she sits, young while the earth is old,
>   And, subtly of herself contemplative,
>   Draws men to watch the bright net she can weave,
> Till heart and body and life are in its hold.
>
> The rose and poppy are her flowers; for where
>   Is he not found, O Lilith, whom shed scent
> And soft-shed kisses and soft sleep shall snare?
>   Lo! as that youth's eyes burned at thine, so went
>   Thy spell through him, and left his straight neck bent,
> And round his heart one strangling golden hair.

Taken from Ruskin's garden, the white roses in the background may seem inappropriate, but they refer to the legend of all the roses in Eden having been white until they blushed at Eve's beauty. The earthy Fanny Cornforth sat for the painting initially, but Leyland, who commissioned it, complained. Rossetti agreed that Fanny's features were too sensual and decided to repaint the face based on the more classically beautiful Alexa Wilding. Not wishing to offend Fanny, he made the amendments in secret at Kelmscott in 1872–73. Rossetti was eager to please Leyland and so changed the painting without charge, but commented: 'I have often said that to be an artist is just the same thing as to be a whore, as far as dependence on the whims and fancies of individuals is concerned.'

PLATE 24

LA PIA DE' TOLOMEI
———— 1868–80 ————
Oil, 41¼ x 47½ in / 104.8 x 120.6 cm
Spencer Museum of Art, University of Kansas

Commissioned by Leyland for £800, this painting took its subject from Dante's *Purgatorio*. Rossetti may also have been introduced to the story by a play of the same title by Charles Marenco that ran in London in 1856. La Pia was imprisoned in a fortress in marshy Maremma by her husband and was left to die without receiving absolution. On the frame Rossetti quoted the words her suffering spirit speaks to Dante in the fifth Canto of *Purgatorio*:

> Ah! When on earth thy voice again is heard,
> And thou from the long road hast rested thee
> (After the second spirit said the third),
> Remember me who am La Pia; me
> Siena, me Maremma, made, unmade,
> This in his inmost heart well knoweth he
> With whose fair jewel I was ringed and wed.

Here the languid and melancholic Jane Morris touches her wedding ring. In earlier sketches, for which Alexa Wilding posed, La Pia's head was tilted back, but this configuration was altered to emphasize the hands and wedding ring. In 1868 Swinburne described how 'her pallid splendid face hangs a little forward, wan and white against the mass of dark deep hair... In her eyes is a strange look of wonder and sorrow and fatigue.' Rossetti obtained sketches of the Maremma swamps by Fairfax Murray, and Frederic Shields was asked to supply photographs (an aid that Rossetti often employed) of ivy, representing life in death, growing on a wall. The fig tree symbolizes fruitfulness, the sundial, embellished by a wheel of fortune, refers to life's unpredictable changes. Living up to her name, La Pia has a rosary and prayer book beside her, indicating her piety.

Proud of his model, Rossetti held a dinner party to celebrate the beginning of this overwhelmingly symbolic picture. However, he was still racked with guilt about Lizzie's death and the resulting insomnia gave him severe eye strain, which hindered his progress on the painting.

MARIANA

——————— 1868–70 ———————

Oil, 43 x 35 in / 109.2 x 88.9 cm
Aberdeen Art Gallery and Museum

His ultimately – almost inevitably – doomed relationship with Jane Morris, and the common knowledge of its intimate nature, dominated the last decade of Rossetti's life, and the strain was reflected in his work. *Mariana*, bought by William Graham for £500, is an unrelievedly melancholic depiction of Jane, yet one that has a rich sensuality. She wears the vivid blue dress seen also in *Portrait of Mrs William Morris*, begun contemporaneously in 1868. The subject is taken from the opening scene of the fourth act of Shakespeare's *Measure for Measure*. Rossetti conceived of Mariana as having been working on a piece of embroidery but being distracted by the boy's song, which is inscribed on the frame:

> Take, O take those lips away,
> That so sweetly were forsworn;
> And those eyes, the break of day,
> Lights that do mislead the morn:
> But my kisses bring again,
> Bring again;
> Seals of love, but seal'd in vain
> Seal'd in vain.

The song of the petulant pageboy, here a portrait of Willie, the buyer William Graham's son, reminds her of her lover Angelo's broken promise of marriage. Rossetti's interest in the subject may also have been inspired by Tennyson's poems on the story.

PLATE 26

LA DONNA DELLA FIAMMA
———————— 1870 ————————
Coloured chalks, 39⁵/₈ x 29⁵/₈ in / 100.7 x 75.3 cm
Manchester City Art Galleries

This is a finished drawing in coloured chalks for a painting that was never executed. This medium was the least problematic for Rossetti, whose eyes were particularly troublesome at the time (Degas similarly turned to pastels when his eyesight began to fail). The study was originally bought by the dealer Leonard Rowe Valpy and then sold to Clarence Edmund Fry (the Fry of Elliot & Fry, one of the leading Society portrait photographers of the nineteenth century). The picture concentrates intensely on Jane, ethereal yet at the same time imposing, whose right hand releases a winged figure of love in flames (possibly inspired by William Blake). On her left wrist is a circular mark. Again our attention is drawn towards the elegant model's hands. The theme of fiery love, also prevalent in Rossetti's poetry at this time, was derived from the passage of Dante's *Vita Nuova* in which Beatrice's capacity to engender love is described:

> Whatever her sweet eyes are turned upon,
> Spirits of love do issue thence in flame.

Like other works from this period, such as *Mariana* and *La Pia de' Tolomei*, the pose here is based upon Rossetti's 1865 series of photographs of Mrs Morris. Her fragile health at the time resulted in languid and subsequently introspective poses.

PLATE 27

DANTE'S DREAM AT THE TIME OF
THE DEATH OF BEATRICE
———————————— 1871 ————————————

Oil, 83 × 125 in / 210.8 × 317.5 cm
Board of Trustees of the National Museums and Galleries on Merseyside
(Walker Art Gallery, Liverpool)

This was Rossetti's last major subject from Dante connected to the theme of *Beata Beatrix*. It was taken from the passage in the *Vita Nuova* in which Dante dreams of the death of Beatrice and the women who cover her with a white veil. The figure of Love was posed by Johnston Forbes-Robertson, later a famous actor. In 1869 Rossetti wrote to the ailing Jane in Germany to ask her to sit for the piece:

'I also want awfully bad to...do the Beatrice in the big picture...a nice easy sitting. But a thousand times more than any work do I desire your renewed health, dear Janey, and you know how anxiously I await all tidings on the subject.'

This was Rossetti's largest painting, measuring approximately 7 by 10½ feet, and was based on an 1856 watercolour commissioned by Ellen Heaton. This version, commissioned by William Graham in 1869, proved too large for a domestic setting and was therefore exchanged for a smaller version with additional predellas (supplementary pictures). In 1873 Valpy acquired the large painting but he returned it later on his retirement to a small home in Bath. He too bargained for smaller works in exchange but at exorbitant and troublesome terms. Rossetti complained about this in a letter written in September 1878 to Jane: 'I have got into rather a hobble with Valpy – who is a vampire in his requirements – as to the Dante exchange business.' Eventually, with the help of the tireless Thomas Hall Caine, the painting was acquired by the Walker Art Gallery in Liverpool.

PLATE 28

VERONICA VERONESE
—————— 1872 ——————

Oil, 43 x 35 in / 109.2 x 88.9 cm
Delaware Art Museum: Samuel and Mary R. Bancroft Memorial

Veronica Veronese was commissioned by Leyland and bought in 1872 prior to its completion; Rossetti later painted *A Sea Spell* as a companion piece. Modelled by Alexa Wilding wearing a green velvet dress belonging to Jane Morris, the painting depicts a woman as an icon of creativity. Here Rossetti used unusual flower symbolism. The daffodil is a member of the narcissus family and thus alludes to the narcissistic temperament of the creative mind. The primrose, significant to February, tells us in which month the painting was completed. The literary source of the painting, inscribed in French on the frame, was, according to William Rossetti, written by Swinburne and can be translated as:

'Suddenly leaning forward, the Lady Veronica rapidly wrote the first notes on the virgin page. Then she took the bow of the violin to make her dream reality; but before commencing to play the instrument suspended from her hand, she paused for a few moments, listening to the inspiring bird, while her left hand strayed over the strings searching for the supreme melody, still elusive. It was the marriage of the voices of nature and of the soul – the dawn of a mystic creation.'

Rossetti explained to Leyland:

'The girl is in a sort of a passionate reverie, and is drawing her hand listlessly along the strings of a violin which hangs against the wall, while she holds the bow with the other hands, as if arrested by the thought of the moment, when she was about to play. In colour I shall make the picture a study of varied greens.'

Rossetti was probably inspired by the book *Iconologia*, written by his friend the artist Filippo Pistrucci, in which Love, Art and Eternity are all female figures in classical green gowns.

PLATE 29

THE BOWER MEADOW
——————— 1871–72 ———————
Oil, 33½ x 26½ in / 85.1 x 67.3 cm
Manchester City Art Galleries

The landscape in the background was originally painted 'from nature' alongside Holman Hunt in Knole Park, Kent in November 1850 for a *Dante and Beatrice in Paradise*. At that time Rossetti wrote to Stephens:

'I have got some trees in the picture which I must set about immediately on completing my design, for which purpose I shall have to pitch my tent at Sevenoaks for some days...the subject which relates to Dante interests me tremendously and requires some consideration...I understand that of course there is a stunning country to paint from there.'

In the execution of the landscape, Rossetti's abandonment of Pre-Raphaelite Brotherhood principles was profoundly apparent. This was expounded in a letter to his friend Jack Tupper:

'The fact is, between you and me, that the leaves on the trees I have to paint here appear red, yellow etc. to my eyes; and...it seems rather annoying that I cannot do them so: my subject shrieking aloud for Spring.'

Rossetti later superimposed four figures on to the landscape: two languid dancers and two women in the foreground playing musical instruments, modelled by Maria Spartali on the left and Alexa Wilding on the right. The symmetry of the figures and their colouring recall early Italian paintings of musical angels.

The Bower Meadow was sold to Pilgeram and Lefevre in June 1872 for £735. Rossetti had been suffering from a sense of persecution, and the high price he obtained for this work somehow further fuelled his paranoid delusions. It was shortly sold on to Walter Dunlop who later regretted it, having exchanged *Le Roman de la Rose* and *Ophelia* for part of the price.

PLATE 30

BEATA BEATRIX

—— 1872 ——

Oil, 34½ × 27¼ in / 87.5 × 69.3 cm (predella 11⅝ × 27¼ in / 26.5 × 69.2 cm)
Art Institute of Chicago, Charles L. Hutchinson Collection

This is a replica of the *Beata Beatrix* that Rossetti painted as a memorial to Lizzie Siddal, who died of a laudanum overdose on 11 February 1862. Begun many years before, the original visionary portrait was taken up again in 1864 and completed in 1870. The iconography in this painting is dense, fusing the artist's personal experience with legendary and literary sources. During the initial stages of the painting, Rossetti explained the imagery:

'The picture illustrates the *Vita Nuova*, embodying symbolically the death of Beatrice as treated in that work. The picture is not intended at all to represent death, but to render it under the semblance of a trance, in which Beatrice, seated at a balcony overlooking the city, is suddenly rapt from Earth to Heaven. You will remember how Dante dwells on the desolation of the city in connection with the incident of her death, and for this reason I have introduced it as my background, and made the figures of Dante and Love passing through the street and gazing ominously on one another, conscious of the event; while the bird, a messenger of death, drops the poppy between the hands of Beatrice. She, through her shut lids, is conscious of a new world, as expressed in the last words of the *Vita Nuova* – "That blessed Beatrice who now gazeth continually on His countenance, who is through all ages blessed."'

Intensely emotional for a secular painting, this immortalization of a woman as almost a spiritual icon shows the development of a trend for half-length female figures in an ecstatic trance. This was anticipated in Rossetti's 1857 wood engraving *Saint Cecilia* in its configuration, as well as in motifs such as the dove and the sundial. The pose was first apparent in the 1851 sketches for his erotic watercolour *The Return of Tibullus to Delia* (1853; Private collection). It is not known whether Lizzie naturally assumed the pose or Rossetti decided to position her in this way. In 1871 William Graham wrote to Rossetti begging for a replica:

'I know the labour of repeating, apart from the delight of invention and the surprise of your discovery, is especially hard to your temperament…the Beatrice, from the first day I saw it, has appealed to my feeling altogether above and beyond any picture I ever saw, and the love for it has only deepened.'

PLATE 31

LA GHIRLANDATA
———— 1873 ————

Oil, 45¹/₂ x 34¹/₂ in / 115.6 x 87.6 cm
Guildhall Art Gallery, Corporation of London

This is one of a group of works executed between 1871 and 1874 depicting musical women, some bought by Leyland whose musical interests probably inspired the pictures. This particular painting, however, was bought by William Graham for £840 as Leyland preferred single-figure compositions. *La Ghirlandata* is an aesthetic study of Alexa Wilding in a forest setting with May Morris (daughter of Jane and William) as the angels. Rossetti described the painting as: 'The greenest picture in the world...the principal figure being draped in green and completely surrounded with glowing green foliage.' The harp has blue wings, symbolizing the flight of time. The garland that gives the painting its title is composed of roses and honeysuckle, which refer to sexual attraction – as they had in *Venus Verticordia*, according to Ruskin. The painting was done at Kelmscott in the summer of 1873. In a letter Rossetti told his assistant Henry Treffry Dunn:

'I wrote to Graham yesterday abt. the big picture. The one I am doing for him now is not *Blessed Damozel* but that figure painting on the queer old harp which I drew from Miss W. when you were here. The 2 heads of little May are at the top of the picture. It ought to put Graham in good humour & I am glad he is to have it as he is the only buyer I have who is worth a damn.'

PLATE 32

PROSERPINE
———— 1874 ————
Oil, 49 ¾ x 24 in / 126.4 x 61 cm
Tate Gallery, London

This is one of many versions of a painting that Rossetti regarded as among his favourites – although its history was such a catalogue of disasters that it is surprising he did not come to detest it. Originally a commission from Howell and Parsons for £550, it had to be done on a total of eight canvases. Of these, the first two were destroyed by the artist himself, and the third was cut down to become *Blanziflore*. Howell and Parsons took the fourth version in May 1873, but it remained unsold and was returned to Rossetti in February 1874. The fifth version, which was completed in the autumn of 1873, and promised to Leyland, had suffered from problems with the lining and had to be relined. It was apparently lost after departing from Paddington Station, on its return from London to Kelmscott, where Rossetti was working, never to be seen again. Its replacement, the sixth version, was found to have been damaged in transit on its arrival at Leyland's home in Liverpool, was restored by the artist and was eventually owned by the misogynist painter L. S. Lowry. Leyland finally received version seven – which is reproduced here. A later, eighth, replica was completed a few days before Rossetti's death.

Although the figure was originally intended to be Eve with the apple, Jane Morris here portrays Proserpine, Empress of Hades, who was confined there with her husband for most of the year because she had tasted one of the fruits of the Underworld, a pomegranate. Rossetti loved this legend, feeling that its theme – a woman granted only occasional periods of freedom from her husband – was analogous to his relationship with his model. He wrote a sonnet about it in Italian, inscribed on the spray of ivy, 'a symbol of clinging memory':

> (Afar away the light that brings cold cheer)
> Unto this wall – one instant and no more
> Admitted at my distant palace-door.
> Afar the flowers of Enna, from this drear
> Dire fruit, which, tasted once, must thrall me here.
> Afar those skies from this Tartarean grey
> That chills me: and afar, how far away,
> The nights that shall be from the days that were.
>
> Afar from mine own self I seem, and wing
> Strange ways in thought, and listen for a sign:
> And still some heart unto some soul doth pine,
> (Whose sounds mine inner sense is fain to bring,
> Continually together murmuring,) –
> 'Woe's me for thee, unhappy Proserpine!'

Rossetti may also have been inspired by Swinburne's *Hymn to Proserpina* and *Garden of Proserpine*, published in 1866, and also by Aubrey De Vere's poem on Proserpine, mentioned by Rossetti in a letter to Allingham in March 1856. The elongated, thin composition of *Proserpine* may have been influenced by Botticelli's *Portrait of Smerelda Bandinelli*, which Rossetti had bought in 1867.

PLATE 3 3

SANCTA LILIAS
———— 1874 ————
Oil, 19 x 18 in / 48.3 x 45.7 cm
Tate Gallery, London

Initially begun as a larger piece for *The Blessed Damozel*, the painting was cut down to a smaller single-head composition, Alexa Wilding posing for the central figure on the gold background. The drapery of her gold dress is incomplete. In around 1873 Rossetti wrote the following instructions to his assistant Dunn:

'What I want done is that you should get Ford and Dickinson's gilder down to Chelsea and make him gild under your directions the parts where the red ground of the canvas is left, both dress and background. This would require nicety around the edges, and where these seem dubious I will mark them with a white chalk line. When gilded, I will get you to re-pack it as it came and return it to me at once to paint on.'

The picture was originally offered to and accepted by Charles Howell (Rossetti's agent and friend), but was somehow given to the Honourable William and Mrs Cowper-Temple by Rossetti as a memento of his visit to Broadlands in Sussex in August 1876.

LA BELLA MANO
————— 1875 —————

Oil, 62 x 46 in / 157.5 x 116.8 cm
Delaware Art Museum: Samuel and Mary R. Bancroft Memorial

Painted at Cheyne Walk, this picture was commissioned by Murray Marks in February 1875 for £1,050 and bought by his publisher F. S. Ellis. The title refers to a series of Petrarchian sonnets of the same name by Giusto de' Conti, although of course Rossetti wrote his own sonnet on the subject:

> O lovely hand, that thy sweet self dost lave
> In that thy pure and proper element,
> Whence erst the Lady of Love's high advènt
> Was born, and endless fires sprang from the wave:—
> Even as her Loves to her their offerings gave,
> For thee the jewelled gifts they bear; while each
> Looks to those lips, of music-measured speech
> The fount, and of more bliss than man may crave.
>
> In royal wise ring-girt and bracelet-spann'd,
> A flower of Venus' own virginity,
> Go shine among thy sisterly sweet band;
> In maiden-minded converse delicately
> Evermore white and soft; until thou be,
> O hand! heart-handsel'd in a lover's hand.

Alexa Wilding sat for the main figure and May Morris again for the angel. The scallop-shaped basin is a symbol of purity, as is the washing of the hands, which here is not a reference to the end of an affair as it had been in the earlier *Lucrezia Borgia*. The iris and the lemon tree are symbols of the Virgin. Rossetti borrowed many of the objects in the picture from Marks, including a blue jar that was later painted out. The toilet castor also belonged to Marks; actually silver, it was gilded at Rossetti's request without the owner's permission and much to his annoyance. Rossetti also appropriated the needlework table cover that he found in Marks's home when visiting his wife. In trying to obtain the exact shade of flowers that Rossetti insisted upon, Marks spent much time and money in the Covent Garden flower market.

ASTARTE SYRIACA
―――――― 1875–77 ――――――
Oil, 72 × 42 in / 183 × 106.7 cm
Manchester City Art Galleries

Commissioned in 1875 by Clarence Edmund Fry for £2,100 (the most lucrative commission Rossetti ever received), *Astarte Syriaca* was painted mostly at Aldwick Lodge in Bognor in 1875–76. This, Rossetti's most powerful and devotional tribute to Jane Morris – just as *Beata Beatrix* had been to Lizzie Siddal – was developed from a portrait of her that he had started earlier, entitled *Mnemosyne* (1881, Delaware Art Museum: Samuel and Mary R. Bancroft Memorial). Astarte was the Syrian Aphrodite and here, more so than Venus, she is a potent embodiment simultaneously of all Rossetti's obsessions – legend, religion, art and love – explained in the sonnet he wrote to accompany it:

> Mystery: lo! betwixt the sun and moon
> Astarte of the Syrians: Venus Queen
> Ere Aphrodite was. In silver sheen
> Her twofold girdle clasps the infinite boon
> Of bliss whereof the heaven and earth commune:
> And from her neck's inclining flower-stem lean
> Love-freighted lips and absolute eyes that wean
> The pulse of hearts to the spheres' dominant tune.
>
> Torch-bearing, her sweet ministers compel
> All thrones of light beyond the sky and sea
> The witnesses of Beauty's face to be:
> That face, of Love's all-penetrative spell
> Amulet, talisman, and oracle,—
> Betwixt the sun and moon a mystery.

Venus Astarte has two torch-bearing attendants in this claustrophobic Mannerist composition with surreal lighting in which the *femme fatale* has become immortalized into a pagan love goddess. The roses and pomegranates in the girdle are symbols respectively of the Passion and Resurrection. Astarte's gesture was influenced by the Medici Venus, which was particularly revered and much copied at the time. Rossetti's glazing technique, which gives this painting its luminosity, was perhaps inspired by Titian. In February 1877 he wrote to Theodore Watts-Dunton: 'I have been glazing it and it is much enriched.'

PLATE 36

THE BLESSED DAMOZEL
———— 1875–78 ————

Oil, 68½ x 37 in / 174 x 94 cm (including predella)
Harvard University Art Museums, Fogg Art Museum,
Bequest of Grenville L. Winthrop

Commissioned in 1871 by William Graham, *The Blessed Damozel* is an illustration for an earlier poem of the same title that had appeared in *The Germ*. It was Rossetti's only painting based on one of his poems (normally the painting came first). The first two verses describe how:

> The blessed damozel leaned out
>   From the gold bar of Heaven;
> Her eyes were deeper than the depth
>   Of waters stilled at even;
> She had three lilies in her hand,
>   And the stars in her hair were seven.
>
> Her robe, ungirt from clasp to hem,
>   No wrought flowers did adorn,
> But a white rose of Mary's gift,
>   For a service meetly worn;
> Her hair that lay along her back
>   Was yellow like ripe corn.

Part of the painting was done during a stay at Broadlands in Sussex with William Cowper-Temple in the summer of 1876, when Rossetti had escaped a heatwave in London. The damozel looks towards earth from heaven, surrounded by angels and lovers, the female lovers resembling Jane Morris. The rhythmic form of the lovers may derive from Botticelli, particularly his *Mystic Nativity* of 1500, which Rossetti had seen in Leeds in 1868. Botticelli's painting depicts pairs of embracing humans and angels in the foreground below a circular dance of angels in heaven. In an inversion of Rossetti's usual deification of living women, here is a truly corporeal heavenly woman, modelled by Alexa Wilding (with his housemaid Mary as the angels). In 1879, at Graham's request, Rossetti added a predella showing the damozel's lover lying under a tree, looking up towards his departed partner.

PLATE 37

A SEA SPELL

———— 1877 ————

Oil, 42 x 35 in / 106.7 x 88.9 cm
Harvard University Art Museums, Fogg Art Museum,
Bequest of Grenville L. Winthrop

Begun in early 1875, *A Sea Spell* was originally intended to illustrate
the lines from Coleridge's *Kubla Khan*:

> A damsel with a dulcimer
> In a vision once I saw.

Modelled by Alexa Wilding, it was completed in 1877, and offered
to Leyland as a companion picture for *Veronica Veronese*. Rossetti later
described the imagery in a sonnet:

> Her lute hangs shadowed in the apple-tree,
> While flashing fingers weave the sweet-strung spell
> Between its chords; and as the wild notes swell,
> The sea-bird for those branches leaves the sea.
> But to what sound her listening ear stoops she?
> What netherworld gulf-whispers does she hear,
> In answering echoes from what planisphere,
> Along the wind, along the estuary?
>
> She sinks into her spell: and when full soon
> Her lips move and she soars into her song,
> What creatures of the midmost main shall throng
> In furrowed surf-clouds to the summoning rune:
> Till he, the fated mariner, hears her cry,
> And up her rock, bare-breasted, comes to die?

PLATE 38

A VISION OF FIAMMETTA
—— 1878 ——
Oil, 57½ x 35 in / 146 x 89 cm
Private collection

In 1861 Rossetti translated three sonnets by Boccaccio and encountered the story of Fiammetta. Fiammetta was the pet name of Boccaccio's lover, Maria d'Aquino, who died prematurely. Untypically, Rossetti painted only one version of this subject straight on to canvas without studies. Here Fiammetta, modelled by Maria Spartali, is overshadowed by the angel of death and surrounded by apple blossoms. Rossetti had difficulty in finding good blossom in London. As he wrote to Frederic Shields: 'I am very anxious about the blossom...mine is not good enough to paint... What I want is a full-coloured red and white blossom, of the tufted, rich kind; and from such I began painting today, only it was not in a good state. I would of course be glad to pay anything for a good blossom.'

On its completion Rossetti was very pleased with this painting, which he described as a 'ripper', though it has remained relatively unknown. It was *A Vision of Fiammetta* that inspired Samuel Bancroft Jr to begin to collect Pre-Raphaelite art. This new patron tried unsuccessfully to purchase the painting throughout the rest of his life, but succeeded only in acquiring a watercolour study for the flowers. Rossetti's sonnet on the same subject was inscribed on the frame:

> Behold Fiammetta, shown in vision here.
> Gloom-girt 'mid Spring-flushed apple-growth she stands;
> And as she sways the branches with her hands,
> Along her arm the sundered bloom falls sheer,
> In separate petals shed, each like a tear;
> While from the quivering bough the bird expands
> His wings. And lo! thy spirit understands
> Life shaken and shower'd and flown, and Death drawn near.
>
> All stirs with change. Her garments that beat the air:
> The angel circling round her aureole
> Shimmers in flight against the tree's grey bole:
> A presage and a promise; as 'twere
> On Death's dark storm the rainbow of the Soul.

La Donna della Finestra
——— 1879 ———

Oil, 39 ¼ x 29 ¼ in / 101 x 74.3 cm
Harvard University Art Museums, Fogg Art Museum,
Bequest of Grenville L. Winthrop

Described by Rossetti in a letter to Jane Morris in August 1879 as his best work to date, *La Donna della Finestra* (The Lady of Pity) was bought by F. S. Ellis for £420. The composition remained similar to that in 1870 studies upon which the work was based; again we see the Venetian half-length configuration. The window in the background was influenced by Dürer's engraving of *Saint Jerome* or a Friedrich Retzsch illustration to *Faust*. In May 1879 Rossetti wrote to Watts-Dunton:

'Today I have got on the background of the Lady of Window, and really the picture is quite transfigured and ought to sell. It looks as if I were not dead yet.'

The subject, yet another derived from Dante's *Vita Nuova*, refers to the 'Lady of Pity' who gazed down sympathetically on Dante from a window after the death of Beatrice. Allegorically the lady represented Philosophy, but to Rossetti she was Gemma Donati, the woman who eventually married Dante. The compassionate lady is undoubtedly also a reference to Jane, the model, in whom Rossetti sought solace after the death of Lizzie. By this time their relationship had become more affectionate than passionate, probably as a result of both Rossetti's chloral addiction and the needs of Jane's daughter Jenny (who had been diagnosed as epileptic). In July 1879 Rossetti wrote to her:

'I have put the fig-leaf foreground to your picture & it looks very well. I am in doubt whether to or not introduce a branch of laurel towards the upper part of the picture but if I do not do this it is now well-nigh finished.'

PLATE 40

THE DAY DREAM
—— 1880 ——
Oil, 62½ x 36½ in / 157.5 x 92.7 cm
By Courtesy of the Board of Trustees of the Victoria and Albert Museum, London

In autumn 1879, on seeing a drawing in Rossetti's studio of Jane Morris sitting under a tree, Constantine Ionides commissioned this oil painting. In his correspondence with Jane at this time, the artist wrote:

'This will be a considerable commission, though I must be moderate in these bad times. Terms are not yet settled exactly. Do you know whether Constantine has bought or is buying any pictures of Ned Jones [Edward Burne-Jones]? Of course that worthy need not know of this matter of mine.'

Rossetti was indeed moderate with his price of £700 as it was clear that the wealthy Ionides would have paid considerably more. Rossetti believed that his modesty would be rewarded with further commissions.

In the earlier drawing the woman embodied Nature's creativity, symbolized by the return of Spring. Mrs Cowper-Temple had visited Rossetti's studio in the summer of 1879 and expressed delight in the study. Rossetti had written to Jane in July of that year, anticipating a commission and observing: 'So the old studies of you may go on being useful yet.'

Rossetti's plans for the painting underwent several changes. Originally it was to be entitled *Vanna* or *Monna Primavera*, referring to Dante's *Vita Nuova*. Snowdrops were initially chosen for the flowers, but were replaced by honeysuckle as the season progressed. The head was the second to be painted on to the canvas, having been altered at the request of Ionides's sister Agalaia, who felt the shadow on the face against the sky was too heavy. Typically, Rossetti subsequently described the imagery in a sonnet, which concludes with the lines:

> Within the branching shade of Reverie
> Dreams even may spring till autumn; yet none be
> Like woman's budding day-dream spirit-fann'd.
> Lo! tow'rd deep skies, not deeper than her look,
> She dreams; till now on her forgotten book
> Drops the forgotten blossom from her hand.

PRINCIPAL PUBLIC COLLECTIONS CONTAINING WORKS BY ROSSETTI

CANADA

Ottawa
National Gallery of Canada

GERMANY

Neuss
Clemens-Sels-Museum

GREAT BRITAIN

Aberdeen
Aberdeen Art Gallery and Museum

Bedford
Cecil Higgins Art Gallery

Birmingham
Barber Institute of Fine Arts, University of Birmingham
Birmingham City Art Gallery

Bournemouth
Russell-Cotes Art Gallery and Museum

Bradford
City Art Gallery and Museums

Cambridge
Fitzwilliam Museum

Cardiff
National Museum of Wales

Carlisle
Carlisle Museum and Art Gallery

Glasgow
Glasgow Art Gallery and Museum

Llandaff
Llandaff Cathedral

Liverpool
Walker Art Gallery

London
British Museum
Guildhall Art Gallery
National Portrait Gallery
Tate Gallery
Victoria & Albert Museum
William Morris Art Gallery, Walthamstow

Manchester
Manchester City Art Gallery
Whitworth Art Gallery, University of Manchester

Oxford
Ashmolean Museum

Port Sunlight
Lady Lever Art Gallery

ISRAEL

Tel Aviv
Museum of Tel Aviv

NEW ZEALAND

Auckland
Auckland City Art Gallery

SOUTH AFRICA

Johannesburg
Johannesburg Art Gallery

UNITED STATES OF AMERICA

Boston, Massachusetts
Isabella Stewart Gardner Museum
Museum of Fine Arts

Cambridge, Massachusetts
Fogg Art Museum, Harvard University

Chicago, Illinois
Art Institute of Chicago

Detroit, Michigan
Detroit Institute of Art

Lawrence, Kansas
Spencer Museum of Art, University of Kansas

New London, Connecticut
Lyman Allyn Museum

New York, New York
Brooklyn Museum
Metropolitan Museum of Art

Toledo, Ohio
Toledo Art Museum

Wichita, Kansas
Wichita Art Museum

Wilmington, Delaware
Delaware Art Museum

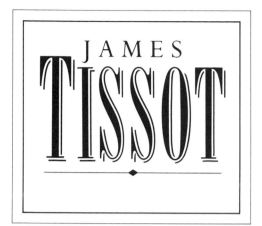

JAMES TISSOT
1836 ~ 1902

A review of the 1879 Grosvenor Gallery exhibition, published in *The Spectator*, remarked that 'Tissot has but one rival in England, and that is Alma-Tadema.' James Tissot and Lawrence Alma-Tadema were born in the same year, 1836, and followed curiously similar careers: both studied and worked in Paris and, as a result of the turmoil of the Franco-Prussian War of 1870–71, the two artists moved to London where they became friends. Unlike short-term refugee painters such as Monet and Pissarro, they settled there, moved in the same social circles and rapidly established spectacular reputations, achieving fame and wealth. When Tissot finally left London, Alma-Tadema bought his house. They had both started painting historical subjects under the influence of the Belgian artist Hendryk Leys before embarking on representations of elegant people going about their daily lives, and they shared a preoccupation with bright colour and minute, almost photographic detail. While many voiced doubts about the two painters' artistic importance, their obvious craftsmanship was widely admired and compared. Both artists were cosmopolitan men of their age, shrewd businessmen who responded to the demands of the picture-buying public by producing works mirroring late nineteenth-century society, but there the affinity ends. Whereas Alma-Tadema's principal subjects were ancient Romans (or rather, 'Victorians in togas'), those that made Tissot's name were very much people of his own era. Tissot excelled in painting fashionable conversation pieces that were once dismissed as 'pretty pictures' (the critic John Ruskin was to call his paintings '. . . mere coloured photographs of vulgar society'), but his works are among the most revealing visual documents of the nineteenth century, brilliantly conveying the mood of the Victorian era while subtly hinting at the routine and tedium of 'the Season'.

Jacques-Joseph Tissot (as he was christened; 'James' was a later affectation) was born in Nantes, a port on the west coast of France, on 15 October 1836, one of four sons of Marie Durand, a Breton, and Marcel-Théodore Tissot, a member of a family of Italian ancestry, who originally lived in Franche-Comté, near the French-Swiss border. Tissot's father was a successful linen draper and his mother and aunt ran a hat-making company. This background, coupled with growing up in the bustling port of Nantes, provided the young Jacques-Joseph with an unusual awareness of two disparate subjects: high fashion and marine paraphernalia, which he was later to combine in his skilful paintings of stylish women in technically precise nautical settings. Marcel-Théodore Tissot was sufficiently successful that he was able to purchase the Château of Buillon, near Besançon, in his native Jura, and retired there, devoting his last years to such dilettanti pursuits as shell collecting.

Tissot's father, who he was later to describe as 'a Christian of the old-fashioned sort', subjected Jacques-Joseph to a devout religious education. In about 1848 he was sent away to attend a Jesuit college at Brugelette in Flanders, then establishments in Vannes in Brittany and Dôle in Normandy. He showed artistic leanings and, while living in these historic towns, devoted himself to sketches of the local architecture. Despite apparent opposition from his father, in about 1856 he finally left his hometown for Paris, enrolling in a studio for a course of formal training designed to equip him to enter the prestigious Ecole des Beaux-Arts. There he met fellow student James Whistler, and the following year exhibited his first painting, a portrait of his mother. After another year he registered as a pupil of Louis Lamothe and Hippolyte Flandrin, painters working in a European version of the Pre-Raphaelite style. There he met Degas, who

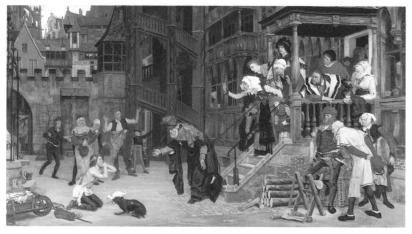

Tissot's 1862 painting *Le retour de l'enfant prodigue* (*The Return of the Prodigal Son*)
places the biblical story in a Leys-inspired medieval setting.

Tissot in an artist's studio, painted in 1868 by Degas, a friend from his student days.

attended the same studio, and remained close friends with him throughout the 1860s. Although Tissot was ultimately to share Degas' enthusiasm for painting modern subjects, he initially fell under another influence: after visiting Baron Hendryk Leys (with whom Alma-Tadema was to work on a series of murals) in Antwerp, Tissot adopted an historical style (even, briefly, archaically signing himself 'Jacobus Tissot') that came so close to that of Leys that he was more than once accused of plagiarism. By 1859, when his work was first exhibited and during a period of anglophilia in France, Tissot anglicized his first name, being henceforth known as 'James', a name as foreign and exotic to French ears as 'Jacques-Joseph' sounds to those of Anglo-Saxons.

In 1860 Tissot exhibited five paintings at the Paris Salon: three history subjects and two portraits of women. In 1861 he exhibited six paintings at the Salon, three of them based on the story of Faust and Marguerite. The Salon reviews of the early 1860s criticized his obsession with medieval costume dramas and continued to regard his work as no more than technically competent pastiches of the better-known paintings of Baron Leys.

In 1862 Tissot visited Venice, where he began work on a series of paintings on the theme of the Prodigal Son, and Florence, which he described in a letter to Degas, noting especially the impression made on him by the works of Bellini, Carpaccio and Mantegna. Back in Paris he lived near the novelist Alphonse Daudet who became a close friend. In 1863 he exhibited three paintings at the Salon: *Le départ du fiancé*, *Le retour de l'enfant prodigue*, and *Le départ de l'enfant prodigue à Venise*. It is possible that he paid his first visit to London in the same year, but information

about this early period of his life continues to remain frustratingly sketchy.

During the mid-1860s, now in his late twenties, Tissot embarked on the stylistic departure that launched him into the mainstream of contemporary art. In 1864 he exhibited for the first time at the Royal Academy, London and may perhaps have visited London on this occasion (the Royal Academy catalogue gives an address in Kensington, but there is no other evidence that he was actually living there). The work he submitted was an untitled medieval subject. In the same year, however, he exhibited two paintings at the Paris Salon: *Les deux soeurs* and *Portrait de Mlle L. L. . . .* – the first of his modern subjects to be shown publicly. Coincidentally, it was in precisely the same period that Alma-Tadema made his break from medievalism, but in his case devoting the rest of his career to subjects based in ancient Rome. Tissot's new artistic endeavours were favourably reviewed and, for the first time, he began to achieve recognition: his two paintings shown at the Paris Salon in 1866 won him an award that henceforth entitled him to exhibit without selection by the official jury. He also gained financial rewards: an increasingly astonished Degas looked on in obvious envy as Tissot slipped apparently effortlessly from his medieval mantle and commanded ever-escalating prices for his avowedly modern subjects. By 1867 Tissot was sufficiently wealthy to have a luxurious house with a splendid studio built in Paris at 64 Avenue de l'Impératrice (later renamed Avenue du Bois de Boulogne), where he remained during the next four years, retaining the property until his death.

Perhaps inspired by his reading of the Goncourts' seminal work on the French Directoire period (1795–99), in 1868 Tissot embarked on a short-lived dalliance with genre paintings featuring men and women in late eighteenth-century costume, an artistic *cul de sac* that was soon to be interrupted by the outbreak of war. Tissot's links with England were also forged at the end of the decade. In 1869 he probably visited England to make his first studies of the subjects of caricatures commissioned by the magazine *Vanity Fair*. Two principal artists, working under the pseudonyms 'Ape' (Carlo Pellegrini) and 'Spy' (Leslie Ward), were regularly employed by the magazine to depict eminent people of the day in humorous style, and over the following eight years Tissot (signing himself 'Cöidé', a pseudonym of unknown origin) joined them, undertaking 62 caricatures. The first of these were foreign heads of state, presumably from studies executed on the Continent, but after his move to London his subjects were exclusively British personalities as diverse as the painter Frederick Leighton and Charles Darwin. Thomas Gibson Bowles, the founder in 1868 and editor of *Vanity Fair*, became a close friend of Tissot and in 1870 com-

'A Special Correspondent', Tissot's portrait of Thomas Gibson Bowles in his 1871 book, *The Defence of Paris Narrated as it was Seen*.

missioned him to paint a portrait of the soldier and adventurer Frederick Burnaby that was to become enormously popular. Other important and lucrative portrait commissions were to follow.

At the outbreak of the Franco-Prussian War, while many fellow artists of varying political persuasions evacuated to England, Tissot remained in France where he joined the Garde Nationale and met up with Bowles who was in Paris as war correspondent for the *Morning Post*. Providing Bowles with accommodation in his Paris home and accompanying him to a variety of incidents during the Siege of Paris, Tissot produced a set of portrait drawings of military personnel to illustrate Bowles' account of the Siege, published

A languid Frederick Leighton in Tissot's 1872 caricature from *Vanity Fair*.

in London in 1871 as a book, *The Defence of Paris, Narrated as it was Seen*.

After the fall of Paris in 1871, Tissot stayed and became involved briefly in the Commune. The actual level of his participation, and whether it derived from serious sympathy or self interest, remains vague, but it proved to be a misguided political allegiance for which Degas and other friends never forgave him. After the collapse of the Commune he fled to London where his earlier hospitality to Bowles was reciprocated when he shared Bowles's London house, Cleve Lodge, near Hyde Park, and resumed his work for *Vanity Fair* by contributing twenty-two cartoons between July and December.

From 1871 to 1874 we learn, partly from correspon-

dence with Degas, that Tissot was beginning to achieve success in London. He was known to have had a well-honed business sense (a 'dealer of genius', as the painter John Singer Sargent called him), and his work commanded high prices. Now that he was also rubbing shoulders with notable writers and diarists, we start to discover something of his personality from his friends' published accounts. As can be inferred from his earlier portrait by Degas, Tissot was something of a dandy, several writers noting his extreme concern with his personal appearance. He was also a master of self-promotion, and we have Edmond de Goncourt's somewhat exaggerated comment, recorded in 1874: 'This ingenious exploiter of English idiocy, was it not his idea to have a studio with a waiting room where, at all times, there is iced champagne at the disposal of visitors, and the studio is surrounded by a garden where, all day long, one can see a footman with silk stockings brushing and shining the shrubbery leaves?' British artist Louise Jopling recalled him with affection, noting that 'Tissot was a charming man, very handsome, extra-ordinarily like the Duke of Teck . . . always well groomed, and had nothing of artistic carelessness either in his dress or demeanour.' In 1890, Edmond de Goncourt wrote again of Tissot, describing him as '. . . this complex being, a blend of mysticism and phoniness, laboriously intelligent in spite of an unintelligent skull and the eyes of a dead fish, passionate, finding every two or three years a new *appassionement*, with which he contracts a new short lease of life.' He was not the only observer to suggest that Tissot was constantly re creating himself: his restless energy directed him readily to adopt new enthusiasms, grafting new branches to his artistic repertoire, from etching to enamel to photography; in his later years he even took up archaeology. Chameleon-like, Tissot was also continually to adopt new artistic styles throughout his working career, from his Leys-inspired historical genre, through Pre-Raphaelitism, a flirtation with Impressionism, a long dalliance with modern narrative pictures to a culmination in religious art.

Tissot's Grove End Road studio as portrayed in 1874 by *The Building News*.

Tissot's friendship with Bowles grew and it is clear that the well-connected publisher opened numerous doors for him in London 'Society'. After concluding his foray into conversation pieces in eighteenth-century costume, Tissot turned to themes associated with the Thames and ships. These perhaps derived from the influence of Whistler, a friend throughout the 1870s among whose works were included several notable studies of the Thames and its bridges.

Tissot's paintings were typically peopled with women, which led to his being dubbed 'the Watteau of Wapping'.

In the spring of 1872 Tissot moved to 73 Springfield Road, St John's Wood. The following year he moved again to 17 (later re-numbered 34) Grove End Road, St John's Wood, where he lived for almost ten years. The house, built in the eighteenth century on the land of the abbey that gave its name to nearby Abbey Road, was situated in an area best known for its houses occupied by courtesans and kept women. It was said that the preponderance of canopied paths to the villas in the area owed their origin to the need for visitors to step out of carriages and enter them discreetly while avoiding the gaze of prying neighbours. There he created a fine studio (though scarcely on the scale of that built by its later occupant, Alma-Tadema) and in the garden erected a splendid colonnade, based on one in the Parc Monçeau (this also featured in several of Alma-Tadema's works, but was sadly later demolished). He exhibited the first of his English 'social conversation pieces', *Too Early*, at the Royal Academy, along with *The Captain's Daughter* and *The Last Evening*. The year 1874, significant in the history of art for the first Impressionist exhibition, saw Tissot visiting Paris once more – although, despite a persuasive letter from Degas, he declined to participate. Notwithstanding his refusal to ally himself with the Impressionists, Tissot remained close friends with many members of the movement: Berthe Morisot visited him in London and commented on his success, and in 1875 he visited Venice in the company of Manet, whose *Blue Venice* he acquired.

There now began a period of Tissot's life that has been the subject of much discussion and speculation, and which has created a unique romantic aura around his life and work. In around 1876, or possibly earlier, he began a liaison with a woman whose identity was to remain shrouded in mystery for over half a century – so much so that she was long referred to as *la mystérieuse*. Many elements

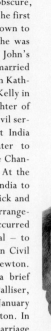

remain tantalizingly obscure, but it would appear that he first met the woman now known to be Mrs Newton when she was residing near his St John's Wood home with her married sister Mary Hervey. Born Kathleen Irene Ashburnham Kelly in 1854, she was the daughter of Charles Kelly, an Irish civil servant in the British East India Company who was later to become Governor of the Channel Island of Alderney. At the age of 16 she went to India to visit her brother Frederick and – presumably by prior arrangement, since the event occurred so soon after her arrival – to marry a widower, Indian Civil Service surgeon Isaac Newton. On the boat she had a brief affair with a Captain Palliser, despite which, on 3 January 1871, she married Newton. In the first week of their marriage her intimacy with Palliser was revealed and she parted from Newton, soon terminated her relationship with Palliser, and returned to England. There, on the grounds of her adultery, Newton sued for divorce, which was granted by the end of the year. A daughter, Muriel Mary Violet, whom she claimed to be Captain Palliser's, was born at her father's home in Conisborough, Yorkshire, on 20 December 1871, and a second child, Cecil George, in March 1876, by which time she was living with her sister. Kathleen Newton bizarrely claimed Cecil as the offspring of her ex-husband, but there is speculation that Tissot was the father (although his lack of a substantial bequest in Tissot's will leaves this in doubt). While frequently visiting the Tissot household and featuring in a number of paintings, the Newton children grew up with their aunt while Tissot and Kathleen Newton lived together in Grove End Road during the next five years. Although some writers, among them Sacheverell Sitwell, have implied that a deathbed marriage took place, it would appear that they did not marry. Both Tissot and Newton were Roman Catholics, and she was probably unable to accept the legality of her divorce.

Tissot's domestic arrangements cannot have been easy. While many artists of the day kept mistresses, few openly resided with them and none were represented in their

In his 1877 etching Tissot portrayed Kathleen Newton as the Irish heroine of the popular song, Kathleen Mavourneen.

A Convalescent (c.1876), showing the much featured colonnade in Tissot's garden.

paintings with the obsessive frequency with which Tissot turned to Kathleen Newton as both his principal model and muse. Conducting his six-year affair with a young divorcée with two illegitimate children and then brazenly exhibiting her on gallery walls, he soon found himself shunned by the very people he aspired to paint. Formerly a naturally gregarious man, he suddenly became an unwelcome guest, in some quarters regarded as a social outcast. He ceased to invite to his home many former friends who might have felt embarrassment at being in the presence of a couple 'living in sin', although his more bohemian and sympathetic associates were still welcomed. He became reclusive and isolated, seldom exhibiting his works and turning more and more to intimate domestic scenes, many of them featuring idealized images of Mrs Newton and her children. He also turned to works other than paintings, such as elaborate *cloisonné* enamels, copper and bronze vases and other objects with enamel embellishments, some based on his paintings, and issued his first volume of etchings. Between 1876 and 1886 he was to publish over eighty prints which, in many cases were derived from his paintings, and which were generally commercially successful.

After his affair with Kathleen Newton began, Tissot ceased to exhibit at the Royal Academy until 1881, although he did show at the newly opened Grosvenor Gallery from 1877 to 1879. In 1877 he exhibited ten paintings at the Grosvenor Gallery, alongside Whistler, neo-classical painters such as Alma-Tadema, Leighton and Poynter and Pre-Raphaelites Burne-Jones and Millais. John Ruskin's critique of the inaugural exhibition was notable for two reasons: firstly, his comments on Tissot's works, of which he declared, '. . . their dexterity and brilliance are apt to make the spectator forget their conscientiousness,' going on to remark that 'most of them are, unhappily, mere coloured photographs of vulgar society' (although he condescended to praise Tissot's *The Challenge*, the first of a planned allegorical series, *The Triumph of Will*). In the same review Ruskin published his now famous attack on Whistler, announcing that he '. . . never expected to hear a coxcomb

ask two hundred guineas for flinging a pot of paint in the public's face.' Believing that as Ruskin had slighted them both he would have an ally in Tissot, Whistler called upon him to act as a witness in his ensuing legal case against Ruskin (which Whistler won, but with the award of a derisory one farthing in damages). Tissot refused, however, as a result of which their long-standing friendship ended. It was not the only occasion on which Tissot acted insensitively where his friendships were concerned: Degas terminated theirs when Tissot sold paintings that he had given to him.

In May 1882 the Dudley Gallery in London staged an exhibition of the four paintings of Tissot's series *The Prodigal Son in Modern Life*, together with a photographic survey of his work since 1859. At the end of the same month Tissot visited Edmond and Jules de Goncourt in Paris to discuss with them the illustration of their novel, *Renée Mauperin*, several of the ten etchings for which were executed from photographs of himself and Kathleen Newton. By now she had been diagnosed as suffering from tuberculosis, and as she began to show signs of the illness, their activities were increasingly proscribed. Her seclusion began to give rise to far-fetched legends, such as that Tissot kept her locked up, a prisoner in his home, where she finally died on 9 November 1882. Within a week Tissot, distraught, abandoned the house, leaving his painting materials scattered on the floor, and travelled to France. Wild rumours of Kathleen Newton's life and death continued for more than fifty years (Arnold Bennett's *Journal*, for example, recording a fanciful story of her suicide after she mistakenly received a letter from Tissot announcing the end of their relationship). For a time Tissot was clearly unable to accept her loss, and it is a measure of his despair that her likeness continued to feature in his works. The house with its memories was too painful and he never lived there again; it was bought by Alma-Tadema, who converted it into a magnificent residence, decorating it in lavish Pompeian style.

The following year, 1883, Tissot had a one-man exhibition at the Palais de l'Industrie, Paris. Included in it were paintings, drawings, and his ever more important prints, as well as *cloisonné* enamels largely dating from his London decade. Although not at this time well known as a watercolourist, he also exhibited with the Societe d'Aquarellistes Français in the same year and subsequently.

Children in a Garden, Tissot's cloisonné *vase based on his painting* The Gardener *(c.1879).*

Tissot's memory of Mrs Newton did not totally usurp his interest in other women. It was said that he competed for the affections of the tightrope walker who appears in his *L'Acrobate*. It is believed also that he planned to marry Louise Riesener, the daughter of a painter, Louis Riesener, and, according to Edmond de Goncourt, added a floor to his Paris house in anticipation of this event before Mlle Riesener finally decided against it. But Kathleen Newton continued to haunt him – almost liter-

ally: early in 1885 Tissot met the professional spiritualist William Eglinton and on 20 May attended a seance organized by Eglinton (one of over 600 he conducted that year) at which, it was claimed by Eglinton's biographer, a spirit guide called 'Ernest' accompanied the ghost of Mrs Newton (euphemistically described as '. . . one whose sweet companionship had been his joy and solace in years gone by') into Tissot's presence. During their meeting, illuminated by Ernest's phantom torch, they kissed several times, then she shook hands with Tissot and dematerialised. There can be no doubt that Eglinton was a fraud, but Tissot was completely convinced, later producing a painting, *L'Apparition médiunimique* (now lost and known only as a print) as a record of the occasion, and providing illustrations for Eglinton's biography, *'Twixt Two Worlds*.

During Tissot's first two years back in Paris he had devoted himself to a series of paintings, exhibited there at the Gallerie Sedelmeyer in April to June 1885 under the title *Quinze Tableaux sur la Femme à Paris*. All but one of the paintings from the same series, under the title *Pictures of Parisian Life*, also appeared at the Tooth Gallery in London, the following year. The series was planned with the intention of publishing etched versions of the works accompanied by specially commissioned texts by distinguished French writers including Emile Zola and Guy de Maupassant. It was to be Tissot's last major venture as a painter of Society, for at its denouement he was plunged into yet another radical revision of his life. When he came to paint the last subject in this important series, *Musique sacrée*, a picture that has since disappeared, he took as his model a woman singing hymns in St Sulpice church. There, as he worked, so he later claimed, Tissot experienced a vision

Pastel portraits such as *Berthe* (c.1882) and his *La Femme à Paris* series represent Tissot's final works before his religious conversion.

of Christ that was to lead him into the final phase in his artistic career – his illustrations for *The Life of Christ* (*La Vie de Notre Seigneur Jésus Christ*) followed by his drawings for an illustrated Bible. This new endeavour clearly coincided with a complete reappraisal of his own life. Consequent to his liaison with Mrs Newton, his dabblings with spiritualism and other occult practices and mystical visions leading to religious conversion were greeted by his friends as interesting but scarcely unexpected. Cynical observers have noted that his conversion coincided fortuitously with general religious enthusiasm and the Catholic revival of the 1880s and 1890s, and the ever-adaptable Tissot certainly made a fortune capitalizing on the trend.

Tissot's aim was to show biblical locations as they really were, rather than as generations of artists had imagined them, and so, on his 50th birthday in 1886, he set off on a journey to Palestine to begin work on watercolour illustrations for his *The Life of Christ*, making extensive use of photography for reference. He returned to Paris in March 1887 and again travelled to the Middle East in 1889. In the same year he won a gold medal at the Paris Exposition Universelle where another 'moral' subject, his *The Prodigal Son in Modern Life* series, was shown and subsequently purchased for the Musée du Luxembourg's permanent collection. Tissot did not completely abandon his earthly interests, however, and in early 1890 was at work on a portrait of the actress Rejane.

In 1894, after eight years engaged in *The Life of Christ*, Tissot had produced 290 drawings, most of which were exhibited at the Salon du Champs-de-Mars in Paris. He showed the complete set of 365 in Paris in 1895 and in London in 1896. The monumental project was published by the firm Mame of Tours in 1896–97 and was an instant best seller. An English edition, *The Life of Our Saviour Jesus Christ*, translated by Mrs Arthur Bell and curiously dedicated to the former British Prime Minister William Gladstone, appeared in two volumes in 1897 and 1898. The watercolours were taken on a successful tour of North America in 1898–99, and in 1900 were acquired by the Brooklyn Museum, New York, where they remain.

To modern eyes Tissot's religious illustrations are of little appeal, and to those familiar with his earlier paintings, this body of work must have come as something of a surprise. However, to the many who were unaware of his previous career, these subjects were a revelation, admired by the religious establishment and the public alike. Tissot received official recognition for his achievement when he was made Chevalier of the Legion of Honour. The 'dealer of genius' earned one million francs for the French publishing rights alone to his *Life of Christ* illustrations as well as taking $100,000 from the North American tour and a further $60,000 for the sale of the original artwork to the Brooklyn Museum.

Though to many these images represented the apogee of Tissot's career, they were not its finale. In 1896 the British illustrator George Percy Jacomb-Hood was commissioned by *The Graphic* as an artist at the first modern Olympic Games in Athens. Inadvertently boarding the wrong ship, he found himself bound for Egypt. On the journey he noted that, '. . . a very interesting traveller . . . a very neatly-dressed, elegant figure with a grey military moustache and beard, always appeared on deck gloved and groomed as if for the boulevard.' He was, Jacomb-Hood later recalled, 'James Tissot, who was returning to Palestine to continue his wonderful series of illustrations of the Bible, to which he was devoting what remained to him of life.' At the age of sixty Tissot was embarking on yet another ambitious scheme, proposing to follow the success of his *Life of Christ* illustrations with a set of Old Testament drawings (now in the Jewish Museum, New York),

The Dead Appear in the Temple, one of Tissot's extraordinary illustrations to *The Life of Christ*.

exhibiting eighty of these, for the first of a projected four volumes, in Paris in 1901. From 1897 to 1902 Tissot divided his time between the Château of Buillon which he had inherited from his father, and his house in Paris, where he lived as a virtual recluse (although it is known that he received visitors, among them Alma-Tadema; Tissot subsequently visited London again and saw the transformation wrought by Alma-Tadema on his Grove End Road house).

He continued to work on his Old Testament drawings, but after producing half the intended total of 400, he died on 8 August 1902 at Buillon and was buried in the private chapel on his estate. Completed by other artists, *La Sainte Bible (Ancien Testament)* was published in 1904.

Born the year before Queen Victoria ascended the throne and dying the year after her, James Tissot's life neatly encompasses the Victorian age and to a remarkable extent mirrors its preoccupations and changes. Ironically, he was not regarded as a 'great' painter until, toward the end of his life, he produced the Biblical paintings that are nowadays his least regarded works. To the modern spectator it is as a painter of late Victorian society that he is without equal, best known for his depictions of elegant women in luxurious costumes. This is especially true of the work he produced during his London decade, a familiarity that is perhaps more a reflection of our own age, and our interest in the luxurious styles of a bygone era, than his. As a survey of his entire oeuvre reveals, his output was both more complex and diverse than these popular works imply. He was also highly prolific. In a working lifetime of some forty years he produced about three hundred finished paintings (albeit that some were replicas painted to capitalize on a successful subject), including many commissioned portraits, as well as some ninety etchings, drawings, book illustrations, caricatures, enamel and sculpture. This compares with the output of one of the nineteenth century's similarly industrious artists, Alma-Tadema, who produced four hundred paintings, but fewer ancillary works, and in a career that was ten years longer. Like Alma-Tadema too, Tissot composed his works painstakingly using models, both professional and amateur, often turning to photography to establish their poses, and with an extensive range of props that comprised a considerable wardrobe of splendid costumes. It is perhaps this later component – itself a product of his awareness of his family's business in the linen trade – that has contributed to the present-day appreciation of Tissot's work. Whether or not a painting contains a 'message', it is almost invariably a vehicle for Tissot to portray pretty women in a multiplicity of beautiful costumes, and often the same dress hat, shawl or other accessory reappears, sometimes in the same painting. His work has thus become a hunting ground for the fashion student, and a trap for the unwary, for although Tissot's paintings to some extent reflect the changing fashions of the age, the artist's own preferences are imposed upon them, and so they cannot be used with certainty as a chronologically accurate monitor of stylistic change.

Tissot's art drew on wide-ranging influences, from his mentor Leys in his early choice of historical and Roman-tic subjects, through Gustave Courbet's Realism, Japonism (Tissot was one of the first Europeans to take an interest in Japanese art) and the work of Manet and other contemporary painters. While admirers of Tissot's work today appreciate his eclectic interest in the diverse art movements of the nineteenth century, ranging from Pre-Raphaelitism to Impressionism, it was this very lack of focus that reduced his credibility among his contemporaries, many of whom thought his work derivative, verging on the plagiaristic. No exploitable motif escaped his attention and every new picture involved a trawling of his memory, his reference files and his catalogue of chic accoutrements, with the result that the charge has often been levelled that every Tissot painting was 'skilfully representative and utterly unimaginative', as Sacheverell Sitwell was to describe them.

It is arguable whether this is fair criticism. It is difficult – perhaps impossible – for anyone brought up in the twentieth century to see a Tissot, or any Victorian narrative painting, quite as it would have been seen by a visitor to a contemporary art gallery. Such a viewer would have been familiar with the nuances of genre painting that are often obscure to modern audiences, and would more readily have been able to interpret them (even if they failed to decipher the visual clues, paintings were generally individually described and their messages explained in nineteenth-century reviews). We also bring to bear our own aesthetic, coloured by the paintings having acquired, in the words of Tissot's biographer James Laver, the 'patina of period charm'. Inevitably our immediate impressions of his works tend to be confined to their surface appeal and the subjects he portrayed. The 'typical' – or rather, to twentieth-century eyes, most appealing – Tissot depicts a woman or women, perhaps alone, perhaps in the company of men, going about some congenial activity. He focuses his gaze on the daily lives of privileged classes to the almost total exclusion of landscapes or still-lifes and, like the modern writer of television drama, creates appropriate settings for social interaction by placing his subjects in precisely those locations where such people naturally gathered. As a result, soirées, balls, picnics, travel by boat and train, cafés, restaurants and the circus predominate in his work.

During his productive years, a debate was raging about whether art should elevate and hence whether it was therefore appropriate to paint such ordinary, everyday subjects, rather than to deal with 'important' themes that might appeal to or excite the emotions or raise moral issues. Tissot's moralizing was limited (he was too commercially minded to offend his Society clients), so the dilemmas he posed might be of the level of a woman torn between two admirers; not for him the raw social commentary of a

Painted for *The Life of Christ*, Tissot's melancholy *Portrait of the Pilgrim* depicts himself as a religious enthusiast.

Courbet. His stand-point – especially in the paintings he executed during his London decade – was rather that of the observer of the social mores of the age, a stance facilitated in the 1870s by his situation as a Frenchman working in London, inside the social milieu, but at the same time an outsider. To him this was an advantage. Tissot, again like Alma-Tadema, was in the position of being able to exploit his foreign-ness; being himself unplaced in the English class structure excluded him from involvement in any sort of debate on the class mechanism and freed him to present on canvas his detached observations of the British social scene.

During Tissot's London period Victorian Society was in a state of disarray. As result of the rapid social upheavals brought about by the Industrial Revolution, the newly rich in particular found themselves uncertain of their place within a much older class structure, nervous about their elevated status and often ill at ease in the social gatherings in which they found themselves, like guests who have turned up at the wrong party, afraid that they are wearing the wrong clothes, or wishing they had not turned up at all. Paradoxically, embarrassed, languid, bored characters occupy some of Tissot's most popular canvases; women wear characteristically vacant expressions and seldom look toward the people they are with, but beyond, perhaps out of the canvas, in an eternal quest for someone, something, anything more interesting. As in works such as *The Ball on Shipboard*, apparently socially well-placed men and women, precursors of the jet set (the steam set, perhaps), who might generally be the subjects of envy, are evidently not having much fun. These are people killing time, scarcely enjoying their leisure, but going through the motions simply because it is expected of them. This, in an often wryly humorous way, seems to be one of Tissot's most characteristic intents. There is a further social comment on the rigidity and awkwardness of etiquette, wittily observed, for example, in *Too Early*, where we are invited to witness the perpetrators of the *faux pas* of arriving unfashionably early rather than fashionably late, and to share in their embarrassment.

Alongside such social commentary, Tissot was primarily a passionate observer of fashionable women. Be they Society ladies, widows, convalescents, discontented wives or the mistresses of older men, women predominate in his work. Their place in Society is constantly re-emphasized through visual tokens of middle-class etiquette: men extending helping hands, women taking their escort's arm, beautiful women as the centre of attention, while the subjects themselves frequently gaze out as if seeking escape from their rigid constraints in this repressed and patriarchal society.

Even if they are light on 'message', a Tissot is always memorable, always displays artistic skill and artifice in compositions that are undeniably pleasing to the eye. The arresting and sometimes enigmatic charm of his work has retained its ability to beguile despite the divide of more than a century, and for this reason alone he has become established as one of the most enduringly fascinating of all nineteenth-century painters.

The fashionable woman in contemporary Society, as exemplified by *At the Rifle Range* (1869).

Like the child that rebels against the values of its parents, the early years of the twentieth century saw a general reaction against the Victorian era. Its fashions, architecture, furniture and especially its art were generally rejected. Paralleling this, Tissot's death, coinciding as it did with the close of the period, was followed by an almost instant eclipse of interest in his work, and for thirty years or more he was consigned to the ranks of the forgotten. A revival occurred with a short-lived vogue for Victorian narrative painting in the 1930s. The first manifestation, in 1933, was an exhibition at the Leicester Galleries in London devoted to Tissot's work. This same exhibition was also to inspire the art and costume historian James Laver to write *Vulgar Society*, the first biography of Tissot, published in 1936. Sacheverell Sitwell's *Narrative Pictures*, published the following year, acknowledged Tissot's importance, while recognizing that much of his appeal lay in what Laver had termed his 'romantic career'. After the Second World War the identity of Kathleen Newton was gradually established, the circumstances of their relationship and her early death adding a further romantic frisson to Tissot's life. Among important post-war exhibitions of Tissot's work have been those organized by the Graves Art Gallery, Sheffield, in 1955, by the Rhode Island School of Design, Providence, and the Art Gallery of Ontario, Toronto, in 1968, and at the Barbican Art Gallery, London, and elsewhere in 1984–85. Allied with the resurgence of interest in Tissot's life and work has come, almost inevitably, a colossal surge in the price of his paintings. As if to fulfil Laver's prophesy that Tissot's art would, in the fullness of time, acquire what he termed the 'patina of period charm', his pictures are now among the most desired, the most admired and the most frequently reproduced of all Victorian paintings.

THE PLATES

~

1 MLLE L. L. . . (JEUNE FILLE EN VESTE ROUGE)

2 JAPONAISE AU BAIN

3 LE PRINTEMPS

4 UNE VEUVE

5 L'ESCALIER

6 JEUNES FEMMES REGARDANT DES OBJETS JAPONAIS

7 A GIRL IN AN ARMCHAIR (THE CONVALESCENT)

8 COLONEL FREDERICK BURNABY

9 JEUNE FEMME EN BATEAU

10 JEUNE FEMME A L'EVENTAIL

11 ON THE THAMES, A HERON

12 LE THÉ

13 M. LE CAPITAINE ***

14 THE RETURN FROM THE BOATING TRIP

15 THE LAST EVENING

16 THE CAPTAIN'S DAUGHTER

17 TOO EARLY

18 THE BALL ON SHIPBOARD

19 LONDON VISITORS

20 READING THE NEWS

21 STILL ON TOP

22 HUSH!

23 THE BUNCH OF LILACS

24 A PORTRAIT (MISS LLOYD)

25 THE THAMES

26 A PASSING STORM

27 HOLYDAY (THE PICNIC)

28 THE CHAPPLE-GILL FAMILY OF LOWER LEA, WOOLTON

29 THE GALLERY OF HMS CALCUTTA (PORTSMOUTH)

30 JULY (SPECIMEN OF A PORTRAIT)

31 IN THE CONSERVATORY (RIVALS)

32 THE LETTER

33 GOODBYE – ON THE MERSEY

34 LE BANC DE JARDIN

35 L'AMBITIEUSE

36 CES DAMES DES CHARS

37 LA DEMOISELLE D'HONNEUR

38 LES FEMMES D'ARTISTE

39 LES FEMMES DE SPORT

40 LA DEMOISELLE DE MAGASIN

MLLE L. L . . .
(JEUNE FILLE EN VESTE ROUGE/YOUNG
WOMAN IN A RED JACKET)
———— 1864 ————
Oil on canvas, 48¾ × 39¼ in / 124.0 × 100.0 cm
Musée d'Orsay, Paris

Painted in February 1864, Tissot's first exhibited work
of a modern subject was shown at the Paris Salon of
that year and marks his successful move away from
historical costume pieces. Like his *Les deux soeurs* (*The
Two Sisters*), which was exhibited at the same time,
Tissot described it as a portrait, presumably to solicit
profitable portrait commissions, but the presence of the
same girl in *Les deux soeurs* and *Le printemps* (*Spring*)
suggests that she was in fact a professional model. While
the pose and other elements of the painting follow established artistic traditions, its principal components assert
its modernity: the girl's jacket, the *veste rouge* of the
title, was currently in vogue but was regarded as a
somewhat 'racy' garment. Known as a Zouave bolero,
it owed its inspiration to the Zouaves, the French colo-
nial troops whose colourful uniforms were later to
feature in works by Vincent van Gogh. The bobble
fringe was also widely used in soft furnishings of the
period, and can be seen here bordering the curtains.
The intellectual background of Tissot's sitter is hinted
at by the collection of artefacts, the clutter of books
and a portfolio of prints (leading one reviewer to
speculate that the sitter '. . . perhaps had blue stockings beneath the folds of her black skirt'). Tucked into
the frame of the mirror a *carte de visite* photograph,
another currently fashionable article, further emphasizes the painting's modernity and heralds Tissot's later
debt to photography.

PLATE 1

JAPONAISE AU BAIN
(JAPANESE GIRL BATHING)
——————1864——————
Oil on canvas, 82¼ × 49 in / 208.9 × 124.5 cm
Musée des Beaux-Arts, Dijon

In a letter of 12 November 1864 the Pre-Raphaelite painter Dante Gabriel Rossetti told his mother that he had visited a shop in the rue de Rivoli, Paris, where a Madame Desoye sold Japanese items, '. . . but found all the costumes were being snapped up by a French artist Tissot, who, it seems, is doing three Japanese pictures, which the mistress of the shop described to me as the three wonders of the world, evidently in her opinion quite throwing Whistler into the shade'. Tissot, like Whistler, was evidently already recognized as an enthusiast for things Japanese, particularly fascinated and influenced by the Japanese prints that were then becoming widely collected. Since no one in Europe was well informed about Japanese art at this time, however, works by artists such as Tissot often presented a quaint amalgam of Western and Eastern art, as in *Japonaise au bain*, where a decidedly European woman poses as a coquettish Geisha amid a jumble of superficially oriental paraphernalia, painted in a totally European style. It was not Tissot's only sortie into Japanese-inspired territory, an interest that was curiously reciprocated when he was later appointed as drawing teacher to the Japanese Prince Akitake Tokugawa, who was studying in Paris in the late 1860s.

PLATE 2

LE PRINTEMPS (SPRING)

———— 1865 ————

Oil on canvas (laid on panel) 35½ × 50 in / 90.2 × 127.0 cm
Private collection

The artistic crossroads Tissot had reached in 1865 was
exemplified by the two works he showed at the Paris
Salon that year: *Tentative d'enlèvement* (*Attempted Abduction*), depicting medieval swordsmen engaged in a skirmish, which represented the last years of his medieval
period, and *Le printemps* which marked his new, Pre-
Raphaelite-inspired transition into modern subjects.
With affinities to *Les deux soeurs* which preceded it,
reviewers also noted its resemblance to a painting by
John Everett Millais, known as *Apple Blossoms* but originally also entitled *Spring*. Whether the similarity is
deliberate or coincidental is uncertain. Millais' painting, which depicts a more crowded scene (it shows a
group of eight girls reclining in an orchard), was sold
by Ernest Gambart, the same dealer who handled Tissot's work in England; but it left his gallery before Tissot's first visit to London, so unless Gambart took the
painting to Paris, Tissot presumably knew it only from
photographs. Tissot's *Le printemps* was also exhibited in
London in 1866.

PLATE 3

UNE VEUVE (A WIDOW)
—————— 1868 ——————
Oil on canvas, 27 × 19½ in / 68.6 × 49.5 cm
Private collection

Painted in 1868 and shown at the Paris Salon the following year, Tissot's image of a young widow is a visual
representation of a popular theme in nineteenth-century literature. Artists such as the Belgian Alfred Stevens
even made a speciality of the subject, which became
one to which Tissot returned. In *Une veuve* the rich
trappings on the tables and the glimpse of the formal
gardens and substantial château behind establish the
widow's wealth, while her dreamy expression indicates
the drift of her thoughts during the tense, prolonged
period prescribed by formal Victorian mourning.
Bouchardon's *Cupid Stringing his Bow* symbolizes her
anticipation of finding a new love. Her position physically between the restless child and tranquil elderly
lady emphasizes her own status and eligibility, lying
somewhere between lively youth and the restraints
imposed by the advance of maturity. As in the works
of the Impressionists, the garden location was to feature strongly in Tissot's subsequent work, and during
his London period had a special significance as a
symbol of his private world.

PLATE 4

L'ESCALIER (THE STAIRCASE)
— 1869 —
Oil on canvas, 20 × 14 in / 50.8 × 35.6 cm
Sutton Place Foundation

A preparatory pencil sketch for this work does not
include the books and letter that Tissot added to the
painting to emphasize the enigmatic nature of the scene.
Images of women at windows were popular themes in
nineteenth-century art, but we have no further clues
as to whether the woman is anticipating a visitor's arrival
or yearning for a departed lover. Painted in Tissot's
grand Paris studio, the bobble-fringed white dress is in
a similar style to the jacket featured in his portrait *Mme
L. L . . .* of five years earlier, and appears again in such
works as *Mélancolie* and two versions of *Jeunes femmes
regardant des objets japonais*.

PLATE 5

Jeunes Femmes Regardant des Objets Japonais (Young Ladies Looking at Japanese Objects)

——————1869——————

Oil on canvas, 28 × 20 in / 71.1 × 50.8 cm
Cincinnati Art Museum, Gift of Henry M. Goodyear, MD

Tissot's interest in *japonisme*, like that of his contemporaries and friends, among them Whistler, Alfred Stevens, Manet and Degas, was manifested in no fewer than three paintings showing young women peering at Japanese objects, two of which depict the same models, one wearing the white dress seen in *L'Escalier*. All were painted in Tissot's house and apparently represented treasures from his own growing collection. During the 1860s Tissot came to be regarded as one of the foremost collectors of Japanese art, then at the height of fashion, but critics commented – and he himself perhaps recognized – the limitations of creating paintings merely as vehicles to display his oriental treasures. As one writer noted, whether it was 'Young ladies looking at Japanese objects or Japanese objects looking at young ladies,' it amounted to the same rather restricted result.

PLATE 6

A GIRL IN AN ARMCHAIR
(THE CONVALESCENT)
———————— 1870 ————————
Oil on panel, 14¾ × 18 in / 37.5 × 45.7 cm
The Art Gallery of Ontario, Toronto,
Gift of R. B. F. Barr, Esq., QC, 1966

Although identified by some authorities as a work
dating from 1872 (and hence after Tissot's move to
London), it seems certain that it was painted in 1870.
The girl wears a dress in a style popular in the 1860s,
and her pallid appearance and melancholy demeanour
have led to the painting's acquiring the alternative title
The Convalescent – thus establishing it as the first of many
Tissot produced on the theme of the ailing woman. The
subject was popular in the works of Pre-Raphaelite and
other nineteenth-century painters and in the literature
of the day, and was to prove tragically prophetic when
Tissot's own mistress, Kathleen Newton, became
terminally ill.

PLATE 7

COLONEL FREDERICK BURNABY
──────── 1870 ────────
Oil on panel, 19½ × 22¼ in / 49.5 × 56.7 cm
National Portrait Gallery, London

Colonel Frederick Gustavus Burnaby (1842–85), a
cavalry officer, was one of the great heroes of the Victorian age, a larger-than-life figure noted for his strength
and intrepid overseas adventures. In 1870, the year
Tissot painted this striking portrait, Burnaby had travelled to Odessa via St Petersburg. He wrote popular
accounts of his exploits, among them *A Ride to Khiva*
(1876) and *On Horseback through Asia Minor* (1877), while
A Ride Across the Channel (1882) recounts his solo
balloon flight across the English Channel. While on
active service in the Sudan, he was involved in the
British attempt to relieve Khartoum, where he died
from a spear wound. In the late 1860s both Burnaby
and Tissot had been closely associated with *Vanity Fair*
(the title of which, taken from John Bunyan's *Pilgrim's
Progress*, Burnaby himself had suggested, and he was one
of the original investors in the magazine). Its editor,
Thomas Gibson Bowles, commissioned this portrait,
although Burnaby was known to be sensitive about his
somewhat coarse and swarthy features and disliked
having his portrait painted. It is clear from contemporary photographs, however, that Tissot flattered
Burnaby's appearance to make him seem every inch the
handsome gentleman soldier. Although a relatively
small painting, its skilful composition and extraordinary detail made it one of Tissot's most popular works,
its success leading to many other lucrative society
portrait commissions.

PLATE 8

Jeune Femme en Bateau
(Young Lady in a Boat)

c.1870

Oil on canvas, 14¼ × 25½ in / 50.2 × 64.8 cm
Private collection

Effectively a riverside reprise of *Rêverie* (private collection), this work similarly depicts a solitary, pensive woman with a pug dog in a pleasingly rich composition. Exhibited at the Salon in 1870, it was one of Tissot's last works to be exhibited before the outbreak of the Franco-Prussian War. While pre-dating it, Tissot's painting is compositionally remarkably similar to Manet's *Boating* of 1874 (Metropolitan Museum of Art, New York).

PLATE 9

JEUNE FEMME A L'EVENTAIL
(YOUNG LADY WITH A FAN)
———————— c.1870–71 ————————
Oil on panel, 31 × 23 in/78.7 × 58.4 cm
Private collection

Jeune femme à l'éventail, like its counterpart *A la rivière* (*On the River*) dates from Tissot's Directoire period, and both feature the same model. The hat with striped ribbon also appears in several other works of the same period, including *Jeune femme en bateau*. Both paintings depict a blend of the *femme fatale* popular in the paintings of the Pre-Raphaelites and other nineteenth-century artists and the free-thinking independent woman sometimes found in Victorian literature, signalling her rejection of the restraints of the era's morality and etiquette by her impudent manner and audacious costume.

PLATE 10

ON THE THAMES, A HERON

————————— *c.* 1871–72 —————————

Oil on canvas, 36½ × 23¾ in / 92.7 × 60.33 cm

Minneapolis Institute of Arts, Gift of Mrs Patrick Butler

Another of Tissot's paintings started soon after he settled in London, its composition owes a considerable debt to his continuing studies of the principles of Japanese design. The bobble-fringed shawl reappears in *A Convalescent* of *c.* 1876 (Sheffield City Art Galleries). It is a measure of Tissot's rapidly growing popularity that while this work was sold at Christie's in 1873 for £598, within a year his paintings were typically fetching in excess of £1,000.

PLATE 11

LE THÉ (TEA-TIME)
1872
Oil on panel, 26 × 18½ in / 66.0 × 47.0 cm
Private collection

Like Alma-Tadema, Tissot occasionally re-worked portions of his successful paintings to create new pictures. *Le Thé* is a modification of the left half of his painting *Bad News* (*The Parting*) (National Museum of Wales, Cardiff), also dating from 1872 and shown at the London International Exhibition that year. By deleting the additional male and female figures that establish the narrative content of the latter work, Tissot here creates a genre painting with no specific 'story'. One of several similar works from the same period, each depicts a city riverscape, characteristically with docked sailing vessels (although *Bad News* is set beside a rural river bank). Other minor details have been altered· the pierced sided silver tray in *Bad News* has been replaced by a flat one with feet, for example, and the design of the teapot has become more obviously Georgian. A pencil drawing of *Le Thé* (private collection), known by the misleading title *Young Lady Pouring Coffee*, was inscribed 'à mon ami Degas' and sent to him as a gift.

PLATE 12

M. LE CAPITAINE ✳✳✳
(GENTLEMAN IN A RAILWAY CARRIAGE)
c.1872

Oil on panel, 26 × 17 in/63.3 × 43.0 cm
Worcester Art Museum, Massachusetts,
Alexander and Caroline Murdock De Witt Fund

The railway featured in nineteenth-century painting as
a symbol of the modern age, in landscapes showing
belching steam trains from Turner's *Rain, Steam and
Speed* (1844) through the works of Impressionists such
as Pissarro and Monet to the narrative paintings of
William Powell Frith and the more intimate genre paintings of travellers in carriage interiors, as in Abraham
Solomon's *First Class* (1854) and Augustus Leopold Egg's
Travelling Companions (1862). Tissot's portrait was
described by the critic Jules Claretie as 'a gentleman
seated in a carriage, dressed as a tourist and reading a
book, *Bradshaw*'s guide or the *Guide Joanne*'. Claretie
went on to comment on what he regarded as Tissot's
'endless tendency to pastiche Millais or Mulready after
having imitated Leys'.

PLATE 13

THE RETURN FROM THE BOATING TRIP
—————— 1873 ——————
Oil on canvas, 24 × 17 in / 60.9 × 43.2 cm
Private collection

The setting for this work, one of several of women in
Thames locations, appears to be on the Thames alongside Maidenhead bridge. The model has been identified
as Margaret Freebody, *née* Kennedy, the wife of John
Freebody, a sea captain whom Tissot befriended in
London. He often painted on board vessels that Freebody commanded and featured Margaret and her brother, Captain Lumley Kennedy, in several paintings. The
splendid black-and-white striped dress is seen again in
such works as *Boarding the Yacht*, *The Captain and the
Mate* and *Still on Top* and the red tartan travelling rug
reappears in various paintings. The lady's raffish boating companion wears long 'dundreary' whiskers, then
fashionable but already becoming regarded as a somewhat comical adornment.

PLATE 14

The Last Evening
— 1873 —
Oil on canvas, 28 × 40 in/71.1 × 101.6 cm
Guildhall Art Gallery, London

In the early 1870s Tissot's knowledge of nautical paraphernalia and his consummate skill in painting stylish women in exquisite costumes were turned to successful advantage with a sequence of works featuring both motifs, set principally in Thames locations. *The Captain and the Mate* and *The Last Evening*, both of which were painted in 1873, are variations on the same general theme of lovers engaged in some unspecified confrontation, with Margaret Freebody and her brother, Captain Lumley Kennedy, appearing as the two principal players in both works. As in many of Tissot's most striking paintings, however, the tense events that appear to be unfolding seem superficially to locate them in the British narrative tradition, but with storylines so tenuous or ambiguous as to leave the viewer questioning what human drama is actually being revealed.

PLATE 15

THE CAPTAIN'S DAUGHTER
————— 1873 —————
Oil on canvas, 28½ × 41¼ in/72.4 × 104.8 cm
Southampton City Art Gallery

The Captain's Daughter was exhibited at the Royal Academy in 1873, along with *The Last Evening*, a painting to which it has certain affinities, but with a more obvious narrative content. To James Laver, the author of the first twentieth-century biography of Tissot, '*The Captain's Daughter* is an extraordinarily competent piece of work. The outwardly composed, but inwardly tormented face of the girl, the reverent yet obviously appraising expression of the young man, the wise, kindly look of the old man, who is obviously urging him to marry her, show Tissot's power of observation at its best.' The setting is probably the Falcon Tavern, Gravesend, the location of *Waiting for the Ferry at the Falcon Tavern* (*c.*1874, J. B. Speed Art Museum, Louisville), and the female model Margaret Freebody, the protagonist from such pictures as *The Captain and the Mate* and *The Last Evening*. At about the same time, Tissot also produced a variation of the painting as *L'Auberge des Trois-Corbeaux* (*The Three Crows Inn, Gravesend*) (National Gallery of Art, Dublin), and later an etching with the same title.

PLATE 16

516

TOO EARLY
—— 1873 ——
Oil on canvas, 28 × 40 in/71.1 × 101.6 cm
Guildhall Art Gallery, London

One of Tissot's friends, the artist Louise Jopling, recalled in her autobiography that when it was shown at the Royal Academy in 1873, *Too Early* 'made a great sensation'. It was, she reckoned, 'a new departure in art, this witty representation of modern life'. Rated as one of Tissot's greatest masterpieces and among his most important 'social conversation pieces', it actually depicts a frozen moment of acute social embarrassment among a handful of guests who have arrived prematurely, before the party is in full swing. Each attempts to mask his or her awkwardness: as the hostess discusses the music with the musicians and servants smirk round the door, women toy with their fans and everyone gazes at the floor or into the middle distance to avoid eye-contact. *Les Demoiselles de province* in Tissot's later *La Femme à Paris* series contains a similar group of figures to those in the centre of this very popular work.

PLATE 17

THE BALL ON SHIPBOARD

c.1874

Oil on canvas, 33 × 51 in/84.1 × 129.5 cm

Tate Gallery, London

Sacheverell Sitwell (*Narrative Pictures*, 1937) suggested to his readers that *The Ball on Shipboard,* one of Tissot's most ambitious and successful paintings, depicted a dance on board the royal yacht, the *Victoria and Albert,* at Cowes on the Isle of Wight in 1873 and featured a woman who might be Queen Alexandra with 'Czar Alexander II; or it might be Lord Londonderry'. In fact, it seems more likely that it is a composite work executed in Tissot's studio, using flags, chairs, costumes and other props that reappear in other paintings. The models recur within the work, the same pair of women appearing no fewer than four times, and the same dresses in different parts of the picture. Tissot's background made him thoroughly familiar with ships and marine accoutrements, and his nautical paintings could not be faulted for their precise detail, but the painting was much criticized when it was exhibited at the Royal Academy, the *Athenaeum* declaring that it contained 'no pretty women, but a set of showy rather than elegant costumes'. Today it stands out as one of the most vivid portrayals of Victorians at play, although one with clear overtones of their boredom: trapped on board the ship, they gaze around looking for diversion, while the actual revelry of the ball is suggested rather than depicted.

PLATE 18

LONDON VISITORS

c.1874

Oil on canvas, 63 × 45 in / 160.0 × 114.3 cm
Toledo Museum of Art, Ohio, Gift of Edward Drummond Libbey

Tissot executed several paintings in which London landmarks served as a theatrical backdrop to some everyday event. In this unusually large painting for Tissot,
we are looking into the portico of the National Gallery
in Trafalgar Square, facing St Martin-in-the-Fields. The
boys are wearing the uniform of Christ's Hospital
school, known as the 'Blue Coat School' from the distinctive coats worn with yellow stockings. Although a
number of critics have noted the painting's detached
quality (one contemporary reviewer writing in the
Illustrated London News referring to its 'arctic frigidity'),
the chill grey London atmosphere is brilliantly evoked.
A second, smaller version of the work (Layton Art
Gallery, Milwaukee), has minor variations (the time on
the clock, for example), while in an etched version of
1878 Tissot deleted the boys and added in the foreground the figure of his mistress, Kathleen Newton,
carrying an artist's portfolio. Shown at the Royal
Academy in 1874, the painting was greeted with in-
comprehension by critics who searched in vain for
what the *Art Journal* referred to as some 'distinct and
intelligible meaning'.

PLATE 19

Reading the News

c.1874

Oil on canvas, 34½ × 21 in / 87.6 × 53.3 cm
Richard Green Gallery, London

This striking composition presents the somewhat puzzling juxtaposition of an elderly Chelsea pensioner preoccupied with his newspaper while an elegant lady poses in a window – in fact, the bay window of Tissot's own house in Grove End Road, St John's Wood, to which he had moved in 1873. In keeping with his custom of repeating successful elements from his paintings, the female model wears the dress that is seen twice in the centre of *The Ball on Shipboard* and a hat that often appears in other works.

PLATE 20

STILL ON TOP
*c.*1874
Oil on canvas, 34½ × 21 in/87.6 × 53.3 cm
Auckland City Art Gallery

While it is clear that *Still on Top* was painted in
Tissot's garden, with its pergola behind the woman in
the familiar striped dress, it is not known whether the
title refers to some topical catchphrase or if the flags
are being raised to celebrate a specific event. The theme
of an elegant woman with a mass of festive flags was
successfully repeated in Tissot's *A Fête Day at Brighton*,
*c.*1875–78 (private collection).

PLATE 21

526

HUSH!

——— *c.1875* ———

Oil on canvas, 29 × 44 in / 73.7 × 111.8 cm
Manchester City Art Galleries

Like *Too Early* and *The Ball on Shipboard*, *Hush!* portrays
a social drama acted out according to the niceties of
Victorian etiquette, but with none of the guests apparently enjoying themselves. The scene has been identified as a factual occasion, a party Tissot attended at the
the home of the Coope family at which Wilhelmine
Neruda (Lady Hallé) played violin, though in the absence
of permission to depict the guests, he produced what
he claimed were anonymous portraits. Nevertheless,
the identities of some of the people have been suggested: the pianist may be Sir Julius Benedict, a friend
of Tissot's, with other friends, the artists Giuseppe de
Nittis and Ferdinand Heilbuth, in the doorway.

PLATE 22

528

THE BUNCH OF LILACS

———— *c.1875* ————

Oil on canvas, 20 × 14 in/50.8 × 35.6 cm

Richard Green Gallery, London

Perhaps the most typical of all Tissot's paintings is that in which a beautiful woman occupies the picture or takes centre stage, wearing a fashionable costume and accompanied by such decorative accessories as brightly coloured flags or, as here, lush vegetation in a conservatory, an exotic bird-cage and a large bunch of flowers. *A Girl in an Armchair* and *In the Conservatory* (*The Rivals*) similarly present luxurious foliage backgrounds.

PLATE 23

A PORTRAIT (MISS LLOYD)
——————— 1876 ———————
Oil on canvas, 36 × 20 in / 91.4 × 50.8 cm
Tate Gallery, London

Originally exhibited as *Miss L . . .*, she has been identified as a professional model, Miss Lloyd, whose dress
was presumably kept among Tissot's properties, since
it reappears during the next two years in other paintings, such as *The Gallery of HMS Calcutta* and worn by
Kathleen Newton in *July* and *Spring*. The same subject,
in reverse, was also published as an etching, with the
extended title, 'A Door Must Be Either Open or Shut'
(derived from a well-known French comedy).

PLATE 24

THE THAMES
—— *c.1876* ——
Oil on canvas, 28½ × 42¼ in/72.7 × 107.3 cm
Wakefield Art Gallery and Museums

Like his earlier *Boarding the Yacht* and later *Portsmouth Dockyard*, *The Thames* is another of Tissot's 'triangular' subjects, with, to the Victorian mind, powerful sexual innuendo lurking beneath the surface: the image of one man with two unchaperoned women, three bottles of champagne and a large picnic hamper hinted at nothing less than a debauched bacchanalian revel to come. 'Thoroughly and wilfully vulgar . . . ugly and lowbred women' was the reaction of the *Athenaeum* when this work was exhibited at the Royal Academy in 1876. The sense of outrage was shared by *The Times* ('questionable material'), the *Graphic* ('hardly nice in its suggestions') and the *Spectator* ('undeniably Parisian ladies' – a euphemism that then amounted to calling them prostitutes). This critical response, together with his newly established involvement with Kathleen Newton, perhaps contributed to Tissot's decision to withdraw from exhibiting at the Royal Academy during the next five years.

PLATE 25

A PASSING STORM
—— c.1876 ——
Oil on canvas, 30 × 40 in/76.2 × 101.6 cm
Beaverbrook Art Gallery, Fredericton, New Brunswick

A Passing Storm is the first of Tissot's paintings defi-nitely to feature Kathleen Newton, with whom he began his liaison in about 1876. The title is one of several similar ones popular in Tissot's work and in nineteenth-century narrative painting in general in which the metaphor of weather is used to refer both to the actual environment and to the emotional background – here, we are to assume, a lovers' tiff. The location has been identified as Harbour Parade (formerly Goldsmid Place), Ramsgate. The same view is employed in his drawing, *Ramsgate* (Tate Gallery, London), which omits the figures, a print of the same title and another paint-ing, *Room Overlooking the Harbour* (private collection).

PLATE 26

HOLYDAY (THE PICNIC)
——————— c.1876 ———————
Oil on canvas, 46½ × 30¼ in / 118.1 × 76.8 cm
Tate Gallery, London

First exhibited at the Grosvenor Gallery in May 1877, this work, which was presumably painted during the late summer of the previous year, excited the displeasure of Oscar Wilde. In his review, published in *Dublin University Magazine*, he referred to '. . . overdressed, common-looking people', and was particularly vehement about the '. . . ugly, painfully accurate representation of modern soda-water bottles'. The old lady in the red shawl recalls the companion painting, *A Convalescent* of *c.*1876 (Sheffield City Art Galleries), a remarkably similar composition which is also sited beside Tissot's colonnaded garden pool. The couple in the background of the painting adjacent to the colonnade echo those who are the subject of Tissot's *Quarrelling* (private collection), which dates from the same period. The distinctive black, red and gold striped caps of two of the men in the painting identify them as members of the I Zingari cricket club. Founded after a match at Harrow in 1845, it became one of the most successful 'wandering' clubs (that is, without a home club base), its name aptly deriving from the Italian for 'the gypsies'. The proximity of Tissot's St John's Wood house to Lord's Cricket Ground presumably suggested their inclusion as guests at this typically English summer gathering.

PLATE 27

THE CHAPPLE-GILL FAMILY OF
LOWER LEA, WOOLTON
-------- 1877 --------
Oil on canvas, 60½ × 40¾ in / 154.6 × 103.5 cm
National Museums and Galleries on Merseyside,
The Walker Art Gallery

Tissot's Society portrait commissions were an important source of his income during his London decade.
This subject, which depicts Katherine Chapple-Gill, her
son Robert and daughter Helen, was painted over a
period of two months at the family's home in south
Liverpool. During Tissot's stay, he reputedly developed
a strong affection for Mrs Chapple-Gill, but was by now
deeply involved with Kathleen Newton. The 'family'
of the title ironically omits Katherine's husband, who
presumably commissioned the portrait.

PLATE 28

The Gallery of *HMS Calcutta*
(Portsmouth)

*c.*1877

Oil on canvas, 27 × 36¼ in / 68.6 × 92.1 cm

Tate Gallery, London

Tissot's final maritime subject was produced both as a painting and an etching. The latter bore the subtitle 'Souvenir of a Ball on Shipboard', implying that the subject represented another part of the vessel featured in his 1874 painting, *The Ball on Shipboard*. Another of his romantic triangles, the viewer's standpoint allows us to see the man's longing gaze directed at the woman in the foreground; since she has deployed her fan, however, neither party can see the other. *HMS Calcutta* was one of the ten paintings Tissot exhibited at the first Grosvenor Gallery exhibition of 1877 which collectively incited John Ruskin to dismiss his work as 'mere coloured photographs of vulgar society'

PLATE 29

542

JULY (SPECIMEN OF A PORTRAIT) (SEA-SIDE)

———c.1878———

Oil on canvas, 34 × 24 in/86.4 × 61.0 cm
Private collection

Kathleen Newton poses against a window wearing the dress familiar from such works as *Miss Lloyd*, *The Gallery of HMS Calcutta* and *A Passing Storm*. Ramsgate lighthouse appears in the background of this version of the painting, but not in another, slightly smaller replica, in which Mrs Newton's hairstyle and other details are also slightly modified, though both were clearly set in the same room used for *A Passing Storm*. The affinity of this work with the classical images of drowsy women painted by Albert Moore has been noted by several art historians, and it perhaps represents the closest Tissot comes to adopting the principles of the Aesthetic Movement.

PLATE 30

IN THE CONSERVATORY (RIVALS)

c. 1875–78

Oil on canvas, 16¾ × 21¼ in / 42.6 × 54.0 cm

Private collection

Costumes from *The Ball on Shipboard* are reprised in this rich work, another of Tissot's forays into enigmatic territory. The original title of the painting is not recorded, but *Rivals*, the alternative title it has acquired, seems apt enough if we are intended to infer that the identically dressed twins are competing for the man who has retreated from the combat zone by engaging in small-talk with their mother. The splendid conservatory, with its magnificent bird cage, repeats elements of *The Bunch of Lilacs*.

PLATE 31

THE LETTER

—c.1876–78—
Oil on canvas, 28¼ × 42¼ in/71.8 × 107.3 cm
National Gallery of Canada, Ottawa

The mysterious letter, a crucial component of many a
Victorian novel, is here the focus of a puzzle to which
Tissot offers no solution, but we are left in little doubt
that its arrival is ominous. The sense of foreboding is
emphasized by the autumnal chestnut leaves for which
Tissot clearly had a particular fondness and which appear
in works such as *October* and provide a melancholy
background to *A Convalescent*.

PLATE 32

GOODBYE – ON THE MERSEY

———————— *c.*1881————————

Oil on canvas, 33 × 21 in / 83.8 × 53.3 cm

The Forbes Magazine Collection, New York

Emigration was a recurring theme in nineteenth-century art, and for Tissot, with his special interest in nautical locations, it must have been irresistible. His *Emigrants* of *c.*1873 (private collection) mirrors the well-known image of the mother and bundled child in Ford Madox Brown's *The Last of England*, placed against a background comprising a complex tangle of ships' masts and rigging. *Goodbye – On the Mersey*, in which Kathleen Newton is the focus of attention, is on a grander scale and contains less pathos, but its broodingly grey sky and sombre colours evoke the sadness of departure. After being shown at the Royal Academy in 1881, the painting was exhibited at the Institute of Fine Arts in Glasgow, a city where the theme of emigration would have held a special poignancy.

PLATE 33

LE BANC DE JARDIN (THE GARDEN BENCH)
—————————————— c.1882 ——————————————
Oil on canvas, 39 × 56 in / 99.1 × 142.3 cm
Private collection

Le banc de jardin shows Kathleen Newton with her
children Cecil George and Violet and her niece Lilian
Hervey. All three children lived with the Hervey family, but were frequent visitors to Tissot's house in Grove
End Road, and he often included them in his works,
but as this work was executed after his return to Paris,
he probably based it on photographs and sketches. After
Kathleen Newton's death on 9 November 1882, Tissot
continued to paint her and attempted to communicate
with her through seances. Although he exhibited it, he
is known to have kept the picture until his death as a
memorial to Kathleen.

PLATE 34

L'AMBITIEUSE (THE POLITICAL LADY)
————————1883–85————————
Oil on canvas, 56 × 40 in/142.2 × 101.6 cm
Albright-Knox Art Gallery, Buffalo, New York,
Gift of Mr William H. Chase, 1909

Between 1883 and 1885, after his return from London
to Paris, Tissot devoted himself to a series of major
paintings with the intention of re-establishing his reputation in France. The works were exhibited in Paris
at the Galerie Sedelmeyer from 19 April to 15 June
1885 under the title *La Femme à Paris* (and, as a slightly different selection, in England as *Pictures of Parisian
Life*). They represented Parisian women of different
social classes engaged in a variety of daily activities,
with subjects ranging from bridesmaids to shop girls,
society beauties to painters' wives. *L'Ambitieuse* was
the first in the catalogue of 15 paintings shown in Paris.
It is a similar composition to his *Evening* (*Le bal*) of
*c.*1878 (Musée d'Orsay, Paris), which featured Kathleen
Newton as the 'political lady'. Both depict a woman
with an older companion, inciting envious glances and
discreet comment from the guests at a high-level diplo-
matic *soirée* where huddles of men are presumably dis-
cussing affairs of state. To modern viewers the woman's
dress is a sumptuous creation, but Tissot's contemporaries criticized it for being outmoded, *La Vie Parisienne*
declaring, 'She can't aspire to being described as elegant, wearing one of those pink dresses that you wish
would finish but never do, of antiquated cut, without
any bustle but with a pointed black girdle like those
worn twenty years ago.'

PLATE 35

Ces Dames des Chars
(The Ladies of the Cars)
—————— 1883–85 ——————
Oil on canvas, 57 × 39¾ in / 144.8 × 100.7 cm
Museum of Art, Rhode Island School of Design, Providence,
Gift of Walter Lowry

This work, of which Tissot also produced a watercolour replica of the left portion (Musée de Dijon), was the second listed in the Paris exhibition of his *La Femme à Paris* series. The later London catalogue emphasized the crude splendour of the scene: 'The magnificent creature with auburn hair who leads the race is a true daughter of Batignolles, a woman of the people. Behind her follow a brunette and a blonde, and if they are not beautiful, at all events under the glamour of the electric light and amid the applause of the amphitheatre they seem so.' The amphitheatre has been identified as the Hippodrome de l'Alma, opened in 1877, where Roman chariot races were often staged. Some authorities have noted affinities between the painting and scenes described in Alphonse Daudet's novel, *Sappho*. Although it was not published until 1884, as Tissot was on intimate terms with Daudet he may perhaps have been aware of it at an earlier date.

PLATE 36

LA DEMOISELLE D'HONNEUR
(THE BRIDESMAID)
——————— 1883–85 ———————
Oil on canvas, 57 × 40 in/144.8 × 101.6 cm
Leeds City Art Galleries

Tissot planned to produce etchings of the works in his *La Femme à Paris* series, for which notable authors were to write appropriate texts – Emile Zola on *La Demoiselle de magasin* and Guy de Maupassant on *Les Demoiselles de province*, for example. François Coppée was commissioned to write the accompanying text for this work, the ninth in the series, but the ambitious venture was abandoned following Tissot's religious conversion.

PLATE 37

Les Femmes d'Artiste
(The Artist's Ladies)
—————— 1883–85 ——————
Oil on canvas, 57½ × 40 in/146.1 × 101.6 cm
Chrysler Museum, Norfolk, Virginia

The tenth work in his *La Femme à Paris* series, it was given the title *Painters and their Wives* when it was exhibited in London in 1886, the exhibition catalogue of which described it as follows: 'In a word, it is *le vernissage* – varnishing day – which at the Salon is more or less like our private view day; and the painters with their wives and friends have taken Le Doyen's restaurant by storm, and are settling down to a *déjeuner* which they will enjoy with true artistic spirit. How gay everyone seems at this moment, when the great effort of the year is over, and when our pictures are safely hung, and are inviting the critics to do their worst and the buyers to do their best!'

PLATE 38

LES FEMMES DE SPORT
(THE SPORTING WOMEN)
——————1883–85——————
Oil on canvas, 58 × 40¼ in / 147.3 × 102.2 cm
Museum of Fine Arts, Boston, Juliana Cheney Edwards Collection

Since Tissot often gave his pictures different titles in
French and English, and the work was shown in England as *The Amateur Circus*, this painting has often in the
past been confused with one variously called *Danseuse
de corde* and *The Acrobat*, which depicts the female
tightrope walker for whose attentions Tissot was reputed to have competed with the writer Aurélian Scholl.
Its probable location was the Cirque Molier where aristocratic amateurs often performed – the men on the
trapezes were said to have been French dukes, and this
cirque du high life, as it was dubbed, was seen as exemplifying the bored existence of such individuals. However, as the London exhibition catalogue pointed out,
'The worst is that dukes and marquises do not make
very good clowns; nor can they perform half as well
on the flying trapeze as Léotard and his kindred.'

PLATE 39

La Demoiselle de Magasin
(The Shop Girl)
——————1883-85——————
Oil on canvas, 58 × 40 in / 147.3 × 101.6 cm
Art Gallery of Ontario, Toronto,
Gift from the Corporation Subscription Fund, 1968

This was the penultimate work in Tissot's series. When shown in London the Tooth Gallery exhibition catalogue described the work: 'It is on the boulevard; a scene full of life and movement is passing out of doors and our young lady with her engaging smile is holding open the door till her customer takes the pile of purchases from her hand and passes to her carriage. She knows her business, and has learned the first lesson of all, that her duty is to be polite, winning and pleasant. Whether she means what she says, or much of what her looks express, is not the question; enough if she has a smile and an appropriate answer for everybody.' The work numbered fifteenth in the French catalogue of *La Femme à Paris* exhibition was the lost painting *Musique sacrée (Sacred Music)*, the picture on which Tissot was engaged when he experienced the religious vision that was dramatically to change the artistic direction of the last years of his life.

PLATE 40

PAINTINGS IN
PUBLIC COLLECTIONS
~

AUSTRALIA
Melbourne
National Gallery of Victoria
Sydney
Art Gallery of New South Wales

BELGIUM
Antwerp
Koninklijk Museum voor Schone Kunsten

CANADA
Fredericton, New Brunswick
Beaverbrook Art Gallery
Hamilton, Ontario
Art Gallery of Hamilton, Ontario
Montreal, Quebec
Montreal Museum of Fine Art
Ottawa, Ontario
National Gallery of Canada
Toronto, Ontario
Art Gallery of Ontario

FRANCE
Besançon
Musée des Beaux-Arts et d'Archéologie
Compiègne
Musée Nationale du Château
de Compiègne
Dijon
Musée des Beaux-Arts
Musée de Dijon
Gray
Musée Baron Martin
Nantes
Musée des Beaux-Arts
Paris
Musée des Arts Décoratifs
Musée du Louvre
Musée du Luxembourg
Musée d'Orsay
Musée du Petit-Palais

GREAT BRITAIN
Birmingham
Birmingham Museum and Art Gallery
Brighton
Brighton Pavilion Art Gallery
Bristol
City of Bristol Museum and Art Gallery
Cambridge
Wimpole Hall (National Trust)
Cardiff
National Museum of Wales
Leeds
City Art Gallery
Liverpool
Walker Art Gallery
London
British Museum
Guildhall Art Gallery
Museum of London
Tate Gallery
Manchester
Manchester City Art Gallery
Oxford
Ashmolean Museum
Examination Schools
Sheffield
Sheffield City Art Galleries
Southampton
Southampton City Art Gallery
Wakefield
Wakefield Art Gallery and Museums

INDIA
Baroda
Museum and Picture Gallery

IRELAND
Dublin
National Gallery of Ireland

JAPAN
Mito
Historical Museum of the
Tokugawa Family (Shokokan)

NEW ZEALAND
Auckland
Auckland City Art Gallery
Dunedin
Dunedin Public Art Gallery

PUERTO RICO
Ponce
Museo de Arte de Ponce

UNITED STATES OF AMERICA
Baltimore, Maryland
Walters Art Gallery
Boston, Massachusetts
Museum of Fine Arts
Brooklyn, New York
Brooklyn Museum
Buffalo, New York
Albright-Knox Art Gallery
Louisville, Kentucky
J. B. Speed Art Museum
Minneapolis, Minnesota
Minneapolis Institute of Arts
New York
Jewish Museum
Norfolk, Virgina
Chrysler Museum
Northampton, Massachusetts
Smith College Museum of Art
Philadelphia, Pennsylvania
Pennsylvania Academy of
the Fine Arts
Philadelphia Museum of Art
Union League Art Collections
Providence, Rhode Island
Museum of Art, Rhode Island
School of Design
San Francisco, California
California Palace of the
Legion of Honor
Stanford, California
Stanford University Museum of Arts
Toledo, Ohio
Toledo Museum of Art
Washington, DC
National Gallery of Art
Worcester, Massachusetts
Worcester Art Museum

PICTURE ACKNOWLEDGEMENTS

SIR LAWRENCE ALMA-TADEMA

The Fountain (1876): Hamburger Kunsthalle; *The Triumph of Titus* (1885): The Walters Art Gallery, Baltimore; *Self-portrait* (1852): Fries Museum, Leeuwarden; *The Phyrric Dance*: Guildhall Art Gallery, London, photo Bridgeman Art Library; Architect's plan: The British Architectural Library, RIBA, London; Egyptian motifs: Birmingham University Library; *A Sculptor's Model*: Private collection, photo © Christie's; *Cleopatra* (1875): Art Gallery of New South Wales, Sydney; *Her Eyes are With Her Thoughts, and They Are Far Away*: Owen Edgar Gallery, photo © Sotheby's; Bronze bust by Onslow Ford: Royal Academy; *A Family Group* (1896): Royal Academy, London

SIR EDWARD BURNE-JONES

The Lament (1866), William Morris Gallery, Walthamstow; *The Bath of Venus* (1873–88), Calouste Gulbenkian Foundation, Lisbon; *King René's Wedding* (1870), Roy Miles Gallery/Bridgeman Art Library; Portrait of Burne-Jones by George Howard and Dante Gabriel Rossetti photographed by Lewis Carroll: National Portrait Gallery, London; Burne-Jones's birthplace and self-caricature of his Red Lion Square home: from *Memorials of Edward Burne-Jones*; *The Annunciation*, *The Flower of God* and *St Martin* stained glass design: Christie's Images; photographs of the Burne-Jones and Morris families and Burne-Jones and his granddaughter: Hammersmith & Fulham Archives & Local History Centre; *Pilgrim at the Gate of Idleness*: Roy Miles Gallery/Bridgeman Art Library; *The Knight's Farewell*: Visitors of the Ashmolean Museum, Oxford; *The Wedding of Sir Tristram*: Corporation Art Gallery, Bradford/Bridgeman Art Library; Portrait of Maria Zambaco: Private collection; *Hope*: Christie's/Bridgeman Art Library; *Phyllis and Demophöon*: Birmingham Museums and Art Gallery; *Evening Star*: Private collection/Bridgeman Art Library; Photograph of John Ruskin: Private collection; *The Adoration of the Magi*: Norfolk Museums Service (Norwich Castle Museum); *Houses at Rottingdean*: Sotheby's, London; Detail from *The Last Sleep of Arthur in Avalon*: Museo de Arte, Ponce, Puerto Rico; Kelmscott *Chaucer*: William Morris Gallery, Walthamstow; Portrait of Katie Lewis: Private collection/Bridgeman Art Library.

LORD LEIGHTON

Acme and Septimus (c.1868): Ashmolean Museum, Oxford; *The Countess Brownlow* (c. 1879): Belton House (National Trust); *The Maid with the Yellow Hair* (c. 1895): Private collection/photo Christie's/Bridgeman Art Library; photograph of Frederic Leighton at the age of 24, by David Wynfield: National Portrait Gallery, London; *The Death of Brunelleschi* (1852): Leighton House; photograph of Leighton's mentor Adelaide Sartoris (1860), by Camille Silvy: National Portrait Gallery, London; *The Reconciliation of the Montagues and Capulets over the Dead Bodies of Romeo and Juliet* (1853–55): Agnes Scott College, Decatur, Georgia; Portrait of Leighton (1881), by G.F. Watts: National Portrait Gallery, London; *Lieder Ohne Worte* (c. 1860–61): Tate Gallery, London; Study for *A Girl Feeding Peacocks* (c. 1863): Private collection/photo Sotheby's; Leighton House, London: Mansell Collection, London; *Venus Disrobing for the Bath* (1866–67): Private collection/photo Fine Art Picture Library; *Psamathe* (c. 1880): Board of the Trustees of the National Museums and Galleries on Merseyside (Lady Lever Art Gallery)/photo Bridgeman Art Library; Portrait by Leighton of Richard Burton (1875): National Portrait Gallery, London; *The Arts of Industry Applied to War* (1878–80): Victoria and Albert Museum; *The Private View of the Old Masters, Royal Academy, 1888* (detail) by Henry James Brooks: National Portrait Gallery, London; Leighton photographed for F.G. Stephens' *Artists at Home* (1884): National Portrait Gallery, London. All colour plates supplied by and reproduced with the permission of the collections listed. Additional photo credits: plate 2, Christopher Wood Gallery/Bridgeman Art Library; plate 23 The Fine Art Society/Bridgeman Art Library; plate 26 Bridgeman Art Library.

SIR JOHN EVERETT MILLAIS

Millais at work on *The Nest*, from a drawing by Charles Paul Renouard, Mansell Collection; Miss Eveleen Tennant (1874): Tate Gallery, London; *The Nest* (1887): National Museums and Galleries on Merseyside (Lady Lever Art Gallery); portrait drawing of Millais by Holman Hunt (1853): National Portrait Gallery, London; *The Disentombment of Queen Matilda* (1849): Tate Gallery, London; *The Wyatt Children*: Phillips, London/Bridgeman Art Library; *Effie with Foxgloves in Her Hair* (1853): The National Trust Photographic Library/Derrick E. Witty; *Two Masters and their Pupils*: Sotheby's Picture Library; *The Rescue* (1855): National Gallery of Victoria; *Only a Lock of Hair* (1857–8): Manchester City Art Galleries; *Red Riding Hood* (1864): Roy Miles Gallery, London/Bridgeman Art Library; sketch for *The Black Brunswicker* (1859–60): Tate Gallery, London; *A Souvenir of Velásquez* (1868): Royal Academy of Arts, London; *The Crown of Love* (1875): Private collection/Fine Art Photographic Library; Millais's portrait of Benjamin Disraeli (1881): National Portrait Gallery, London; *Effie Deans* (1877): Christie's, London/Bridgeman Art Library; *A Yeoman of the Guard* (1876): Tate Gallery, London; portrait caricature of Millais by 'Ape' (1871): National Portrait Gallery, London; *Glen Birnam* (1891): Manchester City Art Galleries; *Speak! Speak!* (1895): Tate Gallery, London. All colour plates supplied by and reproduced with the permission of the collections listed. Additional photo credits: plates 4, 6, 8, 9, 13, 23, 25, 33, 34, 35, 37, 39 Bridgeman Art Library; plate 14 Christie's, London; plate 16 Tate Gallery, London; plate 36 Scala, Florence.

DANTE GABRIEL ROSSETTI

Portrait of Elizabeth Siddal (1850–65): Fitzwilliam Museum, Cambridge; self-portrait (1847): National Portrait Gallery, London; Rossetti's sister and mother (1877): National Portrait Gallery, London; *The Meeting of Dante and Beatrice in Paradise* (c. 1852): Fitzwilliam Museum, Cambridge; study for a portrait of Rossetti by Holman Hunt (1853): Manchester City Art Galleries; portrait of Elizabeth Siddal (1854): Private collection/photo Christie's Images; drawing of Elizabeth Siddal (1855): Hulton Deutsch; nude study for *Ecce Ancilla Domini!* (c. 1849): City of Birmingham Museum and Art Gallery; pen and ink portrait of Annie Miller: Private collection/photo Bridgeman Art Library/Fine Art Society; photo (c. 1860): Hulton Deutsch; Fanny Cornforth in an unfinished version of *Found*: Carlisle Museum and Art Gallery; portrait of Algernon Swinburne (1861): Fitzwilliam Museum, Cambridge; *Money to the House* caricature: Delaware Art Museum: Samuel and Mary R. Bancroft Memorial; *How They Met Themselves*: Manchester City Art Galleries; *Fair Rosamund* (1861): National Museum of Wales, Cardiff; Christina Rossetti depicted by her brother (1862): The National Trust; *Death of a Wombat* (1869): The British Museum, London; photograph of Rossetti in 1862: Hulton Deutsch; drawing of Jane Burden (1858): National Gallery of Ireland; *Pandora*, a chalk study (1869): The Faringdon Collection Trustees, Buscot Park, Faringdon; portrait of May Morris: Private collection/photo Christie's Images; watercolour by Henry Treffry Dunn: National Portrait Gallery, London.

JAMES TISSOT

Study for *The Return from the Boating Trip* (1873): Hazlitt, Gooden & Fox; *October* (1877): Montreal Museum of Fine Arts, Gift of Lord Strathcona and Family/photo Brian Merrett; photographic portrait of Tissot: Bibliothèque Nationale, Paris; *Le retour de l'enfant prodigue* (1862): Private collection/photo Bridgeman Art Library; portrait of Tissot by Degas (1868): Metropolitan Museum of Art, New York; *A Convalescent* (c. 1876): Sheffield City Art Galleries; *Waiting for the Ferry* (c. 1878): Private collection/photo Fine Art Photographic Library; Grove End Road studio from *The Building News*; photographs of Tissot, Kathleen Newton and her children; *The Parable of the Prodigal Son*: Private collection/photos Krystyna Matjaszkiewicz; *Children in a Garden vase* (c. 1878): Musée des Arts Decoratifs, Paris/photo L. Sully Jaulmes; *Berthe* (c. 1882): Musée du Petit Palais, Paris/photo Phohe (c. 1882): Musée du Petit Palais, Paris/photo Photothèque Musées de la Ville de Paris; Portrait of the Pilgrim (c. 1886–94): Brooklyn Museum, New York, Gift of Thomas E. Kirby; *At the Rifle Range* (1869): © The National Trust, 1992, Wimpole Hall; *Waiting for the Train (Willesden Junction)* (c. 1871–73): Dunedin Public Art Gallery. All other illustrations are from private collections. All colour plates are reproduced with the permission of the collections indicated.